PRAISE FOR
I WASN'T READY TO SAY GOODBYE

"As one who deals with unexpected death, I am so pleased to find a truly valuable reference for those souls who are blindsided by such misery. I would characterize this work as thoughtful, thorough and intensely meaningful. The personal passages which share feelings and experiences...are superb. They turn a scholarly treatise into one that will touch those in suffering greatly and help them understand the wide range of emotions that they will experience. Up until now, Rabbi Kushner's reference, *WHY BAD THINGS HAPPEN TO GOOD PEOPLE*, has been my mainstay in such circumstances; I will add this book to my recommended list to loved ones and friends."

> *E. Charles Douville, MD*
> *Cardiothoracic Surgeon,*
> *Providence Portland Hospital*

"I Wasn't Ready to Say Goodbye is a book that is easily related to by anyone struggling to cope with the sudden death of a loved one. I highly recommend this book, not only to the bereaved, but to friends and counselors as well. If you want to experience what the pain of grief is like, to better understand what the bereaved are going through, read this book."

> *Helen Fitzgerald, author of The Grieving Child,*
> *The Mourning Handbook, The Grieving Teen (July 2000).*

"The authors have captured a means of discussing and exploring a very painful life passage in real life, down to earth language and experience. Many thanks to Pam and Brook for having the strength to get through their sudden loss of a loved one, wisdom to understanding the Way, and the generosity in sharing their discoveries to further our healing."

> *Charlotte A. Tomaino, Ph.D., Neuropsychologist*

"This book, by women who have done their homework on grief, offers a companion for others still recuperating. Further, it introduces us to so many others, both famous and ordinary, who can hold a hand and comfort a soul through grief's wilderness. Outstanding references of where to seek other help."

George C. Kandle, Pastoral Psychotherapist

"A well written book about a very difficult subject. I Wasn't Ready to Say Goodbye will be useful for those going through these difficult times."

Bradley Evans, MD
Cardiologist, Providence Portland Hospital

"As an emergency department nurse with 15+ years experience in that area, I have had first hand experience with sudden death. I have always felt that not enough has been written to address the problems and difficulties that face those who have experienced sudden death/loss, and how it differs from a loss that can be anticipated. This book carefully pointed out the many ways we may grieve, but also gently addressed that point at which the grieving process was no longer healthy and that professional counseling was needed. The overall feeling from this book was of gentleness, guidance and a sense of spirituality. The reader is given choices, resources and suggestions to enable them to plan and implement their own grief process. I am planning an in-service education program for the emergency dept. staff (MDs and RNs) on sudden death and grief reduction and will share your book. The list of resources is very comprehensive and it is evident that much time and energy was spent to provide the reader with a very complete guide."

Kathleen Reilly; RN MS CEN

I WASN'T READY TO SAY

Goodbye

surviving, coping
& healing after
the sudden death
of a loved one

also by Brook Noel…

Shadows of a Vagabond

The Single Parent Resource

*Back to Basics: 101 Ideas for Strengthening
Our Children and Our Families*

The Rush Hour Cook

Visit

**www.brooknoel.com
www.griefsteps.com**

I WASN'T READY TO SAY

Goodbye

surviving, coping
& healing after
the sudden death
of a loved one

BROOK NOEL & PAMELA D. BLAIR, PH.D.

CHAMPION PRESS, LTD.

Care has been taken to trace the ownership and obtain permission, if necessary, for excerpts from the works of others. If any errors have occurred, they will be corrected in subsequent printings provided notification is sent to the publisher.

CHAMPION PRESS, LTD.
MILWAUKEE, WISCONSIN

ISBN 1-891400-27-4

Library of Congress Catalog Card Number 00-131036

Cataloging-in-Publication Data
Noel, Brook.
      I wasn't ready to say goodbye : surviving, coping & healing after
the sudden death of a love one / Brook Noel & Pamela D. Blair. -- 1st ed.

      p. cm.
      Includes bibliographical references and index.
      LCCN: 00-131036
      ISBN: 1-891400-27-4

      1. Grief 2. Bereavement. 3. Loss.
(Psychology) 4. Sudden death I. Blair, Pamela
D. II. Title.

BF723.G75N64 2000   155.937

Manufactured in Canada.
30 29 28 27 26 25 24

Cover Design by Kathy Campbell, Wildwood Studios.
Text Design by Calbro Media.

Dedication

For George, who taught me how to let go
and for Steve who taught me how to love again.
- Pamela D. Blair

For 'Samson' who taught me that friendship goes beyond
human dimensions. For Caleb who taught me that love and
kinship go beyond earthly dimensions.
- Brook Noel

Acknowledgements

Pamela D. Blair....

Thanks so much to Dr. Charlotte Tomaino, Kathy Murphy and to everyone in the TBI group. To Gary Leistico, Patricia Ellen, Alyce Branum, Carl & Wilma Machover, Delores, Paddie and Keri for their inspiration. To my children, Aimee, Ian and Rachel for their contributions. To my husband, Steve, with all my heart I thank you for believing in me. My sister, Marilyn Houston for her constant support and input to this book. A great big thank you and hug to my clients who inspired me, and to all those close to me who helped me through a very trying time. Brook Noel, fellow writer and spiritual journeyer, I thank you for your vision, talent and perseverance in seeing this work from its inception, to its completion.

And finally, to all those seen and unseen who have been instrumental in this book.

Brook Noel...

To Sara Pattow—Thank you for being an anchor in my life. Your friendship is one of my life's richest treasures. To Mary Ann Klotz—Thank you for standing by me and walking me through my darkest nights. To Gina Wahl—Your optimism, kindness and friendship is a blessing. To Greg Anderson—as both mentor and friend, I can never thank you enough for the gifts you've given over the past three years. You are wonderful. To Ron Martino—Thank you for your dedication, belief and encouragement. To all of Caleb's friends—especially Rob, Steve and Jeremy--thank you for standing by our family and becoming a part of our family. My heartfelt thanks to Nicole for helping Caleb's memory live on through the waterski tournament. A special thanks to Gregg and Kim Walker whose support, love and friendship has been so positive and influential in our lives. God bless the new Walker---Braeden Caleb (Walker). To Pamela D. Blair—I feel fortunate to have found you and for your guidance, help, input, support and partnership throughout the walk of grief and this book.

And lastly, but certainly not least, for my family. Andy thank you for standing by me through thick and thin. I feel fortunate to share my life with you. I love you. For my little angel Sammy, who reminds me daily of life's beauties. And for my Mother, thank you for your support and love through my trials and triumphs. You are the absolute best. I love you with all my heart and soul.

Do not stand
at my grave and weep.
I am not there
I do not sleep.

I am a thousand
winds that blow.
I am the
diamond
glints on snow.

I am the
sunlight
on the ripened
grain.

I am the
gentle autumn's
rain.

When you awaken
in the morning hush,
I am the swift
uplifting rush
of quiet birds in
circled flight.

I am the
soft stars that
shine
at night.

Do not stand
at my grave
and cry:
I am not there,
I did not die.

- Hopi Prayer

Contents

Part One: Journey through Grief

Part Two: Sharing our Stories

Part Three: Pathways through Grief

Introduction

Each year, about eight million Americans suffer the death of a close family member. The list of high visibility disasters, human suffering and sudden loss is long and will continue to grow. Many include families and individuals we don't see in the media. They are suffering behind closed doors in our neighborhoods, in our own homes, in hospital waiting rooms. They are pacing ICU hallways, watching as life support is discontinued, sitting numb in hard chairs. They are impatiently waiting in a hotel room for a body to be found. They are torn apart by an unexpected phone call. They are grappling with sudden death, a sudden ending, a sudden tragedy. None of them were ready to say "goodbye".

From our very first breath, we are thrust into the cycle of life and death. As infants, we trust our parents to tend to our needs. As children, we trust the good in those around us. We are taught that if we are good to others, they will in turn, be good to us. Soon we become adolescents who are taught cause and effect. We are taught that if we eat nutritionally and take care of our bodies they will serve us well for years. And we grow into adulthood, where we continue to trust these basic cycles. We trust that the sun will rise each morning and set each evening; that our children will outlive us; that there will be many days to cherish those we love.

Then, in a split-second with the news of a loved one's sudden death, the world changes forever. The neat world of predictable cycles ends. We are slam-dunked into an abyss with few tools at hand. No time for preparation. No time to gather what we'll need for our journey. No time for finished business or goodbyes.

Physically, we may be made up of cells and genes and skin and bones, but emotionally, we are composed of thoughts and feelings and memories and pieces of the people we have touched, and who have touched us. After the news of sudden death, we awake less whole with a gaping hole left by the death of the person we loved.

Grief brings that moment where you awake and look into the mirror, and no longer recognize the eyes staring back at you. Though the sun still rises and sets as it always has, everything looks just a bit different, a bit distorted. The shadows cast by grief stretch far and wide.

This kind of death happens across all age groups. According to Sherwin B. Nuland, author of *How We Die: Reflections on Life's Final Chapter*, trauma, defined as a physical injury or wound, is the leading cause of death for all persons below the age of 44 in the United States. It kills approximately 150,000 Americans each year, of all ages. Sixty percent of traumatic mortality occurs within the first twenty-four hours after injury. Drowning kills almost 5,000 people in the U.S. each year. Approximately 1,000 Americans suffer lethal electrocutions each year. The list is endless of the ways we die—suddenly, unexpectedly.

The U.S. Department of Health records more than 2,000,000 deaths each year. About 6 percent of all deaths, 8 percent of all hospital discharges, and 37 percent of all emergency department visits are injury-related. In fact, injuries cause more deaths among youth than disease or natural causes. Motor vehicle traffic injuries, firearm injuries and poisoning are among the three leading causes of injury death, accounting for nearly two-thirds of all injury deaths. Sudden death from situations like stroke, chronic obstructive pulmonary disease and accidents are among the top five causes of death. Every year, more than 11 million adults lose a parent, and by age 62, 75 percent have lost both. Accidents and their adverse effects cause approximately 100,000 deaths each year and suicide over 30,000. Sudden death is a part of the human condition. Yet, when we (the authors of this book) looked for a book on the topic, we found none written specifically for the general public. This book was born from the frustration of that search. As authors, we struggled with the void left from sudden death. For the most part, we went it alone, using trial and error to keep our feet on the path of survival.

According to *Kearl's Guide to the Sociology of Death: Death's Personal Impacts*, the grief associated with bereavement is one of the most profound of all human emotions—and one of the most lethal. Every year about eight million Americans suffer the death of a close family member, disrupting life patterns for up to three years. According to the National Academy of Science, of the approximately 800,000 Americans widowed each year, up to 160,000 are thought to suffer pathological grief.

As a culture, we are inept at handling the grief of those around us. No one teaches us what to do when the foundation we believe in crumbles and we are left in the midst of ruin, while society anxiously awaits our quick and tidy rebuilding. Society has little time for our pain, while we can see nothing outside of it. For example, it is a fact that about 85% of wives outlive their husbands. In *Time Wars*, Jeremy Rifkin notes how Emily Post in 1927 reported that a widow's formal mourning period was three years. Twenty-three years later, this period had declined to six months. And by 1972, Amy Vanderbilt advised the bereaved to "pursue, or try to pursue, a usual social course within a week or so after a funeral." We impose time limits and expectations for how long one must suffer. While over 90 percent of American companies grant official time off for bereavement, most have established three days as the formal bereavement period.

You can not explain the impact of tragic death to someone who does not know its impact firsthand. You can't understand the traps until you've stepped into them. You can't explain the questioning, the disorientation, the helplessness that arrives from facing the world without that piece of yourself that died with your loved one.

Ask any survivor of sudden death/loss if they thought they could cope with that loss (of a child or spouse or sibling or friend) and they will tell you "no." Many will tell you they'd have gone crazy in the face of such tragedy. Yet, these same people are the ones who face the adversity, who climb out of the abyss, who find trust again, who rebuild.

This book includes our stories as well as those we have come to know. Stories of people who are rebuilding through the courage of each other's words. It's through these stories that we recognize ourselves. It's through these stories that we step out of isolation and into a community where others are walking the maze of recovery with us. In this book, we bring you the stories, wisdom and information we wish we would have had access to during our journey. We bring you the work of those who have gone before you in the dark labyrinth of life's night. We bring you the words of those who have hit walls, stumbled in the maze, skinned their knees and gotten back up to emerge in a new place. For as much as the book is about death, it is also about beginning. After losing someone we love, we begin again. We learn it all again. We learn how to take baby steps of courage, how to walk and talk, how to dream different dreams, how to trust again and how to create life anew while honoring the past. We see life a bit differently. More than anyone else, we understand the value of each minute, we understand the importance of saying what needs to be said today, we understand what is truly important.

We weren't ready to say goodbye and there will be thousands who pick up this book who weren't ready to say goodbye either. This book is meant to serve as a touchstone of sanity, for navigating the unknown emotional terrain of sudden death— a terrain full of walls, shrouded in fog where we offer you the words of analyst and philosopher Carl Jung who wrote, "When you are up against a wall, be still, put down roots like a tree, until clarity comes from deeper sources to see over that wall."

Part One
The Journey through Grief

Chapter One
The Starting Point:
notes from the authors

"What we call the beginning is often the end. To make an end is to make a beginning. The end is where we start from."

T.S. Eliot

Pam's Story

I believe no matter how much pain we're in, there is something inside of us stronger than the pain. That something allows survivors of the worst tragedies to want to live and tell their story. You can see it in the eyes of someone who has managed to hang on to their dignity in the midst of adversity. It's a kind of stubbornness. You can call it God, the soul or the human spirit. It is found only when we have been oppressed, or broken, or abandoned, and we remain the one who holds on to what's left. It is this inner something that has allowed me to go on in the face of tremendous loss.

I remember all the vivid, surrealistic details of that morning. The smell of fresh ground coffee brewing lingered in the air as I came to consciousness. I was trying to squeeze one or two more minutes out of warm bed and feather pillow when the phone rang. Grabbing at the intrusive noise, I put the receiver to my ear and heard nothing but the sound of someone trying to catch her breath. I thought it might be one of those weird "breather" calls until I heard LeAnne say, "Pam, George is in a coma.....(long pause).....he had a hemorrhage or something." I felt the molecules in the air begin to thicken as I tried to take a breath so I could talk to George's younger sister. "LeAnne, where are you? What do you mean? I just saw George yesterday afternoon. He looked fine!"

Crying and gasping for air she replied in a thin voice, "You and Ian have to come here—to the hospital. I think it's important that you bring Ian here now." I tried to remain rational as I remembered that Ian, my twelve-year-old son with George, was getting ready to bolt down the stairs on his way to school. I still needed to get up and pack his lunch box. I thought, *Why is LeAnne bothering me with this? I'm sure it's just nothing. After all, George is young and healthy (and handsome). Comas don't happen to people like him. They don't happen to people I know.*

"LeAnne, why don't we wait and see. He'll probably come to. And besides, Ian is just about to leave for school and he has a test today. Why don't you call back in a few minutes after you have more information and I'll bring him down to the hospital later. It's probably not as bad as..." She interrupted my rambling with a bold, deliberate, almost cold intonation in her voice. *"Now.* You have to come now. It's really bad. There's a lot of blood in his brain and he probably won't live."

Blood in his brain. I sat down hard. What was I hearing? Was I hearing that George, the man I had loved as my husband and the father of my child, and who had become a dear friend and loving co-parent after our divorce, was about to leave the earth? Come on. People exaggerate. LeAnne is exaggerating. After all, George means as much to her as he does to me, and his son Ian, and his once stepdaughter, Aimee.

"Okay, LeAnne, I'll take the day off from work and I'll bring Ian to the hospital. Where are you?" She replied in an almost inaudible voice, "The emergency room. I'll meet you there."

My limbs were numb, the blood was gone from my face and neck, and I wasn't sure I could make my mouth work. Steve, my husband of seven years had left for his office in the city and I was alone. I would have to tell Ian myself. I would have to tell Ian that the dad who loved to be with him on weekends, who lived for his son's little league games and karate matches was probably brain dead. I would have to tell my daughter, Aimee. Part of me thought that if I could just see George and tell him loudly how much his son needed him, he wouldn't slip away into death's darkness. That's it. I would scream at him and bring him back to us.

Somehow I made my legs work. One numb foot in front of the other. At the bottom of the stairs I called, "Ian, meet me in my bedroom. I have something to tell you." I kept telling myself, *you will remain calm . . .think logically . . .don't upset the boy too much, just keep calm.*

How do you describe this strange limbo moment where life slows down and everything around you falls away into unimportance? It felt like there was no house with its comfortable furniture around me, no more smell of coffee, no cat rubbing my legs for attention, no appointments on the calendar—all that existed for now were the two small, brown, round eyes of my little boy resting on mine.

I told Ian what little I knew. There, sitting on the edge of my now neatly made bed, he melted into tears. Deep sobs and a lot of "How did this happen? What happened to him?" over and over again. His voice was cracking, rising and falling, the way twelve-year-old boy's voices sometimes do. I comforted him. I knew that was my only role, comforter to my son with no one to comfort me.

I called my daughter Aimee, nine months pregnant with her first child and George's stepdaughter. She agreed to join us. We made our way to the hospital, not talking. Ian looked out the car window and I could tell he wondered why everyone driving past us looked so normal, so unaffected by our plight. Didn't they know what was going on? How could they go about their business knowing George was dying *or dead?* Why are they behaving as if nothing happened? I felt as if I were moving through someone else's movie. Everything felt surreal, in slow motion.

No human being is without feelings. From a baby's first cry to a dying person's last look at friends and family, our primary response to the world around us is colored by emotion. Whether that world seems to us friendly or frightening, beautiful or ugly, pleasant or disagreeable, affects the way we approach others, and indeed influences everything we do. I do not believe that such feelings arise in us solely due to environmental conditions, or to genetic factors, however important these both may be. Members of the same family, placed in the same kinds of situations, react in very different ways. Our emotions are a conscious response to our experience, but they are self-generated and reveal something important about our character.

It felt like I had no emotions and no character that day. I was skin and bones and brain and blood vessels making attempts at movement. Lips in slow motion on a frozen face with unfamiliar arms and legs, a mind repeating over and over, *this is crazy, this is crazy.* George's mother and sister waited with Ian, Aimee and I in the emergency room. We all looked the same as we did last week only now we were more robot-like, sitting and standing and walking and pacing around a room with hard plastic chairs and a TV set hanging from the ceiling. I couldn't look at George's mom with her soft round face and gray hair. A gentle lady of 62 with kind blue eyes—the same kind blue eyes that George had. If I looked at her I would have seen the pain. The pain of a woman who was told she would probably never have children and to whom George was a miracle, a gift from God—her first-born.

To me, the emotions are "real" in the sense that I can perceive them objectively as a luminous atmosphere surrounding every living being. Every time we feel an emotion there is a discharge of energy in the emotional field, whether slight or strong, and this produces a characteristic vibration and a color—the "footprint" of that particular emotion. I could "see" the emotion in the room.

George was brain dead. The doctor said he had suffered a massive cerebral aneurysm. He was dead and he looked like he was sleeping—the machines kept his lungs rising and falling, his heart beating, his face a rosy healthy glow. I encouraged Ian to hold his hand, to say goodbye. He was brave. He did. He cried and said, "Goodbye, Daddy, I love you." Aimee took her private moment with him also. George had, only the week before, stopped by to visit her in her new apartment, to place his hand on her baby-full belly, to say congratulations.

George's wife said I could have some time alone with him. Because I believe that people in comas can "hear," I told him "thank you for our son and for the love you showed Aimee. Thank you for the time we had together." I think he heard me, if not with his ears, with his soul. I asked him to please be an angel in our son's life—to watch over him. The hospital staff began disconnecting the machines as the family encircled the hospital bed, holding hands and praying.

I tell my story because I believe in the power of story to heal. As a therapist and workshop leader, I find it rewarding to help others tell their story. The stories I hear about loss are as diverse as fingerprints—each one slightly different from the next. And yet, when we gather like we did at a recent workshop I conducted, the attendees share and the connection to each other is immediate and profound. Regardless of where we are in the process of loss we become supportive as we relate and recognize each others pain. A sense of community and acceptance is vital to our spiritual and emotional healing.

In her book, *The Fruitful Darkness*, Buddhist anthropologist and depth psychologist Joan Halifax reflects on our collective as well as personal stories when she writes, "stories are our protectors, like our immune system, defending against attacks of debilitating alienation...They are the connective tissue between culture and nature, self and other, life and death, that sew the worlds together, and in telling, the soul quickens and comes alive."

In his classic book, *Reaching Out*, Henri Nouwen writes that though our own story "can be hard to tell, full of disappointments and frustrations, deviations and stagnations . . . it is the only story we have and there will be no hope for the future when the past remains unconfessed, unreceived and misunderstood."

Hopefully, the stories and information in this book will help you feel less alone as you struggle to find the path that will lead you across rivers of grief and through forests of sadness. We hope in some small way that we can be your support network and a touchstone for sanity during a very difficult time.

Brook's Story

It was a day in October that changed my perception of life, and my perception of death, forever. It was the day I lost my brother, who was not only a brother, but in many ways a father, a friend and a lifeline.

The day was unseasonably warm for a Wisconsin October. It was the fourth of the month and the thermometer showed a temperature near seventy degrees. With weather like that, no Wisconsinite would stay indoors. My husband, daughter and I decided to take a trip to Manitowoc, a town about an hour north of our then-home-base in the Milwaukee suburbs. Manitowoc housed a Maritime Museum that we had yet to visit. The main feature was a submarine, complete with tour. That afternoon we walked the streets, looked in the shops, took the tour, and bought our two and a half-year-old daughter a blue hat, which read U.S.S. Cobia. Our daughter posed with the hat, her smile radiating happiness.

We left Manitowoc around five that evening to return home. A dear friend of mine had traveled into town and we had plans to meet at six for dinner. I glanced at my watch as we continued the drive, knowing I would be a few minutes late. The plan was that she leave a message with where she was and I would meet her there. We didn't get home until a little bit after six. My neighbors, Kevin and Mary Ann were outside barbecuing. I stopped over briefly to say hello and let Samantha show off her new hat. I apologized for my quick departure and ducked into the house to check messages and find out where Sara had chosen for dinner.

The red digital display showed four messages. I hit play. The first was from my mother. It said simply to call her right away. The second was from Sara, with the name of the restaurant. The third was from my mother again, this time her voice sounding thick with a tone I couldn't discern, "Brook you must call me right away. There's been a terrible accident." I immediately pushed stop on the machine and dialed my mother's number. Both my brother and mother continued to live in the town where I was raised. It's a small resort town called Manitowish Waters, about five hours north of my then-Milwaukee home. Life is simple there. You work; you ski; you enjoy the woods, the lakes; you "watch the Packers" and enjoy the seasons as they unfold. Outsiders make great attempts to vacation there. Often the northwoods has been dubbed "God's Country", and life is full and fun there.

My mother answered on the first ring. I can still hear our voices to this day and picture myself standing beneath the archway of our guest bedroom. "Mom, it's me. What's up?" I asked inquisitively, never prepared for the two-word response that would vibrate over the phone.

"Caleb's dead."

Immediately my knees gave out beneath me as I shouted "No," before falling to the floor, the questions, the disbelief, lingering around me. I asked how, but did not hear the reply. I crawled into the guest bed with the cordless phone pushed to my ear and curled my body into a tight ball. I could do nothing but sob. My daughter had walked up behind me and was patting me gently on the back. "It's all right Mama," said the innocent two-year-old voice. "It's all right Mama." Andy, my husband, came and took Samantha from the room and I simply mouthed the words my mother had said, *Caleb's dead.*

My mother suggested that I hang up the phone and call her back. I put down the phone while I still writhed on the bed, wanting desperately to escape from the unwelcome reality that had suddenly become claustrophobic. Rising, I walked into the living room. I looked briefly at my daughter and Andy, before running from the house. The points thereafter are somewhat vague and gathered mostly from what I've been told of my response.

I entered into my neighbor's kitchen and fell into her arms as I told her the news. She quickly took me outside and huddled me close. All I remember is her telling me, "You are in shock." I remember my hands trembling violently and my body shaking. Her husband got Samantha from our house to play with their children; and then she and my husband Andy called my mother.

The details unfurled. Caleb and his faithful chocolate lab Samson, had been duck hunting out on a marsh with three friends. They had rowed a boat out about 20 minutes to the site that was thought to have the best potential. While waiting for the official opening time, Caleb was eyeing some geese that were flying over. At that moment he was stung by a yellow jacket just over his eyebrow. Within minutes, Caleb would go unconscious. His friends performed CPR as they frantically rowed back to shore. Unable to fit in the boat, his faithful dog swam across the marsh, unwilling to leave his master. His friends broke into his truck, using his cellular phone to call the paramedics. The local paramedics arrived and were then intercepted by a special team sent from the hospital that was about thirty miles away.

Despite the efforts of friends, paramedics and doctors, Caleb never came to nor responded to Epinephrine or any other drug. My mother was told he had suffered a fatal, profound anaphylactic shock reaction to the sting of a bee. Caleb had been stung by bees before and never had 'but a mild reaction. We, nor he, even knew of this bee allergy.

My brother was a strong and vital young man. He owned a successful printing shop, which he built from the ground up. He was a National Barefoot Water-ski Champion who was in great physical health and a prime athlete. He was about 200 pounds, and in one day, we had to come to understand that a bee, no bigger than an inch, had taken the life from this handsome twenty-seven-year-old man. It is something that I think we all are still trying to comprehend. It is something that I don't think we ever fully will, but we each must find our own way to cope and go on successfully—that is the best tribute we can give to this great man who touched our lives.

When Caleb died, I looked for someone to hold my hand and to understand what I was feeling. I wasn't ready for a support group, all I wanted to do was to curl up in my bed, hide from the world and have something convince me it would, some day, be all right again. I scanned bookstores looking for something I could relate to but found very little coverage on sudden death. The other books didn't understand the unique challenges of facing a death in this way. Eventually, I gave up the search for that book.

As time has passed, I have learned more about what I have endured and what I have to endure to move on with my life. I have spoken with others—some in the recent aftermath and some who lost someone tragically years ago—many of whom are looking for guidance similar to what I had searched for. With these people in mind, I decided to create the book I wish would have been there for me. I met my coauthor, Pam, while working on a book entitled *The Single Parent Resource*. There was an immediate closeness between the two of us, even though we lived two-thousand miles apart. When I decided to write this book, I felt compelled to call her and see if she would consider writing the book with me. Fate must have nudged me to call, since at that point, I didn't know she had experienced sudden loss in her life as well.

We cannot offer you any quick fixes. We cannot give you a tidy outline that will divide grief recovery into a neat and precise process. We cannot tell you that six months from now the world will be back in alignment. We have seen too much to offer such hollow promises. What we can promise, is that in these pages we will do our best to offer you a hand to hold and words to guide you through your maze so that you may come out complete and hopeful on the other side.

Chapter Two
Notes for the First Few Weeks

"And people answered the phone for me.
And people cooked for me.
And people understood for me.
My dearest friends cared for me
when I didn't care."
- Wendy Feiereisen

At this moment, in the direct aftermath of losing someone tragically, there is so little anyone can say. We cannot find the words to offer you peace—though we wish it a gift we could give you. We promise you now that we will give you everything we can to help you make your way through this. We will help you wind a path through the haze, the confusion and the pain that is gripping at your core.

But now is not the time to demand resolution, answers or forward movement. This is simply the time to cope, to get by, to survive.

For the first few weeks, do not concern yourself with what you will do, where you will go or what lies in the future. For now, we ask that you simply follow the guidelines in this chapter. There will be time to cope, to understand, to process—later. Right now, you simply need to take care of *you.*

Look through the brief writings that are contained within this chapter. Read whatever captures your interest. Trust that it will be what you need. Put the book down and come back to it as necessary. In a month or so, when your concentration returns you will be able to read more. For now, just take small steps.

Treat Yourself as if You Were in Intensive Care

You are in the process of going through one of the most traumatic experiences a person can endure. The challenges you have already faced both physically and mentally will leave you vulnerable, exhausted and weak. It's imperative that you focus directly on yourself and on any dependents. Find ways to get your needs met first in these few weeks.

If you have small children, contact friends and relatives to help you care for them. Consider having someone stay with you for the specific task of caring for your children since some children may be further traumatized by separation. In Chapter Nine we cover the specifics of children and grief. While it is human nature to want to help and care for others, we must understand at this trying time we will barely have enough energy to care for ourselves. Even if we want to help those around us, we won't have the resources. It's in our best interest to allow this time for our own grief.

Someone to take Calls

If the person that has died is of your immediate family, you will be receiving many phone calls, visitors and cards. Have a friend come by to take messages, answer the door and answer the phone. Most callers do not expect to speak directly with the family but simply wish to express their condolences. Have someone keep a notepad handy to record the names and messages of callers.

Be forewarned, occasionally you may receive a strange call or a strange card. On one occasion Brook took a message from a caller that offered condolences for the loss of her brother and then in a second breath requested a current picture of her daughter. Pam remembers a caller who said, "I'm sure George's death was easier for you, because you were divorced after all." These thoughts and comments are inappropriate and can be very hurtful, though the caller does not intend them to be. In our society, we just don't know how to handle grief and loss. People cope with grief differently—many people don't know how to cope at all. When you think of it, our world is geared toward *gaining* and *acquiring*, we have few lessons on how to handle *loss*. Occasionally people will ask a strange question or perhaps write a note in a card that seems a bit "out of place". Realize that this is not done to hurt you; these are just people who are inept at handling loss and the thought of loss.

Seek Assistance

In addition to getting help to answer the phone, seek out your most trusted friend to help with any final arrangements that are your responsibility. You may be the person who needs to organize the funeral service or you may have insurance agencies to contact or an estate to settle. While you can, and should be involved in these areas at some level, it is important to find someone who can do most of the calling for you, make trips to the funeral home, find out information and then let you make the final choices. In the direct aftermath of loss your judgment may also be impaired and a trusted friend can act as a guide in decision making. In the Appendix of this book, you will find some worksheets that will guide you and your support person through these processes.

Don't Worry about Contacting People

In the first few days you will make initial calls to immediate family and friends. Beyond that, try to limit the number of calls you are personally responsible for. At this time, you are unlikely to have the energy or the will to make these calls. We have included a worksheet in the Appendix you can give to a trusted friend. This worksheet will guide them through needed calls and arrangements. Additionally, you may want to obtain the deceased's address book and let your trusted friend contact the people within.

Let Your Body Lead You

Grief affects us all differently. Some of us may become very active and busy, while others may become lethargic or practically comatose. Let your body lead you. If you feel tired—sleep. If you feel like crying—cry. If you are hungry—eat. Don't feel you need to act one way or another. There are no "shoulds" right now, simply follow the lead of your body.

One caution: With the shock of losing someone tragically it is not uncommon for people to turn to medication. This can be as minor as a sleep aid or as major as consuming large amounts of alcohol. Try to resist these urges. This will not make the grief easier. If you must engage in some sort of self-medication be aware that this will not take away from any of the grief you are feeling, it will simply postpone it until you cease the self-medication. Natural alternatives are available and we have a comprehensive listing of these alternatives in Chapter 17.

Religious Traditions

If you were married or your loved one adopted a religion you are unfamiliar with, you may encounter traditions that are uncomfortable for you. The religious requirements around death and burial may cause confusion and unrest in the family and among friends.

For example, Marjory comes from a family where a wake lasts for days and cremation is preferred. Since Marjory was the custodial parent, she took her son to Sunday school on a regular basis. When her young son died unexpectedly, her ex-husband, a religious Jew, was adamantly against the plans she was making. Religious Jews are required to bury their dead within 24 hours and believe that cremation is a most undignified method of disposing a body. Also, after the immediate burial, Jews "sit shiva" for seven days with the nearest of kin.

It is so important at a tragic time like this to be caring and understanding of the traditions of both the deceased and the families involved. To honor the deceased, the living must find ways to compromise. In Marjory's case, because most of her family had been uninvolved in her son's life and her ex-husband's family had been so close to her, she decided on burial for her son instead of cremation. Her ex-husband in turn agreed to participate in the Christian-oriented wake Marjory had planned.

If you are unclear about what is best for you, your family or your loved one, seek counsel with a clergy person, family mediator or therapist. In dual faith situations where decisions are difficult, the services of an Interfaith Minister might be helpful. You can contact the Association of Interfaith Ministers for a referral by phone at 203-855-0000 or by e-mail at: aim@interfaithclergy.org

Keep in mind that peoples' needs will be different. When Brook's brother died, they held a small informal viewing for close friends. Many of Caleb's friends chose not to attend. They preferred to remember Caleb as they had seen him last. Others found the viewing helpful. There is no right or wrong way to grieve, it's simply important to be open and respectful of individual needs.

Wills and Arrangements

While those that die a lingering death often have wills and have told the living what they would like as far as funerals, burial, etc., one who dies a sudden death has frequently not indicated to friends and family how they would like to be treated in death. This presents an extra burden to loved ones, since they are required to go ahead with arrangements under assumptions of what their loved one may have wanted. With our emotional and physical levels depleted, these decisions become even harder. You may find it helpful to discuss your options with a group of close friends that knew the deceased. When Brook and her mother were trying to figure out what type of service to hold, they talked to each other first, and then asked Caleb's friends for input and ideas. With the help of others, they decided a celebration in his honor would be the way he would choose to be remembered. Since the decision had been a group effort, everyone felt comfortable.

Expect to be Distracted

During the first few weeks your mind will be filled with racing thoughts and unfamiliar emotions. Many people report having difficulty with simple tasks. Losing one's keys, forgetting where you are while driving and sluggish reaction time are all commonly reported problems. With everything you are mentally and physically trying to process, it's normal to be distracted. Take special caution. Try to avoid driving and other activities where these symptoms may cause injury.

Have Someone Near You

If possible, choose a close friend to keep near you through the first week or two. Let this person help you make decisions, hear your fears or concerns and be the shoulder for you to lean on. Give them a copy of this book. Later as you move through the grieving process it will be very helpful to have someone who has "been there" and understands what you are talking about thoroughly.

The Help of Friends

Our energy is so depleted in the first few weeks after loss, it's hard to even ask for help. We have included a handout at the end of this chapter that can be photocopied freely and given to your inner circle of friends and relatives. You may be reluctant to do this, but please do. Even if we don't think we need people right now, we do indeed. Brook shares her story of friendship...

"When I lost my brother, my friend Sara was my anchor. I never asked her to come over that evening but as soon as she heard, she came (even though I told her there was nothing she could do). She simply sat next to me. Then she went upstairs and packed my bag for the upcoming week. She hugged me when I needed it and sat in the other room when I needed to be alone. To this day, her warm presence brings tears to my eyes. It was an extension of love and caring like few I have known."

If, like Brook, you are too grief-ridden to ask for help, simply show friends this book and let them read these few pages so they have an idea of what you need and how to support you. Friends want to help, but they rarely know how. The cycle of your grief will be more bearable when you hold the hand of a friend. Reach out.

The following two entries summarize beautifully what those who face grief need from the people around them.

"'I'll cry with you,'
she whispered
'until we run out of tears.
Even if it's forever.
We'll do it together.'
There it was...a simple
promise of connection.
The loving alliance of
grief and hope that
blesses both our breaking
apart and our coming
together again."
Molly Fumia, *Safe Passage*

"Needed: A strong, deep person wise enough to allow me to grieve in the depth of who I am, and strong enough to hear my pain without turning away.

I need someone who believes that the sun will rise again, but who does not fear my darkness. Someone who can point out the rocks in my way without making me a child by carrying me. Someone who can stand in thunder and watch the lightning and believe in a rainbow."

Fr. Joe Mahoney, *Concerns of Police Survivors Newsletter*
(This is excerpted from a beautiful book on grief titled *Forever Remembered: Cherished messages of hope, love and comfort from courageous people who have lost a loved one.* Compendium Publishing.)

These days will be long and challenging and there may seem no resolution for any of the pains that plague you. That's all right. It's all right to feel hopeless and like all has lost its purpose. These are natural and normal feelings. Trust that life will go on, and that in time, you will reestablish your place within it. For now, simply take care of yourself. In a few weeks return to this book or refer to it as needed. Trust that there will be light again and know this book will be here for you in a month or so when you're ready to begin dealing and coping more with your journey through grief.

A Guide for Those Helping Others with Grief
(photocopy and give to close friends and loved ones)

Don't try to find the magic words or formula to eliminate the pain. Nothing can erase or minimize the painful tragedy your friend or loved one is facing. Your primary role at this time is simply to "be there." Don't worry about what to say or do, just be a presence that the person can lean on when needed.

Don't try to minimize or make the person feel better. When we care about someone, we hate to see them in pain. Often we'll say things like, "I know how you feel," or "perhaps, it was for the best," in order to miminize their hurt. While this can work in some instances, it never works with grief.

Help with responsibilities. Even though a life has stopped, life doesn't. One of the best ways to help is to run errands, prepare food, take care of the kids, do laundry and help with the simplest of maintenance.

Don't expect the person to reach out to you. Many people say, "call me if there is anything I can do." At this stage, the person who is grieving will be overwhelmed at the simple thought of picking up a phone. If you are close to this person, simply stop over and begin to help. People need this but don't think to ask. There are many people that will be with you during the good times—but few that are there in life's darkest hour.

Talk through decisions. While working through the grief process many bereaved people report difficulty with decision making. Be a sounding board for your friend or loved one and help them think through decisions.

Don't be afraid to say the name of the deceased. Those who have lost someone usually speak of them often, and believe it or not, need to hear the deceased's name and stories. In fact, many grievers welcome this.

Excerpted from "I Wasn't Ready to Say Good-bye: a guide for surviving, coping and healing after the sudden death of a loved ones" by Brook Noel and Pamela D. Blair, Ph.D. (Champion Press, 2000) www.championpress.com ISBN 1-891400-27-4

Remember that time does not heal all wounds. Your friend or loved one will change because of what has happened. Everyone grieves differently. Some will be "fine" and then experience their true grief a year later, others grieve immediately. There are no timetables, no rules—be patient.

Remind the bereaved to take care of themselves. Eating, resting and self-care are all difficult tasks when beseiged by the taxing emotions of grief. You can help by keeping the house stocked with healthy foods that are already prepared or easy-to-prepare. Help with the laundry. Take over some errands so the bereaved can rest. However, do not push the bereaved to do things they may not be ready for. Many grievers say, "I wish they would just follow my lead." While it may be upsetting to see the bereaved withdrawing from people and activities—it is normal. They will rejoin as they are ready.

Avoid judging. Don't tell the person how to react or handle their emotions or situation. Simply let him/her know that you support their decisions and will help in any way possible.

Share a Meal. Invite the bereaved over regularly to share a meal or take a meal to their home since meal times can be especially lonely. Consider inviting the bereaved out on important dates like the one-month anniversay of the death, the deceased's birthday, etc.

Make a list of everything that needs to be done with the bereaved. This could include everything from bill paying to plant watering. Prioritize these by importance. Help the bereaved complete as many tasks as possible. If there are many responsibilities, find one or more additional friends to support you.

Make a personal commitment to help the one grieving get through this. After a death, many friendships change or disintegrate. People don't know how to relate to the one who is grieving, or they get tired of being around someone who is sad. Vow to see your frriend or loved one through this, to be their anchor in their darkest hour.

Excerpted from "I Wasn't Ready to Say Good-bye: a guide for surviving, coping and healing after the sudden death of a loved ones" by Brook Noel and Pamela D. Blair, Ph.D. (Champion Press, 2000) www.championpress.com ISBN 1-891400-27-4

Chapter Three
Understanding the Emotional
and Physical Affects of Grief

"Shock has rearranged our insides. The disorientation comes from
not yet recognizing the new arrangement. Grief is a molting where we shed the
parts of us that are no longer applicable to the new parts.
It isn't a time to understand anything."
Stephanie Ericsson, Companion Through Darkness

The unexpected loss of someone close to us can quickly turn our world into an unfamiliar place. Coping with what used to be routine, becomes exhausting. The simplest task may seem daunting. Grief affects us not only emotionally, but also physically. When we can understand how grief affects us, we are better equipped to deal with its grip. While we wish we never had to learn or understand these emotions, being aware of them may offer us comfort in our own times of sorrow. A common feeling of people dealing with tragic loss, is the feeling of going crazy. The emotions are so strong and intense, those grieving often think they are the only ones to feel that way or that their feelings are wrong. In the pages to come, we have included many of these emotions. You're not crazy and you're not alone. By understanding these emotions, we take the first step toward realization and thus our first step on the pathway of healing.

In her book, *A Journey Through Grief: Gentle, Specific Help to Get You Through The Most Difficult Stages of Grief*, Alla Reneé Bozarth, Ph.D. writes, "While you are grieving, your emotional life may be unpredictable and unstable. You may feel that there are gaps in your remembered experience...You may alternate between depression and euphoria, between wailing rage and passive resignation...If you've experienced loss and are hurting, it's reasonable that your responses will be unreasonable."

In this chapter, we will explore many of the levels on which grief affects us. Some grievers report feeling many of these pains early on, while others report experiencing them later and still some report few of these experiences. Your relationship to the loved one will make your individual dance with grief different.

Exhaustion

Perhaps the most commonly reported symptom of grief is utter exhaustion and confusion. In her book *Surviving Grief,* Dr. Catherine M. Sanders explains "we become so weak that we actually feel like we have the flu. Because of our lack of experience with energy depletion, this weakness frightens and perplexes us. Before the loss, it happened only when we were sick."

Little things we used to do without thinking, like mailing a letter, can easily become an all day task. Getting a gallon of milk can seem monumental. The thought of getting dressed, driving a car, getting money, paying a cashier, carrying the gallon, driving home—just these thoughts alone, can leave a griever hungry for sleep.

Brook sought the help of a psychotherapist in working through grief. The psychotherapist had a valuable viewpoint on exhaustion.

"When I first went to a psychotherapist to work through some of my own grief issues, her first words to me were simple and powerful. I mention them in the chapter on coping in the first few weeks, but they are so important that I will mention them again here. 'Brook,' she said, 'What has happened here has the same affect on you as if you had gone through major surgery. Consider yourself in intensive care and treat yourself as if you are in intensive care.' Her point hit home. Although emotionally I had experienced a 'triple bypass,' I expected myself to return to jogging the day after. My body was carrying it's own messages of what it needed—and that was rest and extra care."

There are many remedies for exhaustion. People may prescribe vitamin combinations, exercise, eating well, staying busy and more. The suggestion of the psychotherapist is perhaps the most important: *You are in recovery. Give yourself some time to grieve and let the emotions work through you.* If you jump to stay busy now, or sidetrack part of the grieving process, it will only resurface down the road. It's all right to be exhausted and to rest. Take your time to heal. If, however, you have any suicidal thoughts, are not eating, become dehydrated of are suffering any additional serious symptoms, seek professional help immediately. Alternative treatments for fatigue are also listed in Chapter Seventeen.

Days of Distraction

Most people function well in their daily lives. We know how to get things done, stay organized and accomplish what we set out to do. After experiencing a sudden death, it's like we lose the most basic of skills. Those things that we once did with ease become difficult and challenging. Brook found distraction to be a major challenge for her during her first few months of grieving.

> "I remember shortly after Caleb's death, I needed to weigh two envelopes to take to the post office. I have a postage scale in my home office and I always use that to avoid holding up the line at our one-clerk, small-town post office. Well, that day I could not find the scale.
>
> I walked through my office; through my living room. I even checked the kitchen, bedroom and bathroom. Nothing. Off and on throughout the day, I would repeat my search. For three hours, I scanned the house for that scale. Finally, in frustration, I threw my hands up and decided just to have the items weighed at the post office.
>
> When I returned, I walked into my office and there on my desk was the scale. It had been sitting there the entire time, covered by nothing. It was in an area I had stared directly at for hours, yet I had not seen it. This is the type of distraction that often accompanies grief.
>
> I noticed on these days, I didn't always feel down or sad, but when I was trying to cope with grief and didn't have an

outlet, situations like this would occur. Many of these "days of distraction" occurred a couple of months after Caleb's death. They became an alarm for me. During these days, I would quit trying to do so much and instead, relax and work through my grief.

I had a similar challenge one day while trying to pay a bill. For an hour, I couldn't find my checkbook. When I finally found my checkbook, I had lost the bill that I wanted to pay. The cat-and-mouse search continued a few more times and before I knew it an entire day had passed while simply attempting to mail out a single payment. When at first this happened, I would push myself and try to keep going. By the end of the day I was often near tears from frustration."

These moments of distraction are signals from your body that you *must* slow down. No matter how small the task, it is too much for you right now. Be careful not to overburden yourself. Lower your expectations. Know that you will be able to function like you once did—but it takes time—it takes recovery.

Grief Knows No Schedule

In today's world we have grown accustomed to scheduling so much of life. Most of us own at least one organizer or appointment book. Yet grief is one thing that will never fit in an appointment-square. You may find there are times when you are in the midst of a normal, pleasant activity and suddenly a wash of grief comes over you. Know that this is common and that grief can surface at any time, without notice. Both of us experienced the common "ambush" of grief.

"I remember watching a television comedy with my husband. I had been laughing throughout the show and it had been a while since I shed tears over Caleb's death. Then there was an ad to solicit funds for needy children—the theme song was *Amazing Grace.*

The day before we cremated Caleb, we held a small viewing for his closest friends and family. We had given the pastor no instruction and the pastor sang that song. I had been driven to tears then, and I was driven to tears again as I watched the ad on television. A year and a half later, I was walking on Bourbon street in New Orleans when I heard a street performer singing *Amazing Grace*. I had tears in my eyes then as well."

Pam had a similar experience...

"George was a Beatles fan. Many months after he died, while in a fast food restaurant and mid-bite of my hamburger, the piped-in music started with John Lennon's *Imagine* and a nail went into my heart."

There is so little of life we control. Grief's timing is among the uncontrollable. Expect experiences, similar to these, frequently over the first three to six months (the frequency is often based on how close you were to the deceased). Over the course of a year, they will lessen, but they may still happen from time to time.

Physical Symptoms

When grief covers us with its dark wings, it is much like a serious illness. We will be emotionally and physically depleted and a variety of symptoms will follow. It is important to be aware of these symptoms, however, so we don't think we are going crazy. These symptoms will pass as we work through our grief. If you find any symptom to be overwhelming or unbearable, contact a professional. Here are some of the commonly reported symptoms:

chest pain	dizziness
sleep difficulties	dry mouth
poor appetite or overeating	crying
shakiness or trembling	exhaustion or weakness
numbness	shortness of breath
disorientation	listlessness
migraines or headache	heart palpitations

Grief and Dreams

Some people have dreams of the deceased and others do not. Each of our subconscious minds cope with life differently. You probably know people who remember their dreams and others who rarely remember a thing. Similarly, how grief affects us in our dream world varies. If you don't have dreams of the deceased, don't worry.

If You Don't Dream

In *Intuition* magazine, Marlene King wrote an article entitled, "The Surrogate Dreamers: One couple's gift to a grieving friend." Marlene invited a couple she knew over for a casual Saturday night barbecue. The next night, Stephen, the 44-year-old husband of the couple died of heart failure while dancing with his wife. Over the next week Marlene helped her friend with details surrounding the tragic death. Marlene writes, "It was during this period that Janice told me she hoped to connect with Stephen through her dreams, but no dreams had come. Knowing that emotions often block us physically, I reassured her that her dreams would return, when she was less emotionally fragile."

A few days after this conversation, Marlene dreamt of Stephen. She saw him dressed in a tuxedo. She felt this odd, since Stephen usually dressed casually. She goes on to say, "I reported the dream to Janice...the absolute silence and lack of response on the other end of the phone made me question whether I was right to tell her about the dream. Unknown to me, she had elected to have Stephen cremated the day before, and had chosen to dress him in the same clothing he wore in my dream. For a while after that, it was as though my husband and I became Janice's 'surrogate dreamers.' Our love for her seemed to open us up to the dream communication that was temporarily unavailable to Janice due to her shattered emotional state."

If you find that you are not having dreams, know that this is normal. Our emotions can be so turbulent during these times that we are cut off from our dream source. Listen to others close to you. Listen to family and friends. What dreams are they having? If they don't bring it up, ask if you like. These dreams can carry messages for you as well.

If You Do Dream

Consider keeping a dream journal. Many people believe that dreams following closely after death are the deceased making contact. These dreams may be ones that you want to cherish and hold. If you remember your dreams, spend ten minutes each morning jotting down thoughts and impressions in your dream journal. If you only remember pieces of your dream, jot those down. Often just a few notes will spur other recollections.

Dreams of your deceased loved one can open up new avenues to healing, but you may not be aware you are having dreams or they may be hard to remember. One way to keep the dream upon waking is to keep still—don't move a muscle—don't get up to go to the bathroom or turn on the light. Start with any dream fragment that comes to your conscious mind and try to piece the entire dream back together. Or, simply write down the dream fragment and the rest may come back later in the day. In her book, *Nature's Prozac*, Judith Sachs offers the following thoughts on remembering dreams, "Before you go to sleep at night, put a pad and pen on your bedside table. Tell yourself you are going to remember your dreams (this suggestion may take a few nights to penetrate.) As you relax in bed, give yourself permission to explore all the areas of your mind that you don't pay enough attention to during the day. We tend to be in REM sleep just before waking, so it's best to set your radio alarm to a soft music station rather than to the news or hard rock. This way you can wake slowly and take stock of what's going on in your mind."

Troublesome Dreams

Some grievers report nightmares or troublesome dreams. These dreams may involve a direct conflict between the dreamer and the deceased. Other times the dreamer may envision the deceased dying or in pain.

With sudden death we often have very little information. Dreams are where our subconscious mind works things through. If you awake from an unpleasant dream, realize it is your subconscious mind prompting you. Recall as much as you can. Try to fill in the blanks. Examine the dream the best you can. If you find it hard to face these dreams or have problems being objective, ask a trusted friend or psychotherapist to review them with you. Keeping a dream journal can also help you to make sense of troublesome dreams.

Another way to handle disturbing dreams is to try to "re-program" them. Think through your upsetting dream. Try to find the point within the dream where things become upsetting. Choose a different ending that would make you more comfortable. Visualize the dream playing out this way in your mind several times, especially before going to sleep. This can help change or diminish the dream's impact.

If nightmares are a problem, over-the-counter or prescription medications could be the cause. According to medical researcher, Judith Sachs, if you are taking sleeping medications such as barbiturates or benzodiazepines (for anti-anxiety) these can give you nightmares. Additionally, some people have reported anti-depressants as causing vivid and shocking dreams. Also, getting off drugs can give you nightmares. So make sure you withdraw under a doctor's supervision and mention any side effects.

Communication Dreams

If you are a person who does dream, keep in mind that these dreams can be quite varied. Some may be peaceful and others may be disturbing. As you move through the process of grief your subconscious mind will respond in varied and surprising ways. Brook had an intriguing dream shortly after her brother's death...

"I had my first dream three weeks after Caleb's death, which I was told was surprisingly soon, and I have had many since. I think that since I try so hard to be the foundation for others, I work through a lot of my grief and feelings in my sleep.

Three weeks after Caleb's death, my book on single parenting was due. In an attempt to meet the deadline I took three days to curl up in a hotel and get some solid writing done. I usually stay up until one or two when I'm on my writing escapades. Yet on this night, I had an overwhelming feeling to lie down and read some of my notes. I plopped onto the bed, my feet propped up on the pillows and my head near the bottom. I still had my contact lenses in, and being only 9:00pm I knew I'd get at least five more hours of work in before calling it a night.

The next thing I knew it was 6:45 a.m. I was in the exact same place on the bed and I had dreamt of my brother.

We were in our childhood home in northern Wisconsin. Our rooms, as in reality when we were kids, were directly across from one another. I was in my room, as I had been during the week I had stayed up north after Caleb's death. In the dream I was fully aware that my brother was dead, and I was grieving it with my entire soul.

Suddenly there was the familiar thud of footsteps down the hallway. Caleb's, no doubt. At first, I peered out my door a bit nervously. I could see Caleb standing in his room. Every detail of his face, body and clothing were clear to me. Caleb was wearing the clothes he had been cremated in. He was rutting around in his room with a sort of frustrated look. Then he saw me, 'Brook, where are all my clothes?' he asked, peering into his duffel bag.

I stood rigid. I knew he was dead, yet I knew he was there. 'Caleb, you're dead.' I said simply.

He looked up and said he knew that, but that he had to take care of a few things. First, however, he wanted to change his clothes.

'Where are you going?' I asked.

'I'm just going to see a few people,' he said grabbing something off his desk, though I couldn't tell what it was.

'Caleb,' I said gently, 'I don't think that's a good idea. Everyone thinks you're dead. And, well, you might scare some people.'

'Really?' He asked, with his head titled in an inquisitive look.

'Caleb, don't leave without hugging me,' I said, tears filling my eyes. My brother took me in his strong arms. 'You cannot go,' I repeated; 'Everyone thinks that you are dead. Please don't go—I'll never see you again.'

He tilted my head up toward his and wiped a wisp of hair away from my face. Staring straight into my eyes with his little smirk he said, 'You poor little children.' In that moment I knew he was saying he lived on, though I never understood in what way.

Feeling somewhat foggy, I got up and slowly moved around the room. I had this feeling of incredible closeness with Caleb—so close I was tingling. Over the course of my writing weekend I had brought one large box that I wanted to go through during my breaks. Inside were photos, papers and other miscellaneous things from Caleb's desk drawers. I wanted to sort through and divide up the photos for his friends and find any estate paperwork. At that point, I had yet to open the container.

I walked over and opened the box. I reached in and pulled out a picture of Caleb. I reached in again and pulled out a card. On the inside of the card was a quote in Caleb's handwriting. The quote was taken from Jonathan Livingston Seagull:

'If our friendship depends on things like space and time,
then we have already destroyed our brotherhood.

But overcome space and all you have is here;
Overcome time and all you have is now.

And in the middle of here and now
Don't you think we might see each other once or twice...'

To this day, when I recount this dream, people ask me what I think it meant. Many want to know if I feel I had actual contact with my brother or if that was Caleb trying to speak to me. All I can say is that for a night when we should have been the furthest apart—separated by death and the unknown—I had never felt closer to him."

Feeling the Presence of the Deceased

Feeling the presence of the deceased is similar to a "phantom limb" syndrome, which is experienced after someone loses a limb. Many grievers feel like they have lost a part of themselves. Some spouses feel the deceased's presence in bed. Hearing footsteps, smelling that person's scent, hearing a voice or seeing a fleeting image of the deceased is common during the grief process. Often this occurs as we try to rationalize and understand what is happening. Is someone sending us a message? Are we being told something? Are we "losing" it?

In her book *Surviving Grief*, Dr. Catherine M. Sanders writes about the flicker phenomenon, "a perception seen at the outside edges of our visual field as a flickering shadow. Immediately, thoughts of the deceased come to mind, but when we look directly at that area, nothing is there."

These sightings or feelings may well be the deceased trying to comfort us, trying to get through somehow. When we try to rationalize and make sense of these experiences, we rob them of their magic. Just as we don't understand why these unexpected deaths occur, we must try not to overanalyze these moments—simply let them offer comfort.

The World Becomes Dreamlike

Many people who have lost someone suddenly, find the world becomes a surreal place. It's almost as if we are floating without seeing or comprehending. Everything becomes a blur as the concept of time disappears. Days are measured by: one day after he died, two days after he died...all standard concepts fade away. Some have described it as slogging through molasses, a slow motion movie, a feeling like they are not in their body. Perhaps this is nature's way of slowing us down to heal.

Helen Fitzgerald, author of *The Mourning Handbook* writes, "During this initial period of grief you will feel a numbness and a disassociation with the world around you. People who are going through this often tell me that they feel as if they are watching a play in which they are but spectators. Others feel that what has happened is only a bad dream from which they will wake up to find everything back to normal." Know that this is part of the body coping with tragic loss. Our bodies and minds know better than to dump us back into reality after such an intense blow. Therefore we are nudged slowly, step-by-step, back into day-to-day life. Much of the world will remain out of focus, allowing us to gather our bearings one step at a time.

A Time to Withdraw

Many people will experience a state of numbness while moving through grief. The world may take on a dreamlike quality or seem to go on separate from them. Often experiences or people that once evoked joy and happiness evoke nothing at all. Activities once enjoyed seem foreign.

Some people spend a relatively short time in this numb state, as short as a few days, while others find it lingers. This is part of how our bodies help to protect us from the overwhelming emotions caused by our loved one's death. We become numb and filter through information as we are able, instead of all at once. The feelings will come back, but it will take time.

Hand-in-hand with exhaustion, performing our day-to-day activities, even if they are ones we used to enjoy, may seem overwhelming. Most people are not able to maintain a variety of interests immediately after this shock. Do not make expectations for yourself to do everything. Instead, look at your commitments and try to minimize. Contact event or group coordinators to let them know that you will be taking some time off, indefinitely. For example, if you are part of your child's home and school program, a softball coach or part of a regular bowling league—take a break. At this point you need only focus on working through these hard times. Minimize the expectations on yourself to avoid adding to your stress.

This advice runs contrary to what many will say. Many people will urge you to "stay involved," "take on more," "try something new," or "get back in the swing of things." Yet this advice doesn't make sense. If you don't have the energy or focus to take care of yourself, why should you be taking on additional responsibilities? Sure, they may take your mind off of your grief for a short period—but you still have to do your grieving. There simply is no bypass.

Impulsive Living

While some grievers withdraw, others will compulsively pursue activities. The thought process often goes like this, "Life is short. I'd better do everything now that I always wanted to do... spend all the money, sell the house and move to Hawaii, write that book, divorce my wife, etc." Others will take unnecessary risks.

It's imperative to carefully monitor your behavior during the first year. Do not make impulsive decisions. Do not sell your house, change locations, divorce a partner., etc. Wait until the fog has lifted and you can clearly see the options available to you.

Instant Replays and Obsessive Thoughts

At some point in our grief work, we are likely to find ourselves recounting the days with our loved one in our minds. We may also play out different scenarios of the death, trying to understand what has happened. For some, the review completely preoccupies the mind, and despite our wishes we can think of nothing else.

As is the case with post traumatic stress disorder, you may find yourself living and reliving the experiences you had with your loved one during the days, hours or minutes just before the death occurred. "If only I had not taken that road...If only I had said 'don't go...' If only I had been there I might have prevented the accident..." and on and on.

With the first news of loss, our mind acts as a filter. It immediately sifts through the facts and details offering only the barest to keep us informed. Too much detail would be more than we could bear. So our mind filters and filters until our bodies and hearts can cope with a little more. At some point, when the body has recovered somewhat, the mind lets larger blocks of information in. At this point, by human instinct, we look for resolution. We struggle to make sense of what has happened and that is where the instant replay begins. We explore every option—even the outlandish. These explorations are what allow us to slowly internalize the fact that life, as we once knew it, has changed.

This is a pivotal point in the grieving process. At this point, or close to it, we are finally acknowledging the death in reality.

The "If Only" Mind Game

"If only" is the game of guilt that plagues many survivors. The "if only" questions surface intensely in cases of unexpected death. The situation is so "out of control" that our human nature fights and searches for a way to control the uncontrollable. As we yearn to make sense of the senseless, often the only route of control we find is to blame ourselves.

"I should have known," or "If only I had talked to him for two minutes longer..." are sentiments that those who grieve may say to themselves. Realize this guilt is a way of trying to gain control over the uncontrollable and then work to let it go. Each time it enters, remember that this is our longing for control, but don't give in to the guilt. You cannot change what has happened and odds are you couldn't have changed it beforehand. No one knows these things are going to happen—no one has that much control. Brook found that she ran on the "I should've known" treadmill.

> "I have talked with many of the people surviving the loss of a loved one and in every situation the one who is grieving can somehow tie blame to themselves. Even with my brother's case, where it was such a freak accident, we could all find ways that we "should have known" or "should have been able to prevent it." Yet as each of us told our stories of prevention, others could see there were simply too many holes. None of us could have stopped what occurred."

Don't run yourself around this wheel of pain. If you find that you cannot stop trying to tie the blame to yourself, relay your story to a professional counselor, therapist or pastor. *While we grieve, we are not objective.* These professionals can help us to see how unrealistic and unfounded these thoughts are.

Anger

Who wouldn't be angry when someone they loved so dearly is suddenly taken from them? Anger is natural in this situation and is actually a healthy part of the grieving process. Yet anger takes different forms, some of them healthy and some of them unhealthy.

Let's examine the types of anger that are natural, though unhealthy. Some of us will express anger when we are not getting the support we need from friends, family or work. While intensely wrapped in our grief, we usually don't think to ask for support. Instead we lash out at those close to us with hostility, irritability and anger. If we can recognize this anger for what it is, we can use it in a healthy way. This can be our cue that we are not receiving the support that we need. We need to ask for more or seek out other support networks.

Displaced anger is simply misdirected anger. We want someone to take responsibility for what has happened. We need someone to blame and to be held accountable. We may scream or yell at those who cared for the person at the hospital. We may become angry with those who were with the person when he died. Displaced anger is completely natural and will lessen as you learn to accept what has happened.

Anger can also surface when we recall past moments or turmoil, pain or unresolved anger within our relationship with the person we have lost. Suddenly we are forced to realize we will never share another physical interaction with this person. When that happens, memories flood through. Within these memories there are bound to be recollections of feisty exchanges, arguments and past hurts. Wishing we had more time with the loved one, we may over-criticize ourselves for any time there was conflict in the past. It is unrealistic, however, to expect perfection in any relationship. Immersing ourselves in the "should haves" and "could haves" of the past will only prevent us from dealing effectively with anger in the present.

Anger also occurs when we suppress our feelings. Anger is not the most accepted emotion in today's culture. In fact, many people don't even recognize anger as part of the grieving process. Depending on our support network and situation we may be encouraged not to show our anger. When this happens, the anger still exists and needs to be released, so it is released inward. This can cause a variety of problems. We may become sick, depressed, have chronic pain or begin having nightmares. Begin to look at healthy alternatives for releasing this anger.

Anger is especially common with tragic deaths. Since we could do nothing to stop or prevent the loss, and are left only to interpret it, we may become frustrated and develop feelings of helplessness. Bouts of crying are the most common release for this anger. It's easy to not release this anger and to turn it inward. If you suspect you may be doing so, talk to a friend or counselor to help release these feelings.

Appropriate anger is the point that we all hope to get to eventually. In this phase we can take our anger, in whatever form, and vent it. There are many ways to release anger appropriately. Here are a few...

- beat a pillow
- create a sacred space where you can go and not be heard or seen to let the anger out of your system
- use journaling to record and release your angry feelings
- take a walk out into an unpopulated area and scream until you are exhausted
- talk with a friend, therapist or counselor
- see the appendix for other ideas

Fear

Throughout our grief work, fear can be debilitating. Some people experience fear in a small number of areas, while others are overwhelmed by it. It is perfectly natural to be fearful. We have experienced the most unexpected tragedy. Common fears include: fearing any situation that remotely resembles how the loved one died, fearing that others we love will be harmed, fearing we will be unable to go on, fearing we will die ourselves and fearing the simplest activities will lead to tragedy.

Fear serves several purposes. In the initial stages of grief it gives us something to focus on besides the death that has taken place. It also offers potential control. If we fear that riding in a car could kill us, and choose not to ride in a car, we create the illusion of control. As explained earlier, with tragic death it's common to seek any control we can find. Most of the time, fear will run its course naturally. If you find that you have any fear that is, or is becoming, debilitating, talk to a professional.

As you think about this chapter, remember that grief will be a unique experience for each one of us. If you experience symptoms that aren't listed here, or less symptoms, that is okay and normal. What is important to remember, is that you need to work through these feelings. Sometimes we will require another person's help. Monitor yourself on the path through grief. You know, in your heart of hearts, whether you are walking down the path or stuck at the beginning or middle. There are many things we must face in life alone, grief need not be one of them when we reach out to one another.

Chapter Four
The World is Upside Down

"The doorbell rang at around eight-thirty. I wasn't expecting anyone, so a strange feeling came over my heart. I peeked out the keyhole, and saw my brother, Denver, and sister-in-law, Allison, standing in the hallway. I let them in. There was a deep silence, and I knew from my brother's eyes what had happened. He didn't even have to speak. He took me in his arms, and my world changed forever. My eyes moved to a picture of my son as a child, his red hair cropped close to his head, and his big blue eyes looking out at me. My world was turning to darkness, and I would never live in it the same again."
- Singer Judy Collins on the death of her son, Clark

"I can remember staring at the sun that day and watching it fade behind the trees. I remember wishing with everything in me that the sun wouldn't go down. I knew this was the end of the last day where I had known my son alive," said one mother. Yet as the sun sets on our days with our loved one, the world takes on a new look and we are forced to question our place within it.

Many grievers report feelings of everything feeling "upside down" or "wrong." In a matter of seconds, we learned that the world has changed and will never again be the same. A stage of shock follows. Unlike a terminal death where people may prepare affairs and make arrangements in advance, those facing sudden death are forced to deal with all of these things immediately. Questions and loss of purpose follow as we are forced to interpret and understand death at a time when we are not remotely prepared to do so. Spiritual questions and reassessment of one's religious faith may also occur. In this chapter we will look at the ways in which our world is turned upside down and some ideas on how to cope during this confusing time.

Assumptions are Shattered

When we grapple with sudden loss, we are forced to reconsider some assumptions about ourselves. We may begin to feel vulnerable and a sense that life is tenuous. We may begin to question whether or not the world is meaningful and orderly. We may see ourselves as weak and needy for the first time. Those who haven't had to deal with the trauma of sudden death may also come to question these assumptions, but they are not *forced* to question the basic truth of these assumptions in the same way a survivor must.

We are all forced to confront our mortality. Most people deal with this issue in mid-life. It is then that we begin to see signs of our own aging or we face the imminent death of our parents or grandparents. This is the natural order of things. However, as survivors of sudden death we are forced to confront our mortality at the time of the trauma—regardless of our age. A heightened sense of the fundamental fragility of life quickly emerges—usually within minutes, hours or days of the death.

Aphrodite Matsakis, Ph.D. says in her book, *Trust After Trauma*, "...although it can empower them to try to make the most out of life, it can also be frightening and overwhelming not only to themselves, but also to others who, quite understandably, prefer to avoid confronting the inevitability of their own deaths."

You may have thought, "It can't happen to me." But it did happen and you may no longer feel the world is a safe place. Feelings of vulnerability can bring on a sense of doom or an expectation that your own future may be foreshortened. You may also experience an intense fear that the trauma may repeat itself and another family member, lover or friend will die.

Dr. Matsakis goes on to say, "The just world philosophy cannot explain what happened to you. You used to think that if you were careful, honest, and good, you could avoid disaster. But the trauma taught you that all your best efforts could not prevent the worst from happening. Perhaps you saw others who were also innocent die or be unfairly injured. So, while you would like to believe that the world is orderly, and that good is rewarded and evil is punished, you had an experience that contradicts these beliefs."

When our foundation is swept from beneath us, we begin questioning the fundamentals of life. As crazy as it seems, this shattering of assumptions is necessary in grief. *We must re-evaluate what we once held as true, move through the ruin and create a new foundation based on what we have learned.*

When Faith is Shattered

If our spiritual faith has been shattered, perhaps all we can expect from the grieving process is some form of transcendence. Gail Sheehy describes this beautifully in her seminal work entitled, *Pathfinders*, where she writes, "Transcendence is a realm beyond all the negative emotions of mourning, beyond even the neutral point of acceptance. When it happens that a life accident creates a pathfinder, the person is able to transcend his former self as well. A positive self-fulfilling prophecy is made as one comes out of the dark hours. And around a new work, idea, purpose, faith, or a love inspired by the accident, one's goals are realigned. Transcendence is an act of creativity. One creates a partial replacement for what has been lost. The light at the end of mourning is glimpsed, and it is cause for new joy."

It's common to question God in these dark times. We may lose faith in God, a faith we thought would never change or waiver. In *The Grief Recovery Handbook*, John W. James and Russell Freidman write, "We have to be allowed to tell someone that we're angry at God and not be judged for it, or told that we're bad because of it. If not, this anger may persist forever and block spiritual growth. We've known people who never returned to their religion because they weren't allowed to express their true feelings. If this happens, the griever is cut off from one of the most powerful sources of support he or she might have."

For most of us, this loss of faith is temporary and if we ask our clergy person or faith community, they should willingly help us with this struggle. It is common for grievers to yell, scream at God or lose faith. One should not feel guilty for such emotions. Like many other aspects of grief, this is part of our need as we work through the process. Even Pam's faith was tested during her experience with sudden loss…

"I remember walking up and down the halls of the hospital where George lay on life support, shaking my fist at Heaven, yelling at God. Someone who overheard suggested that I not be angry with God and that I control how I speak to Him. I replied, 'My God can handle this anger. And I know if I get angry at God, God won't desert me.'"

The following anonymous poem can be comforting to recite when we are feeling lost and our faith is being tried.

Prayer of Faith

We trust that beyond absence
There is a presence.

That beyond the pain
there can be healing.

That beyond the brokenness
there can be wholeness.

That beyond the anger
there may be peace.

That beyond the hurting
there may be forgiveness.

That beyond the silence
there may be the Word.

That beyond the Word
there may be understanding.

That through understanding
there is love.

- author unknown

Loss of Purpose

Many grievers feel a loss of purpose. After all, we've known a life that is certain. We were certain that a person would be there, we never questioned. Suddenly, all we have left are questions—questions like: Why did this happen? If a person can die so suddenly—what is the purpose of trying to accomplish and trying to live? Brook battled this concept in the wake of Caleb's death.

"I have always been an over-achiever. I scheduled and organized my life so I could climb mountain after mountain in search of reaching some higher place. When Caleb died, I wondered what the purpose of all the climbing was. I suddenly realized there was no guarantee I would live to be seventy—or even another week. So what was the purpose of all this sowing—if the chance to reap could be taken away?

Lost inside this question, I turned to a wonderful friend and my local pastor, Jeff. We often had lunch together and I always found comfort in his words. I stared at him across the table, and said simply— 'What does anything matter?' He relayed a sentence, which was a riddle in itself. He simply said, 'Because nothing matters, everything matters.' I tried over lunch to comprehend the sentence as it twirled through my mind. Finally, I asked him to interpret further.

Jeff explained that looking long term or planning ahead cannot matter. Sure we need to be somewhat prepared for the future, but to become overly preoccupied is foolish since life can disappear so quickly. 'Everything you do at this very instant is what matters,' he explained. 'You should be living life, right now. Anyone who lives for tomorrow is a fool.' At the time, I had been juggling a few thoughts on where to go with my writing career and what project to pursue next. The thought of having a whole book in front of me seemed daunting and purposeless. I was scared to start something, scared perhaps that I would never finish it. Jeff asked me what mattered most at that very moment. "Getting by," was my reply. As our eyes met, I knew that was what mattered. I would write about getting by because that meant something to me, and if life went away tomorrow, I would be content in where I was today."

Since nothing of the future matters, everything in the here and now does. To learn to live in the present, to reap the gifts of the moment is the best tribute we can give to anyone, much less ourselves.

Redefining Ourselves

When we lose someone, we often lose a piece of ourselves. The closer our relationship with the person, the more of our self we have to redefine. Much of our identity comes from our relationship to others. Take the woman who has called herself a wife and mother for 30 years and then loses her family in a plane crash. This woman whose identity was wife and mother, is left without a husband or children. Defining ourselves by others can bring fullness to our lives, but when faced with loss it also means we must redefine the resulting emptiness.

One of the first things to remember as you seek your own redefinition is that you don't need to know all the answers now. No one will force you or hold "a clock to your head" asking you to redefine yourself over night. This is a process. It involves soul-searching, courage and rediscovery. It takes time. Realize that you don't have to let go of who you were—you just need to adapt for the future. In the case above, the mentioned woman will always know what it was like to be a wife and a mother. For the rest of her life, she will act as a wife and mother in her thoughts and actions because that is what she was for 30 years. Even though life turns itself upside down and our role may change suddenly, we can't deny the way we have lived in the past.

Simply stated, the question becomes, "Now what?" After expecting life to take a certain course, it has chosen it's own, far from your plans. Again, take it slow. Choose one thing that you know for certain. If you have always loved to paint, know that in the future you can still be a painter. Focus on what you do know about yourself. Look at the things you've always wanted to try and pick one to focus on. Take it one step at a time, and as you're ready, add another "piece" to yourself.

For some this rebuilding takes months, for others it can take a lifetime, but piece-by-piece you can rebuild. When you are ready to begin the rebuilding process, turn to the Exercises Chapter for ideas to get you started.

What Matters?

Earlier in this chapter, we looked at the question of purpose and the paradox of how all that matters is the very present. With that being the case, we must then turn to our priorities, goals and dreams in order to find a way to live a content lifestyle.

Many people wonder "What's life for anyway?" after losing someone tragically. All the dreams and goals we make for tomorrow seem pointless if we focus on the fact that they can be torn away without notice. "Why live for tomorrow, when it may not exist?" asked one man. In some form or another, many of us can relate to his question.

Each of us is forced to venture down our own soul path and do our own exploring. We must re-evaluate our priorities. If spending time with our family is important, then we should start now. We shouldn't work so hard in hopes of that "better day" when family can be our only focus. Instead, we must learn to incorporate our priorities, needs and dreams into our daily lives.

What are your priorities? What matters? How could you live differently? Most importantly, how could you make every day count? In many ways, the best tribute we can give to the deceased is to allow them the impact of permanently changing our lives. Allow your life to fluctuate in form. Allow your priorities and loves to surface—and then live by them. When we do this, we are offering the greatest tribute to the one we have lost. In this way, we are showing them that though they have gone, they have changed our life and allowed us to live more fully. Think about that. If you were to die tomorrow, could you think of any better legacy to leave behind than the power of helping others live more complete lives?

Finding a Beginning, Middle and End

Questions abound, when we lose someone tragically. Unlike those who lose someone through a terminal illness, we have little or no time to question doctors, understand a diagnosis, struggle with our faith or say our goodbyes.

Yet through our upbringing we learn to understand life in terms of cycles. We understand the cycle of age. We know the cycle of schooling.

We know the cycle of work. We know the cycles of diet and exercise. Almost everything can be understood as a cycle with a beginning, middle and end. Our minds will immediately try to do the same with our tragic loss experience. Our mind will look for the beginning (What happened?), the middle (How did he/she feel, respond, progress?), the end (Was he in pain? Did he have any last thoughts or words?) Yet unless we were present, we are left with question after question. In order to get to a place where we can think about the experience in its entirety, we must know as much of the cycle as possible.

This is why it is so natural to talk with others about our loved one's last moments. Over and over again, grievers tell their stories, attempting to make sense of them, attempting to understand the cycle. Often, there are ways to get more information. Police, witnesses and doctors can all offer clues to what happened. When we have enough clues we can piece together a story that will allow our questioning to lessen. As our questions lessen, we create more room to heal.

Dr. Ann Kaiser Stearns, author of *Coming Back: Rebuilding Lives After Crisis and Loss* offers the following suggestion: "Make a conscious effort to identify what is not making sense to you about your loss or crisis. You might ask yourself: What is it about the situation and/or about his or her death that is most puzzling or troubling to me? What part of grief is troubling me? What other things are troubling me?"

Before seeking your own beginning, middle and end, this can be a useful exercise. Confront your questions. Explore your feelings and record these thoughts. Use this as a guideline to gather the information you will need.

Brook found that she and her mother had many questions.

"For starters, my mother and I had never heard of the term anaphylactic shock—we couldn't even pronounce it. Our initial disbelief was so strong, not a single question was asked at the hospital. But as the days went by, the questions came one after the other. *Caleb had been stung a month before—was this a cumulative effect of venom? A long time ago he had chest pains that went undiagnosed—could his death be connected to that? Had any blood been drawn and a firm allergic reaction determined? If his death certificate said 12:54 and his friends said he was unconscious at 11:15—what happened between then and 12:54?*

I did as much research as I could and then I called the doctor. I immediately put him at rest by letting him know that I trusted he had done everything in his capacity, and I did not, in any way, question his ability. I let the doctor know that my questions were more about figuring out the order of events. We talked for close to an hour.

After combining his comments with my research, I was able to confidently assume that Caleb did die from a fatal reaction to a bee sting. He was dead before the ambulance arrived, or minutes after, and unconscious long before that. He was not pronounced dead until 12:54 because the doctors were praying for a miracle. Being so young and healthy, they worked extensively on him in the E.R. trying anything they could to revive him.

I also was able to learn that bee allergies are typically not hereditary. However, I also learned, those who know they are allergic can carry an Epinephrine shot, that can possibly reverse the reaction or allow more time to get treatment.

With this knowledge and for my own peace of mind, I went to a specialist in the allergy field. I asked the allergist to test both my three-year-old daughter and myself. He took our blood and sent it to the Mayo clinic for analysis. The tests came back negative. Yet, since this allergy can develop at any time, he gave us both adrenaline kits so that we would feel more at ease. While only 40-60 people a year die from fatal reactions to insects, it was important for me to have that comfort."

Talking to others will help you get the information you need to find your own beginning, middle and end. This information-gathering can be a major catalyst in moving past the grief of "what happened?" to the process of rebuilding. It allows the mind to cycle through the event in its entirety, instead of stopping to question and get lost in the who, what, when, where, why and how.

Why did this happen?

Every griever is bound to question fate and the heavens, wondering: Why did this have to happen? There are, of course, no concrete answers. We can speculate. We can try to create reasons to offer comfort to ourselves and our family—but in the end, we just don't know. Perhaps this is one of the hardest parts about losing someone so unexpectedly. In our Western world we are so accustomed to having the answers. We know $2 + 2 = 4$. We know that we can send a spacecraft to the moon and back. We know that our 401K possesses X value or that our gardens will certainly begin to bloom in May. We are a culture that seeks answers and rarely rests without them.

Yet here, we face the challenge of accepting that there is no answer, at this point in time. To leave it be "only questions" is one of the most challenging demands of grief work. As poet Rainer Marie Rilke eloquently states, "Live the questions now. Perhaps you will then gradually, without noticing it, live along some distant day into the answer."

Brook eventually garnered the trust that someday she would understand.

"Many have asked me where that trust was birthed. It came from many nights of trying to figure it out. I mapped out every possibility, every sequence of why this might have happened. None of them brought answers. In fact, few of them brought comfort. Eventually, I realized I was getting nowhere. The only way to get somewhere was to surrender to the fact that I did not know the answers. It is hard to surrender, to quit seeking, to accept the unknown.

One night I simply laid my heart at the foot of the universe. I said to the earth, to the world, 'I do not understand this and I am ready to quit trying to understand. I am ready to accept that the universe knows more than I, and that I will understand as I am ready. Until then, I ask that I am granted peace.'

Peace didn't come overnight, but it did come. And with it came a renewed faith. But it was a different faith than what I had once known. It is a faith that someone is standing by me or over me and will lead me to what I must know as I must know it. It is a faith where I surrender the unknown without expectation. I trust the process and that all will unfold in its own time."

Chapter Five
The Stages of Grief

"We don't 'get over' the deepest pains of life, nor should we. 'Are you over it?' is a question that cannot be asked by someone who has been through 'it,' whatever 'it' is. It's an anxious question, an asking for reassurance that cannot be given. During an average lifetime there are many pains, many grieves to be borne. We don't 'get over' them; we learn to live with them, to go on growing and deepening, and understanding..."
Madeleine L'Engle, Sold Into Egypt

It's hard to acknowledge that healing or recovery of any kind is possible when you find yourself on an emotional roller coaster. The stages of grief are confounding in intensity and different for everyone. Our wish is not to talk to you or at you, but to be with you...as people who have made the journey—from loss to self discovery—from acute to managed grief—from one end of the maze to another. We hope you will gain some acceptance of yourself in reading this chapter and that as a result, you will feel less crazy and more normal.

The five stages of grief commonly referred to are based on the work of Elisabeth Kübler-Ross and describe a dying person's reality as they go through the process of death. The stages are:

denial and isolation

anger

bargaining

depression

acceptance

These stages only partially apply to a survivor of sudden death. In addition to these stages, the survivor of sudden death will experience many more stages and rages that need to be worked through. Yet, grievers usually experience the five stages as well, in one form or another. We will begin by explaining these stages but be aware that you won't necessarily experience every stage and you may not experience them in a linear or sequential fashion. In the initial stages you may find that you bounce around among a variety of different emotions.

The research shows, and is corroborated by our observations, that the active grieving period when you have lost someone to a lingering death lasts about two to five years, depending on the work one does in recovery. In lingering death there is pre-death grieving, so that by the time the actual death has occurred, family and friends have already been grieving for a period of time. Sudden death presents a different scenario. With sudden death the various stages can be compressed into a single hour, minute or day.

In reality, grieving is more like a maze of emotions than an elevator that starts at the bottom and arrives at the penthouse of joy. Like in a maze, we go forward a bit and then back over the same territory. If we learn to love and accept ourselves even as we are emotionally "a-maze-ing", we may begin to see our humanness and our brokenness as a threshold to personal growth. In any case, it is important to assure yourself, no matter how "crazy" and lost in the maze you may feel, that you do come out on the other side, and that you are not alone.

Shock...the first step in recovery

In the first week or so you will probably feel stunned and overwhelmed. You may also feel numb or hysterical. Your emotional system shuts down providing temporary insulation from the full impact of your loss. You will go through the motions, it will look like you're coping well sometimes.

In her book, *The Worst Loss*, Barbara D. Rosof writes, "In shock you may be unable to move or speak coherently; people report that they cannot think. Shock responses may also be active and intense; you may have screamed, or run from the room, or physically attacked the bringer of the news. All of these behaviors are means of shutting down, or distancing yourself from a reality that you do not yet have a way to deal with. As you look back, your behavior may seem bizarre and totally out of character for you. Remember that your entire world had been knocked out from under you. You were in free fall, and your first task was to find any way to stop the fall."

When the funeral is over and your relatives and friends have gone home, the shock begins to wear off. It is important not to make any decisions that will have a lasting impact on your life (i.e. sell the house, give away the person's belongings, etc.) while you are in shock.

Denial... "There must be some mistake!"

We are not usually conscious of our denial, it happens below the level of our awareness. Denial is sometimes characterized by immersing one's self in fantasies such as, "He's just away on a trip," or "She'll be walking in the door any minute," or "He can't be dead, we have plans to go away this summer and he wouldn't let me down that way."

Denial is a natural, instinctive, protective response that actually gives us time to grasp reality. Barbara D. Rosof tells us that "as shock fades, and your mind and body reclaim their control, you start to take in the news. But it still may be too much; you may move in and out of denial. Lasting for hours or sometimes days, denial is another way of retreating from a reality too painful to bear....As irrational as it may seem to others, denial serves a necessary purpose. It is a psychological emergency measure, a temporary forestalling. You are not yet ready to confront your loss head-on."

For some, the passage through the denial phase will be accelerated by reading the obituary, seeing pictures in the newspaper or reading the death certificate. Caregivers should not prevent their loved ones from seeing these things.

Denial can be helpful for short periods of relief, however, you must move through it into the painful reality of the loss and begin to feel the feelings. If you find yourself stuck in the stage, you may need professional help to move on.

Depression...or is it appropriate sadness?

Do not confuse depression with sadness. If you are crying a lot because you have lost someone through tragic and sudden death, you are *sad*, not depressed. If you find yourself immobilized, unable to concentrate, sleeping too much or too little, you are *grieving*, you are not depressed. Some other characteristics of this stage are:

- weakness and feeling drained
- loss of appetite
- extreme fatigue
- extreme irritability
- unresponsiveness
- inability to focus or concentrate
- feeling hopeless or powerless
- aches and pains
- lack of personal hygiene
- a feeling that the world is not a safe place

In her book *The Courage to Grieve*, Judy Tatelbaum writes, "So much of our energy is tied up inside that little energy is available for the action of functioning. We may be moody. At times we may feel pain and weep, and then at other times we may feel detached and without emotion. During this period we may be withdrawn and unable to relate to other people. Negativity, pessimism, emptiness and a temporary sense of meaninglessness of life are all symptoms of depression. 'What's the use?' or 'Why bother?' are typical feelings. We may be acutely restless and then become immobile. The essential thing to remember is that the pain of grief is never constant and does not last forever. Throughout this middle phase of mourning, the myriad of feelings of grief come and go in waves, with lessening intensity as time goes on."

Again, if you feel stuck in this stage, you may need professional intervention. For most, however this stage can be described as situational depression, meaning it should subside after a time.

Anger...a normal response

Sarah, a young client of Pam's once said, "I am very angry at my fiancé. It feels like I'm angry all the time. I mean, he was killed one month before we were to get married and it wasn't his fault. So, why am I angry at *him*?"

The death of someone we care about and who made promises to be there and love us forever, turns us upside down and inside out. It affects our equilibrium. We think and feel things we never imagined we were capable of.

In addition, women are especially uncomfortable with anger because we have been acculturated to be "nice" and to seek solutions other than confrontation. In her book *The Dance of Anger*, Harriet Lerner, Ph.D. writes, "Women, however, have long been discouraged from the awareness and forthright expression of anger. Sugar and spice are the ingredients from which we are made. We are the nurturers, the soothers, the peacemakers and the steadiers of rocked boats." Men, on the other hand, are usually quicker to experience anger but have a harder time with sadness.

Feel your anger, acknowledge it and know that it is a normal part of the grieving process. If you don't express your anger, holding it in will cause you to become depressed. Anger turned inside out is depression. You might also seek a trained professional who will help you diffuse your anger by encouraging you to express it safely. Find a safe way to express this normal emotion and you will begin to feel less "crazy" and more at peace.

Acceptance...is really acknowledgement

Acceptance is the hardest concept to understand. When someone is dying slowly, you have an opportunity to reach acceptance—*slowly*. When someone is gone suddenly, acceptance is extremely difficult. Pam had a client in her practice that questioned acceptance.

> "I once had a client who said to me, 'Why do you keep saying acceptance is the final phase in my recovery? The word acceptance feels like a permission giving word. It feels like I've said that the death is okay with me, that I have given my approval. I have *not* given my approval. The death of my husband will *never* be okay with me....so what is meant when the final step in the grieving process is acceptance?"

The *American Heritage Dictionary* says acceptance means:
1. *The act or process of accepting.*
2. *The state of being accepted or acceptable.*
3. *Favorable reception; approval.*
4. *Belief in something; agreement*

Let's not refer to this stage as "acceptance." It is better defined as "acknowledgment." Acceptance is too close in meaning to "approval" and how can one approve the sudden loss of someone? You will probably be ready to acknowledge your loss in about three to six months, though it may take a year or more. There will be times when you are tempted to return to denial for a while—just to feel a little better. Yet the route to healing is through the pain of acknowledgment.

Complicated Mourning

In *The Treatment of Complicated Mourning*, Therese A. Rando offers an order of processes one goes through when facing sudden loss. This list makes an interesting addition to the Five Stages of Grief. This list is organized into what is called "the six R processes of mourning."

1. Recognize the loss.
Acknowledge the death.
Understand the death.
2. React to the separation.
Experience the pain.
Feel, identify, accept and give some sort of expression to all the psychological reactions to the loss.
Identify and mourn secondary losses.
3. Recollect and re-experience the deceased and the relationship
Review and remember realistically.
Revive and re-experience the feelings.
4. Relinquish the old attachments of the deceased and the old assumptive world.
5. Readjust to move adaptively into the new world without forgetting the old.
Revise the assumptive world.
Develop a new relationship with the deceased.
Adopt new ways of being in the world.
Form a new identity.
6. Reinvest.

The six R processes are more in tune with the experiences of those who have lost someone to sudden death. These are the stages that we move through, one day at a time, in order to "reinvest" in the world and in our lives. The work you do throughout this book will help lead you from the first step of recognizing the loss to eventually reinvesting.

The First Year

In addition to the stages of grief, each year has its own challenges. The following entries offer guidelines of what these years may involve. Keep in mind that like many areas of grief, these experiences are not always linear.

The first year is characterized by disorientation, numbness, denial, sometimes a burst of happiness followed by deadening guilt, acute periods of pain and then a return to numbness. The roller coaster ride of grief in the early stages can also include periods of euphoria (i.e. "how nice to be alone") followed by deep lows (i.e. "I can't believe she's really gone.") During the first year, some people describe themselves as robots that are going about the business of living without real joy.

It is easy to remember the hallmarks of the newborn's first year. There is the first step, the first smile, the first coo, the first word, the first tooth—and many others. When we lose someone, it is common to experience an overwhelming number of "firsts." We experience a first trip to the beach without our loved one, an Easter dinner where he isn't present, a trip planned without him, a Christmas morning where he won't open presents. Each of these experiences can be emotionally challenging and physically draining. Please find a way to share these experiences. By joining or creating a support group, you will be with others who have gone through these "firsts." You can share your hardships and heartbreaks and seek solace from others who have walked your path.

There are healing processes that can begin as early as the first year. Seeking information and finding answers to the questions you hold is a solid starting point. However, if you don't feel ready, don't push yourself. Other grievers find comfort from getting their affairs in order. There is something about this process that can help you feel a bit more in control in a situation that is out of control. A lawyer can help you with some of the details. There are now many commercial resources also available. Reading and learning more about grief can also be helpful in the first year. The more you are able to read, the more you will recognize yourself in others. This will help you normalize the experience.

The Second Year

Reorganizing and reexamining ones life characterize the second year. Where do I want to live? How will I support myself? Which car will I sell? How will the children be cared for while I go back to work? What do I do with my son's clothes? What do I do with my mother's empty room? It's a busy time which affords little opportunity for sitting still in one's grief. However, it is essential that you set aside some time to feel your grief and sadness as this is the most necessary part of the healing process. Even if you've done quite well with moving through your grief, coming to terms with the full loss may take a lifetime.

At this stage, some people are ready to begin making new plans. They are ready to identify their individual goals, hopes, fears and dreams. People are often ready to move forward, and long for a pathway out of the darkness. It's unrealistic however, to expect complete recovery in year two. Days will be brighter—but the night still comes. You will be stronger. If you haven't already completed the exercises and reading in Part Three, this is a good time to set goals and begin to work through some thoughts, memories and emotions.

The Third Year

In the third year, there may be longer periods of relief and longer periods of time in between emotional ambushes, but they still come at unexpected moments. You may cry or feel sad once a week instead of once a day—followed by once a month. You will have mostly reorganized your life. You know you will make it through the grief and that you will live. You may have overcome your reluctance to trust the world again.

In the third year you will hopefully be well into your grief work. You will be confidently moving down the path of redefining and rediscovering yourself and your world. You may have found, or are working on, a way to transform your tragedy into a meaningful memorial. If you have yet to begin recovery work, it's important to start now or to examine why you haven't started. The longer the work is delayed, the longer it will take to feel confident and comfortable with life. You will need at least three years to regain your equilibrium, for others it may take longer.

Multiple Grief

Some people have multiple situations they are dealing with on top of their grief. Perhaps an elderly parent is ill, you are sending a child off to college, you are going through menopause, or a career change, or completing college or some other challenging life situation. These kinds of situations can halt, delay or complicate the grieving process. When we have many stressful experiences, much of our emotional energy is funneled into these stressors. We are left with little reserve. Yet, in order to heal we must find a way to cope with these stressors while still feeling and exploring our grief. The idea of grief sessions relayed in the book can be helpful for those in this situation. See the Exercises Chapter for guidelines.

Will I Ever Get Over It?

Recovery from a major, sudden loss is a lifetime process. It's true that the pain lessens with time, but expect to be ambushed by grief occasionally. You may be ambushed by grief on the date of your anniversary eleven years from the date of the death; ambushed by grief the year your son or brother would have graduated from high school; ambushed by grief when you see couples meandering through the park or children playing in the sand box; ambushed by grief even after you are happily remarried—and on and on. In a letter Sigmund Freud wrote to a man who lost his son, he stated, "Although we know that after such a loss the acute state of mourning will subside, we also know we shall remain inconsolable and will never find a substitute. No matter what may fill the gap, even if it be filled completely, it nevertheless remains something else. And actually this is how it should be. It is the only way of perpetuating that love which we do not want to relinquish."

Expect that when you do find happiness, the joy you feel will be intense. It will just be different. Expect that the good days will out number the bad and they will. Expect a new sense for the importance of life to emerge. The way grief changes is conveyed well in Wendy Feiereisen's poem entitled, "Grief."

> You don't get over it
> you just get through it

you don't get by it
>because you can't get around it

it doesn't "get better"
>it just gets different

every day…
>grief puts on a new face.

In Gay Hendricks workbook, *Learning to Love Yourself*, he offers another way to look at painful events and emotions. "…think of a painful feeling as being like a bonfire in a field. At first it is hot, unapproachable. Later it may still smolder. Even later, you can walk on the ground without pain, but you know there is an essence of the fire that still remains. Take your own time, but be sure to walk over the ground again. You must do so because whatever you run away from runs you."

Warning Signs

As you work through your grief, it's important to monitor yourself and your stages. The following list can help you discern healthy grief from distorted grief. If you feel you may be suffering unhealthy grief, seek the help of a support group, clergy person or therapist.

- **Extreme Avoidant Behavior** – If you are avoiding friends and family for a prolonged period of time (over three weeks) you will want to talk to a professional. People need other people to work through grief.
- **Lack of Self-Care** – In order to have the energy and emotional capacity to work through grief, one must first take care of his/her basic needs. If you are having problems meeting basic needs, this is a warning sign to seek help.
- **Prolonged Denial** – If months have passed and you are still in denial, you will most likely need a support group to help you move through this stage.
- **Self-Destructive Thoughts** – These thoughts are not unusual during grief but we can expect them to pass quickly. If they are

persistent or obsessive it is best to consult a professional for guidance in working through them.

- **Displaced Anger** – With few emotional outlets available to us, it is common for anger to be displaced. However, this can become problematic if your anger is hurting you in personal or professional areas, or hurting others—seek help immediately.
- **Prolonged Depression or Anxiety** – Like denial, prolonged and immobilizing depression or anxiety are signs to seek help.
- **Self-Medication** – If you are using substances in excess to self-medicate your pain, i.c. food, alcohol or drugs, seek the help of an organization that specializes in such disorders or the help of a professional.

The stages and procedures we have outlined in this chapter serve only as guidelines. We will each experience and manage grief differently. Take that which is useful to you and let the rest go. Perhaps most importantly, know that with time and some conscious effort on your part, life will get easier and more manageable.

Chapter Six
Myths and Misunderstanding
of the Grieving Process

"Grief doesn't have to be a passive thing that happens to you.
Grieving is first and foremost something you do to heal your wounds
after experiencing a terrible loss in your life."
Bob Deits, *Life after Loss*

It is the rare school or family environment that teaches what to expect either emotionally or pragmatically, when life collapses in tragedy, especially with the advent of sudden and unexpected death. A sudden loss can put one into a whirlwind of emotions and visceral responses, twisting and turning us until we are set down in a place that feels as foreign as another planet. Like a hurricane, there is nothing like it, and nothing can prepare us. We can only follow suggested guidelines, i.e. evacuate, board up, etc. However, unlike a hurricane where there is often advance warning, with sudden death there is no such warning—no way to prepare.

We are ill-prepared to handle sudden death because we don't expect life to be so tenuous, so fragile. However, once our lives are touched by the experience of tragic loss, we never look at life in quite the same way. We become acutely aware of the delicate nature of the human organism, and life becomes precious in a way it never was before.

You can consciously shift from feeling grief is "something that happens to you" to "grieving is something you do to heal." Remember, when life feels out of control, and it's bound to during this time, that you *do* have control over *how* you will grieve and this can be very empowering.

In this chapter we will cover many of the common myths that people hold today. You may have encountered some of these already or been feeling pressured by them yourself. By examining the myth we can create a more well-rounded picture.

Myth #1
Death is death, sudden or long term and we all grieve the same way.
Of course there will be some commonalties in the grieving process. Truth is, depending on our life experiences, age, sex, resiliency, number of previous losses, health, cultural expectations and relationship to the deceased, we will each "do grief" in our own unique way. No two of us are exactly alike in our histories and in our relationship to the deceased.

Another misunderstanding is we, those of us who have lost someone with no warning, are expected to grieve and recoup in the same way, at the same pace, as someone who experiences loss as the result of long term illness or injury. How easy it would be if all of us grieved the same, and we could just print a rulebook, but that isn't the case. It's not important to explain to others that your grief will be different, it's simply important that *you* understand your uniqueness and know that it is okay.

Myth #2
By keeping busy I can lessen or eliminate my grief.
In an attempt to avoid the pain, grievers may choose to keep busy. We may find ourselves cleaning the house, dusting bookshelves, cleaning closets and engaging in other non-important tasks. However, you will find this "busyness" is simply a sidetrack that will only work for a short time.

There is clearly no way around grief. Keeping busy may temporarily alter your mood (as does alcohol, drugs or overeating), but you will eventually need to face the reality that someone you cared for deeply is *gone*.

Myth #3
I am going crazy and I'm afraid I will stay that way.
Sudden death creates trauma for the survivors on many levels. Trauma victims may not behave as people would expect. Many people report feeling numb and indifferent. Those around you, may expect you to be

more openly distraught and you may hear comments like, "My, you sure are taking this well," or "I expected to find you in a more disturbed state." You may find yourself walking around in a fog with an inability to make decisions. You may behave in a matter-of-fact way and you may appear to be functioning at a rather high level. Blank stares are common as the mind tries to grapple with the unimaginable. You may not weep, cry or wail for some time. All of these behaviors may puzzle onlookers and family members, and all of these behaviors are *normal and temporary.*

Myth #4
I will need to make sure I don't grieve for too long—one year should be enough.

Sometimes societal and religious beliefs impose rules like time limits for grief, what we should wear, how we should behave, when and where we should talk about the death and to whom. With sudden death, as with any death, we must find our own way through to embrace life again. Most recoveries from sudden death take at least two years, and in some ways we never "get over" the loss completely. Our expression of grief needs to come out of our need to make meaning or sense from what feels like meaningless tragedy, and no time limit can be set on that.

Myth #5
If I express too many feelings, my family and friends will think I've gone crazy.

In some native cultures it is perfectly acceptable to "go crazy." Yet, in our modern culture, we medicate people to protect them (and their families) from their feelings. Why are we so afraid of feelings? Doctors have been known to prescribe medications, especially for women, to get them through the hard time, to get them over the difficult period. What they are doing in essence is delaying the normal grieving process. Going crazy (within limits) is perfectly acceptable.

Myth #6
If I express my anger at God or the circumstances of the death, I am a bad person and will "pay" for it.

Anger is an extremely uncomfortable emotion for some of us, but it is one of the most important ones to express. If you become angry with God, don't judge yourself too harshly. As Earl Grollman writes, "It's okay to scream at God. He can take it." The Psalms are full of raging at God about injustices. We believe God can handle anything we throw his way. However, if you find your anger is becoming out of control (i.e. breaking valuables, threatening or preparing to kill someone, wanting to burn the church or hospital down or you have suicidal thoughts) immediately seek appropriate professional help and guidance.

Myth #7
I must wear black for a designated time period or I will dishonor the person who died.
The custom of funeral black is ancient. It originated back in the days when people felt that spirits, some of them ill willed and ill tempered, hovered around a corpse. Black was worn to make the living inconspicuous and less apt to be bothered by evil spirits.

By the 19th century, definite rules were in place concerning the length of mourning and the clothing one was to wear during each phase. Two years of deep mourning was expected of widows—no more, no less. According to *Death in Early America* by Margaret M. Coffin, "During the Victorian times a woman mourning the death of a father or mother or one of her own offspring wore dark clothes for a year. This mourning period lasted half the time a wife traditionally mourned her husband, but the garb was similar. Mourning garb was worn for six months for grandparents, for brothers and sisters, and for a friend who leaves you an inheritance. Mourning for an aunt or uncle or for a nephew or niece was an obligation of only three months, and white trim was allowed throughout."

Fortunately, American mourning customs have changed considerably and the depth of our loss is no longer measured by the blackness or the luster of our clothing. Further, the clothing we wear has a definite effect on how we feel about ourselves—brighter colors will help lift our spirits and the spirits of those around us. So don't hesitate to wear whatever clothing makes you feel best.

A woman that Pam knows wore red, white and blue at her husband's funeral and for many months (on and off) during her mourning. Her husband had served in Vietnam and was an American patriot when he died suddenly. Her choice of clothing clearly helped her to honor him.

Myth #8

I won't have to grieve as much and I will feel better if I use alcohol or medication to alleviate my sadness.

Some survivors will use, or increase their use, of alcohol or antidepressants. By doing this however, they distance themselves from what they need to feel to heal, and they distance themselves from their family members and support systems. The grief simply goes underground and waits to be expressed. They may mistakenly believe that "If I drink (drug) to get over it, then the grief will be gone when I'm sober." Nothing could be further from the truth. Some will need the temporary relief that medication can provide in order to function and a competent therapist should help make this decision. You may want to consider some of the natural remedies we have included in Chapter 17.

Myth #9

If I talk about my loss I'll feel worse.

You cannot move through your grief unless you experience it. Hiding it or denying it will only prolong it. Meeting and talking with other people who have been through this process will help you. Ellen Sue Stern writes in *Living with Loss: Meditations for Grieving Widows*, "It's essential to allow yourself to talk as much as you want; healing is hastened by reminiscing about your husband [or loved one] processing the last days of his life, the funeral and any other details surrounding his death. For now choose only to spend time with people who are supportive and understanding, who can lovingly listen as long as you need to talk." For ideas on support, please see Part Three of this book.

Myth #10

I've done something wrong because some of my family and friends are turning away from me.

There will be times when family and friends turn away from you because they are experiencing their own grief. They may believe that if they interact with you by expressing their feelings they will needlessly compound your grief. Others simply want you to "move on"—they don't want to see you hurt any more. If your family and friends cannot be supportive you will feel uncared for and angry. Don't try to make them do or be what they are incapable of—look for support elsewhere. See Part Three for ideas.

Myth #11

After a while I won't think about it anymore.

You may be ambushed by grief when you least expect it. To believe you can forever put the loss and the circumstances surrounding the death "out of your mind" is a completely unrealistic expectation. You will, from time to time, throughout your life, re-experience feelings associated with the loss.

Myth #12

I should be relieved that they didn't suffer a long and lingering illness.

You may hear some say "well at least he died quickly—be happy for that." Perhaps you are thinking this way if the person you lost suddenly was much older or had been suffering. But for most of us, the sudden death was an untimely one—one that occurred way too soon for the person and those left behind. There may be little, if any, relief in the knowledge that they died quickly.

Myth #13

Someday I'll have another (spouse, child, parent, lover...) and that person will erase the pain and replace what I have lost.

Yes, you may some day have "another," but to expect that person to be a replacement for what you have lost not only places an unfair burden on them, but is an expectation that will also set you up for further pain. It is a healthy and hopeful attitude to take comfort in knowing you will love and form similar relationships in the future and at the same time to face the realization that no one can be replaced by another.

Myth #14

Once I am done with one stage of grief, I will simply move on to the next.

With the popularity of the well-known "Five Stages of Grief" (Kübler-Ross,) some people mistakenly believe that grief is a linear process. Like we said before, recovery is not like an elevator that takes you from the basement of despair to the penthouse of joy. It is more like a maze where you go forward a bit, move back a few steps, cover the same ground again and find yourself at the beginning. Like a fun house hall of mirrors, you see yourself over and over again, distorted and misshapen until you come out the other side.

Myth #15
If I relive the good times, I'll stay stuck in the pain.
There are memories that keep us blocked or stuck and those that can move one forward into life. Over time you will learn to recognize the difference. For now, don't be concerned that your memories of your loved one will keep you stuck.

Myth #16
Children really don't understand death and probably don't need to be included in the funeral plans or memorial services.
As we mention in Chapter Nine, Helping Children Cope with Grief, depending on the developmental stage of the child, many children do understand death and feel the loss deeply. When the death is sudden and unexpected, a child's trust in a safe world is altered. By all means, depending on age and ability, try to include the child in the funeral plans or memorial service. Invite them to write a short note or draw a picture about how they feel to be placed in the casket. Some small children may be frightened by the sight of a dead person and you will need to honor this fear. Don't ever push a child to do something that frightens or disturbs them. Likewise, if they are clear and coherent in their requests to be included, do not hold them back. It is certainly in the child's best interest to encourage participation in a way that offers them closure and a small measure of control in this out of control situation.

Myth #17
To properly honor the deceased, I must have the standard wake and burial.

While many people will choose, and be comfortable with a standard funeral, there are many other options. When Brook lost her brother, the thought of a funeral didn't seem right to her family. They felt that Caleb would rather have a party or celebration in his memory. They chose to throw a party at his favorite pub and restaurant in town. Over 400 people came and businesses from all over town donated food and beverages. Instead of a tombstone at the local cemetery, Brook and her mother chose a bronze plaque with a favorite quote mounted on a rock at Caleb's favorite lake. Do what feels best to you. Don't let the funeral home or your clergy person talk you out of creating a wake, memorial service or funeral that better fits what you feel the deceased would have wanted. See the Appendix for forms that may help you plan these arrangements.

Myths, like the grief blocks we discuss in the next chapter, can prohibit the process of recovery. When faced with a troubling myth, return to this chapter for guidance.

Chapter Seven
Grief Blocks

"It comes to all. We know not when,
or how, or why. It's always been
a mystery, a frightening thing,
enshrouded in the silencing.

When suddenly a loved one dies
we seem to sort of paralyze,
to just stop still within our track.
And oh, how much we want them
back."

from When A Loved One Dies,
by Dolores Dahl, Suddenly Alone

Grieving is like a foreign land to most of us; a land where we find ourselves speaking and hearing an inner language we cannot comprehend. Because it can help to have a guide in a foreign land, this chapter will describe ways we commonly avoid grief and why we do so.

I don't want to talk about it.

You've got to talk about it, and talk about it, and talk about it some more. Find someone who will listen and talk until you can't talk anymore...at least for the moment. Then when you need to talk again, start all over with your story. Talking about it is an extremely important task, if you try to skip it, you will be blocked indefinitely. It is a task that will help you come to terms with the death and move you past the denial stage.

Help! I'm stuck on instant replay!

One of the horrors of instant replay is the persistent questioning of the choices we made. For example: Could I have called the ambulance sooner? If I'd known CPR would it have made a difference? Were there warning signs of the condition that I missed? Could I have done anything at all to prevent it? This kind of constant replay over an extended period, blocks acceptance and closure.

Instant replay is the mind's way of coming to terms with the unfathomable. Some instant replay is necessary, but too much can keep us stuck. If your own instant replay is becoming an obsession, make an effort to do what therapists call, "thought stopping." This is a technique whereby you consciously stop the thought, and deliberately change the subject. This is not a complicated task and is easier to do than you might think.

If the deceased's death was particularly troubling you may be replaying it over and over in your mind. If you have a horrible image of your loved one's last minutes or hours that runs over and over like a bad movie, first acknowledge the horror, then try shifting to an image of when you first met. Replace one image with the other.

Paul G. Stoltz, Ph.D., writes in his book entitled, *Adversity Quotient: Turning Obstacles into Opportunities:* "Arm yourself with STOPPERS. Whenever a crisis strikes, anxiety is a frequent—and useless—response. It also spreads like an emotional wildfire making it impossible to apply rational steps to better cope with the problem. Soon you start to "catastrophize" and feel helpless and hopeless. You squander energy and time worrying. To avoid imagining the worst will happen, use what I call "stoppers" to regain control.

- "When you feel overwhelmed, slap your knee or any hard surface. Shout, "Stop!" The sting will shock you into a more rational state. Some people leave a rubber band around their wrist. When they feel anxiety, they stretch it six inches and let it go.
- Focus intently on an irrelevant object, such as a pen, the pattern of the wallpaper or a piece of furniture. If your mind is removed from the crisis, even for a moment, you can return with the calm you need to take effective action.
- Take an activity break. Just 15 or 20 minutes of brisk walking or other exercise will clear your mind, raise your energy and flood your brain with endorphins—chemicals that put you in a more optimistic mood.

- Put yourself in a setting where you're dwarfed by your surroundings. Catastrophizing makes problems larger than life. A shift in perspective will cut them down to size. Drive to the beach and look out over the ocean...stand at the base of a large tree...gaze up at the clouds...or listen to a great piece of music and let the grandeur wash over you."

I'm obsessed with revenge and retribution.

If you are stuck in revenge your loved one most likely died a violent death. The death may have been caused by malice, carelessness or someone's irresponsible behavior. Keep in mind that obsession is a way we avoid feelings and consider moving from obsession to some constructive actions like a memorial fund, volunteering for an organization such as MADD, etc. See the Resource Chapter for other organizations.

One way to slow or stop thoughts of revenge and retribution, is to realize how much energy, and how much of yourself, you are giving to the person with whom you are angry. When we realize how that person begins to control our thoughts and our lives, we can take the steps to let go of these destructive thoughts. In the exercises chapter of this book, there is a visualization exercise that can be helpful for working through revenge. Focus, instead, on how you can commemorate the life of the one you lost. If the death was unintentional, the surviving person involved is most likely suffering their own pain and guilt.

In the book *Get Out of Your Own Way* by Mark Goulston, M.D., and Philip Goldberg, the authors tell the story of a client whose daughter was brutally murdered. The client was preoccupied with thoughts of suicide and anger. The author urged her to get on with her life. "I can't go on until I get over this," she said.

"It's just the opposite," the author replied. "Unless you go on with your life, you won't get over it." I explained, "that only by pushing herself into activities and building new memories would she be able to dilute the impact of the excruciating thoughts that hounded her day and night."

I never saw the body.

When the deceased's body is never recovered, it can be extremely difficult to begin, much less complete, the grieving process. If you were unable to see the body because of its condition, or because it was never recovered, the process is complicated even further.

When the body of your loved one has not been found or was unrecognizable, or you were in some way prevented from seeing him/her, it is difficult to find complete closure. You may find yourself in denial much longer than if you had an opportunity to see the body or some of the remains.

Helen Fitzgerald, author of *The Mourning Handbook*, offers this: "If you have lost a loved one under circumstances where there is no body to view or bury, you may be left with lingering doubts as to whether that person really died, complicating your grief and possibly delaying your recovery...In your case, if there is no body, you may not want to have a memorial service to publicly mourn the loss. You may not want to give up all hope that your loved one could still be alive. Still, you do need to put some closure on this part of your life, and you have the right to have a memorial service when you are ready. Far from an act of disloyalty to the deceased, such a service can help you celebrate your loved one's life and to put closure on your relationship with him or her...You can also include in your memorial service a cenotaph, which is a monument erected to honor the memory of someone whose body is elsewhere. It can be placed in a cemetery, if you wish, or on your own property."

If there are no remains, a memorial can be built. A bench in a park with a plaque, a carved stone or stack of stones placed by a beautiful lake, a statue, a scholarship fund, something visible and real is very important. A memorial like this offers an anchor for our grief.

Anne Marie had a tree planted in a public garden. Her brother, who died at sea and whose body was never recovered, loved the outdoors. With the park's permission, she had a plaque placed at the foot of the tree. She visits the tree when she needs some comfort. It also makes her feel good that others can enjoy the beauty of the tree, as well as read the plaque associated with her brother.

This kind of thing doesn't happen in my family.

Your life experience to this point, may have been death free and now you are suddenly dealing with violent or traumatic death. You may be thinking, *We live in a good neighborhood, we never took drugs, we were church going, God-fearing, so how come this kind of thing happened in my family?*

This is another example of people trying to get control. We are applying what appears to be logical thinking to an illogical situation. This kind of thinking is also a form of denial. The best way to work through denial is to continue working with the situation, absorbing reality little-by-little as you are able.

A great book about this is *When Bad Things Happen to Good People* by Harold S. Kushner. Rabbi Kushner writes, "Laws of nature do not make exceptions for nice people. A bullet has no conscience; neither does a malignant tumor or an automobile gone out of control. That is why good people get sick and hurt as much as anyone."

I can avoid the whole grieving process if I'm medicated.

Some of you will want to take medication (or turn to alcohol) as a way to numb your feelings. However, please be aware that when you stop taking these mood altering drugs, you must start the process of grieving where you left off. It just doesn't work!

Of course it isn't difficult to find a doctor willing to prescribe a sedative and it's easy to buy a bottle of gin, but ultimately, being medicated does more harm than good. It will add to your confusion and stall the process of your recovery. However, if you are experiencing extreme anxiety or depression and are totally dysfunctional, then medication with psychotherapy is indeed your best choice. If you're unsure if you need medication, consult a professional for a consultation. In our chapter on self-help you will find a list of natural, herbal remedies that many people have found helpful.

As Bob Deits says in *Life after Loss*, "To take control of your grief, you must face your loss head on with all your senses working. You can't do that while you are blissfully tranquilized."

I'm not crying.

There must be something wrong with me—I'm not crying. Everyone else is, but not me. Maybe I didn't care as much for him/her as I thought!

You may not be crying, but this doesn't mean you have no heart. If you are not crying, you may be blocked by the fear that once you start crying, you will not be able to stop. You may have been taught that strong people don't cry in public, or your cultural upbringing may have something to do with your inability to shed tears. In any case, you may need to learn how!

Shedding tears can help you release sadness that might become "stuck" in your body. Crying has been referred to as "the oat bran of the spirit and the cleanser of the soul." There are sound scientific reasons for the relief and calmness that follow the shedding of tears. Research has shown that healthy people cry more. When you cry, your tears release chemicals that help you cope with stress and pain. According to doctor's reports, tears contain encephalins, which can dampen physical or emotional pain and release ACTH, which has a calming effect.

I keep judging myself and my behavior.

Here is a sample of some internal, self-judging statements: "I'm not grieving right. I should be doing it differently. Perhaps I went back to work too soon. If I really loved him (or her), I'd be more devastated!"

This kind of self-judgment can block grief and is self-defeating at best. Perhaps you are looking at the way others grieve and are comparing yourself to them. Just as no two people are alike on this planet, no two people will "do grief" in exactly the same way. Some people will function at a very high level and some will not function at all. Some people will become introspective, others will cry, rant, scream and rage at the drop of a hat. These differences are largely influenced by the stage of grief you are in and your personality type. Cultural differences are also at play here, and men have a tendency to grieve differently than women. Another important variable, is the number of losses you have experienced in your life. Multiple losses compound and will influence how you handle your grief. We've said it many times, we all grieve in our own unique way. Stop the judgment and remove this block to healthy grief.

I feel so guilty.

In this case, you may be blocked by self-blame and you may be suffering from what is called, "survivor guilt." In *Survivor Guilt* author Aphrodite Matsakis, Ph.D. writes that "Survivor guilt involves asking the existential question of why you suffer less than someone else, or why you lived while others died."

Of all the blocks mentioned in this chapter, guilt may be the strongest of them all. Struggling with the question, "Why them, not me?" can create so much anxiety, pain and self-doubt that you stay stuck in your grief, much longer and more intensely than needed. You may feel that guilt is the way to "pay penance" for surviving, or that intense guilt is a way to honor your lost loved one. However, they want more for us, much more. Process your guilt with a trusted friend, therapist or clergy person. The best way to honor the deceased is to move through your guilt, put down the stick you use to beat yourself with and move on.

I must be crazy—I feel so angry toward him.

Angry feelings directed at your loved one can be the most upsetting of all emotions. Yet, if you do not express your anger, it will keep you blocked. It may surprise you, but expressing your anger at the unexpected loss can ultimately help you feel less angry. Your spiritual and emotional growth is at stake if you believe there is no room for anger and hateful feelings. You are human. In addition, holding onto anger and keeping it submerged is extremely draining and you need all the energy you can get during recovery. I suggest you express your anger and consider it a blessing that you can. This promises to bring in a new flood of energy and will promote or contribute to your well-being.

I feel like I'm "holding on," maybe I should just get on with my life.

You can choose to hold on to the memories of love received, of lessons learned and gifts imparted. You can continue to love the deceased in a special place in your heart. As opposed to what your family and friends may be telling you, the desire to hold onto an important part of your history will not keep you stuck. One example is Brook's mother. She will always say she is the mother of two children—but one of her children is deceased. *A death does not erase the person nor his or her impact from our life.* Remembering the deceased and reliving special times will still enable you to get on with your life. Although the "I choose not to forget" stance may seem contradictory to the concept of letting go, it will actually help enhance your recovery and give you some control over a situation that feels out of control.

After a while, your friends and relatives may, in an effort to have you start living again (according to their schedule), encourage you to "let go of the past and move on with your life." They mean well, and they are partially right. However, you may have some unfinished business to do first. We suggest you hold on to the feelings you have about the deceased, that you continue to treasure the memories—that you hold on to the past as you honor the present and move into the future.

This is too much to handle so I'm "shutting down".

My son is leaving for college, my mother is ill, I have a major work deadline to meet, I'm having a serious operation, my grandmother just died...

You may have other "stuff" going on and feel you don't have time to grieve. Since grief is cumulative this one death can be the one that is just too much. A typical case of "overload" happened to Mary. Mary's mother died of a heart attack, her grandmother died in a nursing home, her best friend died of cancer and her husband died suddenly of a stroke all in the same year. When one loss follows the other, there is no time in between to recover. For this reason, it is important to grieve each death separately or you will feel too overwhelmed to grieve at all. If you are faced with too many circumstances to handle effectively, consider seeing a counselor that can help you work through the maze of emotions. Seeing a counselor is never a sign of weakness, it's a sign that you are committed to moving on, moving through and getting your life on track.

Consider whether you may be trying to avoid difficult emotions. You must make time even in the midst of other life events. Prioritizing and grief sessions can also be helpful. Try scheduling at least twenty minutes twice each day to experience and work with your grief. Many grievers also find it useful to take a day from time to time, without interruptions, to work through grief. Whatever method works for you is fine, all that matters is that *you make* the time. Without it, you cannot move on.

I'll never be happy again, so why should I try?

With each hardship or loss we face in our lives, it becomes easier to be pessimistic and negative. One man we interviewed reported three deaths in recent years and the loss of a job. He had become detached and resentful and found little reason for trying. He had come to know this dark place intimately, and although it wasn't appealing, it was home. The more familiar something is to us, the harder it is to leave, even if it's a dark and depressing place. However, these feelings are excuses to avoid the pain and work of rebuilding. The rebuilding process is slow and hard, but it will always happen when we dedicate our hearts to it.

Hurtful Self-Talk

Be aware of the following hurtful self-talk that can block the grieving process—keeping you stuck. The following statements are examples of commonly held misconceptions that may run through our minds.

My loved one is with God for a reason, so I shouldn't feel bad

Grief is a mental illness

It is wrong to feel anger at the deceased and it shouldn't be expressed

If I acknowledge the loss, I'm afraid I will die too

I should have died first

If I allow my grief to surface, I'll go crazy

If I grieve, people will think I'm weak

If I appear sad too often, it will bring my family down

If I cry in church, my fellow congregants will think I've lost faith

If my children see me grieving, it will make them feel worse

The deceased wouldn't want me to grieve

I should grin and bear it and put it behind me

If I stop grieving people will expect me to be happy again.

When you find yourself running on the treadmill of hurtful self-talk it is important to come up with a positive statement for balance. Write down your destructive or hurtful thought and then write down a more positive, realistic thought. For example, "The deceased wouldn't want me to grieve," is hurtful. You could write, "The deceased would understand and respect the full spectrum of my emotions." Whenever a negative thought enters your mind, replace it with a positive, more realistic statement.

I feel like I'm holding on and won't ever move forward.

When we lose someone, we have a tendency to want to hold on to every moment and every memory. Many grievers also avoid disrupting the deceased's personal items. Wives may leave their husbands clothes in the closet. Parents may close the door on a child's room. Storing or giving away these items does not mean you are discounting the memories.

The fear of forgetting the deceased or that our memories will fade is a powerful fear, but when we hold on to everything they owned, we stifle, slow and sometimes even stop growth. There is a median. Cherish your special memories, hold them, journal them and don't give them up, but at the same time, be open to new growth.

These are some of the more common blocks to grief that we have discovered. You will discover others in various shapes and forms. Support groups and self-help exercises are most valuable in moving through these blocks and we offer you some in Part Three.

Chapter Eight
Relating to Others

*"Go away. Don't call. And don't try to talk to me. I can't hear you and I'm sure you
won't hear me. If you want to help, bring me food. Otherwise, go away."*
Stephanie Ericsson, Companion Through the Darkness

As we experience grief, and our world changes, relating to others can be
difficult—especially when these "others" have not faced tragic loss
firsthand. Our different view on the world changes us in many ways, and
the interactions that once came naturally may become difficult. Certain
situations are bound to be trying. In this chapter we will look at some of
the mountains we will climb while relating to others.

Too Close to Home
For some time after our loss, situations that are very close to our own may
be hard to deal with. A parent who has lost a child may have a hard time
seeing other parents with their children. A widow may have a hard time in
an environment where other couples are present. It is hard to anticipate
situations that will hit too close to home. Some you might expect, other
times they might surface out of the blue.

One widowed waitress reported that she felt she was progressing well
through her recovery after her husband had died. After six months she had
gone back to work. Then, almost a year after his death, a couple came in
and the man looked about the same age as her husband. He ordered her
husband's favorite wine. "I fell apart right there. I had been fine for
months and suddenly I just couldn't hold it in."

Try not to push yourself into these situations before you are ready for them. There is no "time limit", no set "right or wrong" way to deal with others. Don't let others convince you that you need to do "this or that," instead, follow the cues of your heart and body. If a situation like this surfaces, excuse yourself from the environment and try to get to a place where you can release and vent your emotions.

You are a Different Person

Brook found that she emerged a different person after Caleb's death...

I remember a phone conversation with a good friend of mine, several weeks after Caleb's death. She was telling me about something...though I can't recall what. Then she paused for a moment and said, "Brook, you don't sound like yourself."

My reply came out of my mouth before I could choose it. "I am not the person I was three weeks ago and I will never be that person again."

Surprised by my own response, I relayed it to my therapist who was helping me work through issues surrounding my brother's death. "Of course you're not," she said. "And one of the best things you can do for yourself is to know that you are a different person now."

A fear set in shortly after that, though. I suddenly wondered how I could relate to all my old friends when I now felt so different about the world, life and myself. Things my friends and I had once discussed, seemed so trivial. Their work problems and love life issues that I once discussed intensely, seemed silly. I felt like yelling at them. I wanted to say, 'Trust me, if you're breathing, life ain't so bad.' Though my friends were sorry for my loss, they couldn't fully understand. No one understands the affect of tragic loss unless they go through it firsthand.

I told my mom one night that I didn't think I could keep any of my friends that hadn't known Caleb because they just wouldn't understand. My mom told me to give it time. But I withdrew from friends and didn't call to set up lunches and didn't show up for regularly scheduled activities. I didn't want to pretend to be the person I used to be, "the Brook" I thought they all would expect.

One morning, my dear friend Sara stopped in. She informed me that we were going to have breakfast together and that we could either go out or she would go get a couple of omelets and bring them back. I smiled at her determined attitude. We ended up going out for a nice breakfast and I was amazed at how well it went. We talked about all sorts of things, we talked about Caleb, about work, about my week. We talked and she listened and she absorbed and she was there with me. With the 'new' Brook.

I had other friends who I couldn't seem to cross that bridge with. But what I learned from Sara was that it was so important to give each friendship a chance. Friendship can cross bridges and worlds.

It's Okay to Laugh

In Jacquelin Mitchard's novel, *The Deep End Of The Ocean*, there is an incredible scene. The book is about a family whose son has been kidnapped. The mother, Beth, is sitting in the office of the chief detective, Candy. The two women have become quite friendly throughout the weeks spent on the search. The mother has been grim, depressed and withdrawn throughout the search. In the scene, the detective says something that causes the mother to laugh. She laughs only for an instant, before a look of horror comes over her face—horror, that in the face of misery she laughed. Here is an excerpt from the scene:

> Candy held up the mailer. "Actually it's a padded cry for help."
>
> And Beth, to her horror, laughed, instantly covering her eyes and feeling that she was about to choke. Candy was on her feet and around the desk in seconds.
>
> "Beth, Beth, listen," she said. "You laughed. You only laughed. If you laugh that doesn't mean that's a point against our side. If you laugh, or read a book to Vincent, or eat something you like, it's not going to count for or against us on the big scoreboard of luck." Beth began to cry. "you have to believe me," Candy went on. "It feels like if you watch a movie,

or listen to a song or do anything that makes you feel anything more than like absolute shit, that little moment of happiness is the thing that's going to be punished..."

While this scene details the events surrounding a kidnapping, many of us can relate to these feelings. At times, it's hard to laugh—we feel guilty for "going on." We wonder if our laughing makes our grief less real—if our memories will fade—if people will think we don't miss the deceased.

If only there were rules to grief, how much easier it would be. Laughter and happiness can become haunting. How should we look? How should we act? If we look like we are having fun, what might people think? Is it okay to just forget for a while—to try and escape what has happened?

The answers are all within your heart. There is nothing you need to do, or act like, for the sake of others. Don't worry about how anyone perceives you. It's all right to escape for a while, to watch a comedy—to laugh. Remember, the person who has passed on is one who would wish you nothing but the best. Your laughter becomes their laughter as well.

The Ten-Day Syndrome

In the immediate days following a loss, we are often bombarded with visitors, food, offers to help, phone calls, flowers and condolences. Then we see the ten-day syndrome in action. Most major news stories get about ten days coverage in the media and then its old news—on with the new. The grief experience is often similar. As the days roll by the calls, condolences and comfort lessen. It may appear as if all are trying to get back to "their" world before the tragedy happened. Meanwhile, we are just beginning the long and difficult road of grief—needing more support than ever.

In her book *Suddenly Alone*, Dolores Dahl writes, "Phone calls, visits, food...there was so much activity following your death that I had no time to be lonely, no time to digest the fact that you were gone. I was overwhelmed with the support and the love that filled my home during those first few days of disbelief and confusion. But, as is always the case, everyone returned to their own homes, their own lives, shortly following the memorial service...and I was alone."

It's not uncommon to feel angry with others who continue on as though life is "normal" when for us it is anything but. It's not uncommon to be upset that other's worlds just continue on, while it feels like your whole world has stopped. Brook and her mother discussed this scenario one evening.

My mother had finally gone out to do some mandatory shopping. It was her first outing since Caleb's death. While out, she saw some women friends shopping. They were laughing and choosing items and placing them in their carts. From afar, my mother watched wondering—*How can their lives just go on? Don't they know what I'm going through?*

While on the phone, I reminded her of deaths we had faced in the past; deaths where we weren't the family or the immediately close. We thought about all the people we had known, who had lost someone, before we had experienced loss firsthand. What had we done in those instances? Just as others had done to us, we had sent a card, a call or a condolence and then returned to our own lives.

There is little one can do and life must go on. We are not taught how to handle death—so people do the best they can, usually following the standard of passing on condolences through a call, letter or gift. Only those who have had to walk this painful path will be aware of the agony that waits ahead. Those are the people you need to seek out when the Ten-Day syndrome hits. Whether it be through one of the support networks listed in Section Three or through someone you know, find someone who will walk with you long after ten days have passed.

Repeating the Story

One of the most challenging aspects of grief is the retelling of what has happened. We may find ourselves moving through the healing process and having a great week—only to run into someone who doesn't know of our loss. Brook's mother encountered this several times. The rural Wisconsin town where she lives is a summer home for many. Caleb's death occurred in the fall. The next summer, many returning acquaintances asked, "How are your son and daughter?" The grief of the past moved full force into the present as she recounted the cold events of the previous fall and winter.

Unfortunately, there are no ways around this bump in the path of grieving. The best you can do is to decide how you'd like to handle these situations in advance. If you don't want to talk about it, it's fine to say so. "I lost my son over the winter but I'm not ready to talk about it today." It may seem short or abrupt but it is your right. Others find that telling the story brings comfort.

Awkward Questions

Family is openly talked about in society. "How many children do you have?" or "Do you have any brothers or sisters?" or "Are you married?" are questions we encounter frequently. How to respond can be difficult. Brook experienced this when she moved from Wisconsin to Oregon....

"I live in a very community-oriented neighborhood with lots of neighborhood get-togethers and functions. Since I was the "new kid on the block" many people would ask where I moved from, where my family lived and if I had brothers or sisters. This was their attempt to make friendly conversation and get to know me. The first time I answered, "I had a brother but he died six months ago," and the woman with whom I was speaking just quit talking. We had stepped into an awkwardness that neither of us knew how to step out of. After a couple more minutes of small talk she excused herself. I knew that sharing something like this so soon would cause the other person to be uncomfortable—but what was I supposed to say—she had asked the question!

The next time I was asked if I had brothers of sisters, I simply said, "No." Then the person asked me, "What was it like growing up an only child?" Then I had to explain that I didn't become an "only child" until my mid-twenties.

I finally devised two responses that felt natural to me. I would either say, "I have one brother but he's far away and I don't see him that much anymore," or "I had one older brother who died a year ago—but I still feel very close to him." Both of these answers seemed to put the questioner at ease.

Non-Traditional Relationships

You may be the ex-wife, "other woman" or stepchild of the deceased. You may not fit into a traditional category. Real wives, real mothers, real children, seem to be paid more attention to by relatives and friends. They are seen as more authentic members of the family. And yet, you have your needs as well. Pam's experience is an example of one of these non-traditional relationships,

> "George was my ex-husband at the time of his death. We had developed a close friendship and co-parenting relationship since the divorce. When he died, I felt I had no legitimacy in my grief. Some uncaring individuals even voiced their disbelief at my strong reaction to his death. I found no support group category into which I fit. So, I grieved on my own—in isolation."

If you cannot find support because your relationship to the deceased was out of the ordinary, you will need to find ways to grieve on your own. The self-help exercises in this book may be especially useful to you.

If there is a non-traditional relationship within your grief circle (and it doesn't compromise your values) do what you can to be considerate of this person's feelings and experiences.

Going Back to Work

Depending on your circumstances, and company policies you may find that a week or two is all you can get off from work. Before returning, explore any other options you have. If you have savings or any other sources that can help you secure a four to six week break, consider using it. If that is impossible, take some time to discuss what you are going through with your boss or supervisor.

We strongly suggest setting up a meeting or lunch with your employer before returning to the work environment. Ask if any part time options or shorter days could be arranged for a few weeks. If not, ask for their support and understanding. Let your supervisor know that you are low on energy and very emotional. Ask for his patience and tolerance. Let them know you will not use grief as an excuse not to get your work done, but you will need a little leeway as you figure out how to work, while also working through your grief. Many supervisors will be accommodating when they understand what you're going through. Let your co-workers know that you could use some extra support as well. (You may want to use the handout we offer in Chapter Two). Many times people are unsure if they should treat you "the same as always," or if they should be careful about discussing certain things. Only you know how you want to be treated. Don't keep it to yourself. Tell others, many will be willing to stand by you and support you if given the chance.

Some companies offer bereavement leave. Make sure to check with the Human Resources Department (if your company has one) to see what is available to you. There is also information that can be valuable to companies and employees. The AARP – Widowed Person's Service publishes a brochure entitled, *When an Employee Loses a Loved One*. Bereavement Publishing provides a "Grief in the Workplace" program to help corporate America understand the needs of grieving employees. See the resource section for information and addresses.

At a time when we likely want to curl up and be alone, it is important to relate to others as we are able. Often this is best achieved one person at a time. Take a step out and talk to someone. Go at whatever pace feels right for you. Don't feel shame or guilt for not being able to "jump back into life". Regaining our equilibrium takes time. Go easy and be easy with yourself.

Chapter Nine
Helping Children Cope with Grief

"In one of the stars
I shall be living
In one of them
I shall be laughing
And so it will be
As if all the stars
Were laughing
When you look
At the sky at night"
The Little Prince
Antoine de Saint-Exipéry

To help you understand what you might encounter with your own children or those you care for, we have roughly divided children into age groups ranging from babies to young adults. This should give you some guidance as to what to expect and how you can be most helpful depending on the child's stage of development at the time of the death.

As children grow, they will need to re-experience the loss at each stage of development. For example, at age five a child's understanding of death has moved from fantasy-based to reality-based. As they learn and understand more, they may need to review and re-experience the loss. When children realize the finality of death, they need to re-interpret what the death means to them. It's important to know this so that you don't feel you are "taking two steps backward," if your child becomes preoccupied with the loss at different stages of his/her development.

One of the biggest challenges for children is the loss of their assumption that childhood is a safe place. Until this moment, young children believe they are immortal and invulnerable. Nothing could hurt their friends, parents or siblings. This deep trust is destroyed when they experience tragic loss at a young age.

A child's actions may change. It is not uncommon for a child to emotionally and physically regress during the grief process. The child may lash out, throw temper tantrums, do poorly in school, become shy or introverted, perform badly at once perfected skills, have nightmares and the like.

Patience and love are the keys to helping your child move past regression. This patience and love is only possible if you are doing your own grief work and renewing yourself emotionally.

Babies (birth to eighteen months of age)

Naturally, babies can't ask questions, however they do experience a visceral response to loss. They feel it in their bones and sense it in their environment. An infant's view of the world is self-centered and they believe that all things exist for them and because of them. You may experience the baby as more cranky and irritable. This will depend upon their relationship to the deceased. Naturally, babies will feel more of a loss if it is one or both parents, than if it is an uncle or other close relative that died.

Babies often become fussy, hard to calm, and fearful of separation. They may develop sleep problems or night terrors. By maintaining children's regular patterns, we help offer a safe parameter within which they can experience their grief. During this time, it's important to offer extra comfort, holding and soothing time. Keep in mind that older babies often understand what you are saying, even if they are unable to speak. Offer soothing statements and avoid talking of the death within earshot.

Immediate physical comfort and a commitment to help the child cope as he/she ages are the best actions you can take. If you are the primary caretaker of the infant, it can be challenging to care for the baby's needs as well as your own. If at all possible, find someone outside the family to assist you in caring for the infant so you can give yourself the necessary time to organize your life and to grieve.

Toddlers (eighteen months to three years)

During this phase of development the parents' or caregivers' main task is to set limits with the child. If your world is upside down because of a sudden death in your home, it is hard to keep up with previous limit setting. However, it is essential to the child's well-being. Toddlers may also regress and become extremely fearful of separation from their caregivers. If the toddler was toilet trained at the time of the death, they may have a setback. You may experience them as unduly demanding, whining and needy. They may not want to eat the way they had previously or they may not sleep well. Keeping children on a regular schedule will help to alleviate these fluctuations.

Toddlers know something has occurred in their lives, but they have few, if any words to express themselves. They have no concept of death and expect the loved one to come back. They will worry about their adult caregivers and may cry when you cry. It is okay to put words on your experience and to tell the child, "I am sad because _____."

It is also important to answer any questions openly and honestly. Telling a child that the dead person is "just sleeping" or "God came and took him," can create enormous fear and anxiety. The child may be afraid to sleep or fear he will be snatched away by God. It's okay to use the word dead and to look for ways to illustrate the point.

Direct questions from toddlers are also challenging. At a time when you may be emotionally drained, direct questions can be hard to cope with and answer. Brook's daughter went through an intense phase of questioning.

"Samantha was three when my brother died. At first, she didn't ask many questions, but a few months after the death they started coming. 'Why are you and Gramma Wendy sad?' 'Why did that bee bite Caleb?' 'What's 'lergic' (allergic) mean?' 'Is a bee gonna bit me?' 'You and me don't have to die, right?' I found the best way to answer these questions was honestly. I explained that usually people die when they are older, but sometimes people die when they are young. I explained that she wasn't allergic—we checked with a doctor. When she asked where dead people went, I told her that I didn't know but I thought it was a good place."

For toddlers, the concept of death is hard to grasp. They have experienced nothing that will prepare them for the concept. In their favorite cartoons, characters "die" and then return in the next episode.

Finality is unfamiliar. Until now, death has been something that just happens in movies or in cartoons. Nobody *really* dies. That illusion is shattered when a child faces their first loss experience.

One of the best things we can do is to use age-appropriate materials to help our children understand what has happened. In the resources section, you will find a list of books that can help guide your child through the questions and emotions of grief.

Young Children (three to ten years)

Until children are about four-years-old, they cannot conceptualize death, and because developmentally they believe the world revolves around them, some will even worry that they may have caused the death. Sometime between the ages of five and nine, children begin to understand death, and realize its finality. They will feel abandonment quite keenly and will worry that their needs may not be taken care of, i.e. Who will feed me? Where will I go? Most adults begin the first stage of mourning almost immediately and children usually begin mourning several weeks or months after the death. According to Dr. Roberta Temes in *Living With An Empty Chair: A Guide Through Grief,* "Children should not be criticized for caring, selfishly, about their own personal needs at the time of parental death. The child who asks 'But who will take me to the ball game?' or 'Who'll braid my hair for me each morning?' or 'What's for dinner?' when everyone else is weeping, is not being unduly selfish. She is responding as a child should respond."

Children between the ages of three and six do much of their learning through repetition. For this reason, it's common for children to ask the same question over and over or to alter it slightly. While this can be draining for you, take the time to answer the questions. Keep in mind that the child's peers will have little information on death and will not have the emotional maturity to help their friend. The only support children of this age group can get is yours—or other support you provide.

Adolescents

Pam's son Ian was 12 when his father died. She shares her story...

"My twelve-year-old son, Ian, was anxious to show his dad the new braces Dr. Mathews had installed that day. This was a new experience, a right of passage if you will, and Ian needed to share it with his dad. Although George and I had been divorced for many years, we were friends and joyfully shared in the day-to-day life of our son. I drove Ian to his dad's office, he smiled broadly at his dad, showing off his new hardware, and George embraced him. It was the last embrace. George was dead just one day later. Ian, at age 12, was at least able to communicate and express his sadness and anger verbally, although minimally. Imagine experiencing all the intense emotions of a sudden loss, without the ability to express your feelings in words. This is the younger child's plight."

Adolescence is a time of mood changes, and under the best of circumstances, a challenging time for all involved. Add to this the sudden death of someone close when they are least prepared and it's no wonder children find themselves wondering about the meaning of life.

Peer support is extremely important to the adolescent. If the adolescent child has lost a close friend, they should be encouraged to meet with and spend time with their peers and to use the time constructively.

A grief support group comprised of children experiencing the same type of loss will help immensely. You will need to help the child develop a safe way to express his emotions, especially anger. If there aren't any existing support groups, encourage your child to start one through school or church. Pam saw the benefit of school support with her son.

"We were fortunate that our school system had provisions for one-on-one grief counseling for Ian. He attended sessions with a school staff social worker faithfully for almost two years after his father died—most of them without my prodding. I believe the school's awareness and intervention was responsible for Ian's coping as well as he did. However, there were times when he acted out his anger in the home. With no words to express his enormous grief, Ian acted out physically, as many boys do, on the day of the funeral. Without saying a word, he left our house with a religious book his stepmother had given him. I watched as he threw the book onto the rain soaked street and kicked it for over an hour. He walloped that book over and over again until it broke from its binding in shreds. One final blow sent the soggy book sliding into the sewer. When he came back to the house, he looked spent—and relieved. Fortunately, he didn't hurt himself or anyone else."

Another challenge of this age group is the need to be independent. It is around this age that children begin pulling back from their parents seeking their own identity and independence. Barbara D. Rosof writes in *The Worst Loss*, "In order to grow toward psychological independence, [adolescents] must loosen the ties of dependency that have bound them to parents all their lives. This is a long process, one that proceeds by fits and starts over the next ten years. As they begin to pull away, the prospect of sharing with you the intense and painful feelings that the death of a sibling [or other close person] stirs up may feel dangerously regressive: It threatens to pull adolescents back into the very dependency they are working so hard to outgrow."

For this reason an outside support person becomes essential. If you cannot organize a support group through church or school, talk to a school counselor or other professional about being the support person for your child.

Teenagers to Young Adults

Teenagers and young adults may experience a sense of unfairness, i.e. he/she was supposed to be at my wedding, at the birth of my first child, at my college graduation. They will also experience a keen sense of their own mortality and may worry that they will die in the same unexpected way as their parent, friend or close relative. Again, a support group of peers can be extremely helpful in preventing the submersion of intense feelings, which can erupt in impulsive or destructive behaviors.

"At age 19, Ian is a well-adjusted young adult entering his second year of college who recently asked, 'Mom, I wonder what kind of man I would have turned out to be if my father hadn't died when I was 12?' Choking back tears, I answered the only way I knew how, 'I don't know how you would have been different, I only know he would have been proud of the way you turned out.'"

Teenagers experience many of the same stages of grief as adults. However, they also have experiences unique to their age. These include:

Private Grieving
Teenagers often aren't as familiar and in tune with their emotions. For this reason, many grieve privately. They may cry in their rooms or in the shower.

Unhealthy Anger
Teens may choose unhealthy venues for releasing their anger. They may destroy things or engage in self-destructive behavior. It's important to remember that teens do not have as many healthy outlets open to them as adults do. For this reason, it is imperative that we offer healthy outlets to teenagers.

Sexual Activity
With the loneliness that accompanies grief, teenagers may be left feeling lonely and scared. They may feel family members don't have the energy or ability to comfort them since they are facing their own grief. For these reasons, it is not uncommon for teenagers to become sexually active in an attempt to ease the loneliness.

Guilty Feelings
From an early age children long to please their parents, family members and those close to them. Often they interpret an argument as their failure to please. Furthermore, they may feel responsible for the death because they didn't behave well, caused too many arguments, were a source of stress or didn't meet parents' expectations. While parents find this reasoning inconceivable, it is common in a teenager's mind. It is important to reiterate over and over again that the teenager was, in no way, responsible for the death.

Physical Outbursts

Since children and teenagers are often not mature enough emotionally, they are much more likely to act out their emotions physically. This can take the form of tantrums, fighting, screaming, tattooing, body piercing or other physical expression. Watch for these physical signs. When you see one, realize it is probably caused by emotional repression. Take this as a red flag to find a support network or professional intervention for your child.

The Need to be Away From Home

When the deceased is a sibling, adolescents and teens may want to be away from the house. There are a couple of reasons for this. First, parents may be so absorbed in their own grief that children do not want to intensify their own emotions and grief by being around their parents. They may feel an obligation to comfort parents, yet not have the emotional energy to do so. Second, the house carries many memories of the relationship with their sibling and they may not be ready to face these memories. While it's important to maintain communication with the child and discuss feelings, offer the child his/her needed space, provided it's safe space.

Suicidal Thoughts

If the teenager was especially close to the person they have lost, they may see suicide as a way to rejoin their loved one. Also, when teens are not dealing with their emotions in a healthy way they can quickly become overwhelmed. Suicide becomes an escape route from these turbulent emotions. When a teenager details *any* part of a suicidal plan this is an *immediate* sign to seek professional help.

Linda Cunningham offers some helpful ideas for adults to help encourage teenagers to work with their grief. In her article entitled *Grief and the Adolescent*, she writes: "Teenagers often give us mixed messages. They tell us that they need and expect our help in providing them with food and a nurturing environment but also tell us, on the other hand, that they can run their lives on their own. Because people do not always know how to respond to teens, they frequently back off, resulting in a teen who is left to grieve alone or with very limited support..."

Some other ideas to help grieving teenagers include:

- Ask to see a picture of the person the child has lost. Ask questions about the person. Ask them to share their favorite stories and memories.

- Be inquisitive about the death. Ask the child what happened. Ask how the child feels about what happened. Often, as a teenager tells their story, we can listen carefully for clues of what they are confused about or feeling guilty for.

- Talk to your teenager about grief and the common emotions he is likely to feel. If it is the child's first time with these intense feelings, they can be extremely frightening. Choose a book or two from the recommended resources list to help the teenager familiarize their self with the emotions of grief.

- Encourage the teenager to make a collage. Help to gather magazines and pictures. Cut out words, pictures and notes that carry special memories. Place the finished collage in a place where the teen can see it often. Consider framing the picture and hanging it in their room.

- Help the teenager identify their needs and relate them to others. A teenager may feel unsupported, but it's hard for others to support him when they don't understand these needs. Identifying what would help most is a way to alleviate the unneeded pain of isolation.

- Encourage your teen to start a support group with other grieving friends. Offer your home as a safe place to hold the meetings. Do whatever you can to help. Perhaps you could car pool and pick up other kids, provide appetizers or beverages, photocopy handouts, etc.

General Guildelines for Helping Children

Below you will find some helpful guidelines to review as you work with understanding your child's experience and help them through their grief.

- Children should not be discouraged from attending the funeral, memorial service or burial. Make sure you, or some other adult, holds their hand or sits close by to offer explanations and comfort.

- Children must be told that the person is dead. Do not say the deceased is on a long trip or in a deep sleep. The child must be told that death is final and that there is no hope of the deceased returning. The child can then start to accept the finality of the situation and begin grieving.
- To help the child begin to mourn, a surviving parent needs to continue the daily routine as much as possible.
- Be supportive, understanding, open and accepting of their behavior.
- Work on listening. Communicating with a different generation can be difficult. Do your best to listen and be present without telling the child what to do. If you have a hard time listening objectively, find someone who can.
- Since a child's world has been turned upside down, it's important to remind them that you will always make sure their basic needs are taken care of.
- Continually express your unconditional love and acceptance.
- Answer questions as honestly as possible. Give as thorough answers as the child's age allows for.
- The child's environment should stay the same—this is not the time for a new school, a new house, or even a new baby-sitter.
- When you sense the child's readiness to grieve, it is okay to pray together, cry and reminisce together.
- Allow the child to talk, and talk, and talk about the death with you. Help him or her to understand that the grief will lessen and that the light will come again.

Remember, that no matter how old the child, they have experienced the worst possible tragedy. They will feel terrible. They should not be encouraged to forget or deny. They must learn, with your help and guidance, that they can overcome emotional catastrophes. Allowing the child to feel the full power of the sudden loss will help increase coping ability for the rest of the child's life.

Chapter Ten
Special Occasions and Challenges

"Traditions are like rules; however well intentioned when it comes down to it, they were made to be broken. As children we lived for the opportunity to break rules and traditions, to strike out on a different path. Why not experience that joy? Change the meal, change the location, make new traditions; your life has changed tremendously and so should your traditions."
Scott Miller, Tips For Those Grieving During the Holiday Season

Holidays, birthdays and other special days associated with the deceased present a special challenge. The loss becomes painfully evident and the feelings associated with the occasion become dulled and gray. Try not to be alarmed by occasional setbacks. This chapter will give you some ideas about what to expect. Knowing what to expect will allow you to create some options for yourself when these situations arise.

The Ambush

Deep pain and sadness, as if the death had just occurred, can surface at odd moments. Just when you think you're coping fine, along comes the dreaded ambush! Up from "no where" the rage resurfaces, the disbelief, the flashback, the horror, the insane feeling, the whatever. Just when you told yourself, and your friends, "I'm finally beginning to feel better."

Ambushes are particularly evident around special occasions such as birthdays, anniversaries, and holidays, or any time you are expected to participate in a celebration of some kind.

You may know exactly what kind of place or event triggers you (i.e. a particular store in the mall, the sound of children playing, the smell of pizza, a certain sporting event...) and you can chose to avoid those situations. However, sometimes the unavoidable occurs—the tears begin to flow and the outrage returns. Pam had this type of experience.

"I remember going to the supermarket and seeing my loved one's favorite Campbells™ soup on the shelf. I dissolved into tears and the mascara ran in streams onto to my white blouse. You might try wearing sunglasses in public. I did and it helped disguise the red, puffy eyes and the raccoon look. I also carried tissues and told strangers that I was dealing with a lousy allergy attack. And sometimes I told the truth."

If practical, stop what you're doing and honor it. Have the feeling, weep the tears, beat the pillows, phone someone or everyone in your support group. Allow the pain to wash through you and deliberately allow it to have it's full force.

A word of caution—if the "ambush" occurs while you are driving a car or other vehicle, pull over where it is safe. Driving with tears in your eyes and rage in your heart can be hazardous.

Birthdays

The deceased person's birthday is a time for remembering. You may feel your loss anew each time their birthday comes for many years.

Your own birthday may seem different. You may wonder why you are still alive and they are not, and it will be difficult to celebrate your own life for a while. For those who have lost an older sibling, the year when you pass your sibling's age at their time of death, can be incredibly stressful. It is an odd feeling to outlive your older sibling.

Many people find a sanctuary by creating a ritual with which to celebrate the deceased's birthday. Perhaps you can surround yourself with other people who were close to the loved one. Perhaps you can go take a walk in nature and just think and cry and rant and talk. In the exercises chapter you will find some rituals that may be useful.

Anniversaries

Some people find that they may do well for an entire year, only to find themselves virtually incapacitated by grief during the days surrounding the anniversary of the death. You wake up one morning with a heavy feeling, not knowing exactly why you feel so burdened. Then it hits you—the anniversary of one or another dates you shared with the deceased in the past.

On the anniversary of the day of death, many grievers report a short-term depression. It's not uncommon to experience discomfort, sadness and depression for a couple weeks before and after the date of death, each year. You may find some alternative solutions like herbs, vitamins and therapy to help you through this trying time. The strength of a support network can also be beneficial. Many people do "fine" throughout the year, only to be knocked off their feet as these significant dates occur.

Some religious traditions have a requirement around the one year anniversary of the death. In Judaism for instance, Judaic law has a prescribed ritual for "death days"—the anniversary of the death. You are expected to need to discharge extra emotions during those days. The headstone is unveiled at this time. Even if your religious tradition does not dictate it, you will feel some deep or extreme emotion on the anniversary of the death. Try to look at the anniversary of the death as another opportunity to grieve—to feel some of what has been unexpressed up until now.

Other anniversaries where you can expect to feel "extra emotions" include:

the last day you saw your loved one alive
the day you first met
the day you were married or engaged
the day the "plug" was pulled
the day you found out they were dead
the anniversary of a trip you took together

Of course there will be others depending on your relationship to the deceased. If you expect these anniversaries to be challenging emotional times you will be less surprised. If you know they are coming and when, you will be better able to cope. If you can, make special arrangements for yourself (i.e. take the day off from work, get a baby-sitter for the kids, find time and space to be alone, visit the grave, etc.) You may want to consider a ritual for the day of death. The exercises section of this book contains several rituals to choose from.

Weddings

If you are mourning the loss of a spouse, weddings can be especially difficult to attend. The bride and groom look so happy, "don't they know it can be all over in a matter of seconds!" The vows are said and you hear "until death do us part," and then the tears well up. If you have lost a young daughter or son, expect to feel anger and sadness that you will never see them married, and that you will not have grandchildren, etc. If you are in the early stages of mourning, it may be better for you to stay away from wedding ceremonies altogether and attend receptions instead. Or send a gift and stay home. This is a day of celebration for the bride and groom and their families. Don't be surprised if they avoid you in an effort to maintain their joy and experience the celebration. Try not to take their actions personally.

If you are the one getting married, expect your wedding day to be filled with a flood of emotions. Anger might be one of them—"Mom was supposed to be here, sitting in the front row. Now I have to look at an empty chair. It's not fair!"—"My sister was to be maid of honor, my best friend was looking forward to being my best man!" Your anger and sadness may seem unbearable.

Expect to have some tears—for joy and for sadness. Make sure you tuck a tissue in your bouquet or your jacket pocket. Let the officiant know what you're going through ahead of time. It would also be appropriate to ask the officiant to honor your lost loved one by requesting a moment of silence during the ceremony, as you light a candle for missing your loved one.

Pam, in her role as Interfaith Minister, does many wedding ceremonies. The following is an excerpt from one wedding where the bride had experienced a recent loss. You may wish to incorporate these words or something similar into your own ceremony:

As we light these candles, we sense the love and the presence of all those who have gone before us—especially Denise's mother, Ruth. We feel her with us today, adding her special blessing to this sacred ceremony. It is my hope and my prayer that the families of Denise and Michael, both seen and unseen, will do all they can to help sustain and nurture the bond of these two as they seek to create their own family.

Holidays

With the loss of a member of your immediate family, holidays and special occasions will be difficult. Holidays are often filled with traditions and memories of closeness. As we face these days without our loved one, the empty space looms large in our hearts. By creating new traditions and understanding the common difficulties faced during the holidays, they can be easier to cope with.

The American Association of Retired Persons offer these tips in their article, "Frequently Asked Questions by the Widowed."

- Plan ahead. It helps to ease the strain.
- Set priorities. This can make it easier to phase out elements less pleasing to you.
- Make new traditions. This new phase in your life deserves some new traditions.
- Include [the deceased's] name in conversation. It helps others talk about him/her.
- Express your feelings. Most people understand and accept your need to cry.
- Find someone you can help. Giving assistance to others is very satisfying.
- Buy yourself something special. You've suffered a great loss. Be good to yourself.
- Cherish your memories. These are yours to keep; they grow more precious over time.
- Be patient with yourself. Allow yourself extra time to accomplish tasks.
- Take time out for rest and relaxation. This will ease the stress of grief."

Most importantly, take your time and be gentle with yourself as you move through the holidays.

Holiday Traditions

Don't try and hold on to the way things were done in the past or your previous traditions. Your family has changed. It's okay to change the way you celebrate the holidays as well. Think of a new tradition. If you always celebrated Christmas at home, consider renting a cabin for a couple of days. If you always put your tree up early in the year, consider putting it up later. If a large dinner was always cooked, go out for dinner instead. Do things differently. The memories will be strong when the holidays come; altering routines is the best way to still find some joy. Brook's family changed their routine after Caleb's death.

"Caleb died two months prior to Christmas. Both my mother and I had done most of our shopping. As Christmas neared and we were still heavily immersed in sadness, we wondered what to do with all the gifts. We decided to give them to Caleb's friends. To change our routine, instead of celebrating Christmas day at my mother's, she came down to my house in southern Wisconsin. Now, she comes out to my Portland home each year. While we always have Caleb in our minds and hearts, we have learned the need to let go of some of the pain and engage in activities and new traditions that can help us move forward with our lives."

When we do what Brook has done we are honoring our lost loved one. It may seem as though we are disrespecting our loved ones or moving away from our memories—but in fact, we are paying tribute by moving on with our lives. Elizabeth was a newly widowed mother when the holidays came. She shares her story...

"The holidays, oh please save me from the holidays...make them go away! I remember my thoughts as a newly widowed mother of two young children sixteen years ago, as I raced around trying to put some kind of Thanksgiving and Christmas together. *Can't we just forget about it this year? Doesn't the rest of the world know how much pain I'm in?* I got together with another sad and lonely woman from my support group. I invited her and her kids to my house to have a turkey dinner for Thanksgiving. It helped to not face the carving of the turkey (which he did, rather poorly each year) alone. Somehow I did it, whatever "it" was, all the while listening to the happy Christmas carolers, fa la la la, la, la, la la.

Christmas day that first year was really strange. I opened the presents with my two children and then sat staring at the tree, imagining how it would feel to hurl the decorations off the deck and set the living room on fire. I must have sat in the green living room chair for two hours after that, not moving."

Where does one go during the holidays?

Does one have to go anywhere? Do you have to pretend to be happy and joyous for the sake of others? Is it okay to celebrate this year if you want to? Like so much of the grief process, we need to listen to our inner guidance in these matters. If you need to be alone, that's okay. You can choose that. You may have to put something together for your kids and that's fine. You might find them a great joy and inspiration and a reason to get out of bed. Other than the practical needs of those who are dependent upon you, you don't need to take care of others by pretending "everything's all right."

If you do visit family and friends during the holidays, feel free to let them know the following ahead of time:

- I may need to leave your home earlier than you expect me to. (I get tired easily these days because I'm under a lot of stress.)
- I may need to take a walk by myself after dinner. (It's hard to be around happy families for too long a time.)
- I may cry unexpectedly when I hear certain music. (I have memories of good times and it's hard to hold back the tears.)
- I may not eat all the food and goodies you offer me. (My appetite hasn't been what it used to be—maybe I'm finding all this "hard to swallow.")

Even without a sudden death in your family or circle of friends, the holidays can bring up all kinds of difficult feelings. Depression is the most difficult feeling of all. You will need to face that it's going to be nearly impossible to stave off depression, especially at this time of year. Everyone seems to be so happy, families are gathering together and there is a hole in your life. Walking through the mall you may see the perfect gift for your deceased loved one and dissolve into a flood of tears. You may have already bought the deceased gifts and there they sit, wrapped, under the tree, unopened. It would be extremely arrogant of us to suggest there is an easy fix for the kind of depression that surfaces around the holidays. Both of us, still suffer from periodic holiday blues. It may provide some relief to volunteer your time to help the needy and hungry. Giving of yourself to another, less fortunate person or to someone who has experienced a similar loss can take your mind off your own sadness—for a time.

This year, be one of the first people you think about during the holiday season. A support group will be especially useful during this trying time of year. Peers can offer rituals and ideas they use to make the holidays easier, or they can offer a shoulder to lean on in your time of need.

Happy New Year?

You may be at a different place right now and your optimism about the future may have begun to emerge. Celebrate! You are moving along in your recovery. For others, especially those in the early stages of recovery (first, second and third year), optimism about anything is a struggle. The first full year without your loved one can be especially difficult to move into. Your well-meaning friends and relatives may have a different opinion. You may hear phrases like, "It's the New Year—time for you to start fresh, get a new lease on life, stop crying and feeling sorry for yourself.." It is important to remember when confronted with their judgments or concerns that your recovery is your recovery. Your time frame for healing is your time frame, not theirs.

You may simply need to acknowledge that it is a new year and leave it at that. If the death occurred two years ago, you may mistakenly believe that since you are now two years into recovery that you *should* be feeling better by now. Don't be fooled by dates.

It's possible the thought of a New Year's Eve celebration (or any celebration for that matter) will bring up deep sadness around the loss of good times with the deceased or memories that are less than pleasant (i.e. drunkenness and unsafe driving). In either case, it is important to honor yourself wherever you are. You might make up your own New Year ritual—light some candles (one for each month/year you have made it on your own), burn some incense (to symbolize the burning away of the old way of being and the sweet smell of a new way), pour yourself a glass of wine or soda and drink a toast to yourself. You may have begun to live! It might be a good time to compare where you are emotionally with where you were last year at this time. (Please see the exercises section for specific ideas to help you do this.) Last year you may have wanted to stay in bed with the covers over your head every day of the week, and maybe now you only think about staying in bed three days a week—without the covers pulled up! These are not small steps. They are large strides on the path of grief recovery and they deserve your praise and recognition.

Looking toward Next Year

Next year it will hurt a little less—next year there will be a little more joy in your life. Next year you may be able to hear the music. Next year you may have more to give. Next year you may even be more ready to help someone else. Wherever you are in the grief process, there is the possibility of new life. We know it's hard—and we also know it gets less hard. The next time a special occasion, anniversary or holiday comes around you will feel a little more in control, a little less pained, the situation will be a little less difficult and you will begin to celebrate life again—one day.

Part Two
Sharing Our Stories

This was by far the hardest section of this book to write and compile. As authors our goal was to create a valuable resource and guide, yet in doing that we were stumped when it came to this section. We wanted to cover the different people we lose in our lives—parents, spouses, friends, children, siblings, etc., but just as there are no rules to grief, there are no rules to handling different types of loss. In reflecting on our own experience, we realized what we needed most was to hear that other people went through what we did, and although changed, came out the other side. We also needed general guidelines, poems, quotes and other materials to serve as a path. We collected stories, quotes, songs, poems and prayers that moved us. We divided this section by chapters of one's relationship to the loved one (parent, child, sibling, etc.).

We encourage you to read through each chapter since relationships are not easily classified into one area or another. A husband can also be a friend. Our siblings can be friends and parental figures, etc. For this reason, we believe you will gain quite a bit from the offerings in each chapter.

Furthermore, we didn't look for inspirational or motivational tales. We looked for real-life stories and real-life grief experiences we thought you could relate to. From there we added the quotes and poems. Additionally, we've included some common emotions and questions that those who grieve often have.

Chapter Eleven
The Loss of a Friend

"There is only one way for you
To live without grief in your lifetime; that is
To exist without love. Your grief represents
Your humanness, just as your love does."

Carol Staudacher

True, deep, abiding friends are hard to come by, and like all sudden losses, extremely difficult to understand. Our connection to friends, newly hatched or life-long, may be more intimate than the connection we have to our families; or a family member may be the closest friend we have.

In later life, most of us begin to ease slowly into the fact that due to death, we will need to let go of those we love and are close to. As we age it's natural to expect that friends will eventually become ill and die. As Judith Viorst would say, our second half of life becomes a time of "necessary losses." However, when we lose a friend through the tragedy of sudden death, the slow process of letting go is aborted.

Many friends fulfill particular roles. A friend is rarely "just" a friend. Most friendships include elements of other relationships. For instance, in cases where we didn't have functional parenting our friend may have become like a parent to us. In this case, the chapter where we discuss losing a parent, will be additionally helpful to you. If your friend was much younger than you when he/she died, it may be that you served a parental role or were a significant mentor. Perhaps some of what is included in the chapter on losing a child will be helpful. If your friend was also your romantic love, the chapter on losing a significant other will give you some insights and support as you grapple with your loss. We hope this chapter will provide you with some ways to navigate the loss of a friend.

I keep reaching for the phone. I want to tell my friend something important or ask her advice.

You may find yourself reaching for the phone to call your friend, to tell them about an occurrence, to invite them to a movie, to sit with you and tell you about their most recent accomplishment. Yet there is no one at the other end of phone—only a dial tone.

When a close friend dies suddenly it is natural to feel cut off from your source of advice and companionship. Slam dunked into the ever-present reality of the moment, there you are with your questions, your fears and your friend isn't there to share them with you. In the past, your friend would have been beside you at a moment like this. A support network, uplifting books and music can be helpful during these quiet moments.

Pam offers a great idea of how we can effectively incorporate the memories of our loved one.

"I had a therapist years ago tell me that the goal of therapy was to internalize the therapist's voice and make it a part of my own inner dialogue. Perhaps you can do this with your friend. Close your eyes, imagine their response to your call—you may feel them with you—internalize them—make them part of your life for the rest of your life.

I received a card from a friend when my father died and in it she wrote, 'Now you will have him with you—always...' I believe that's true."

What can I say to the family that will convey what my friend meant to me?

Almost more than any other person, your relationship with the deceased was unique. He probably revealed to you more of his true nature than to anyone else, including his family. Your reminisces and impressions of who he was will be more valuable because he was so real with you. In fact, you may know him better than his family because you spent more time with him over the years. What can you say? You can offer to share your stories. Brook's family found this extremely comforting.

"Caleb had more friends than anyone I've ever known. When he died, our house was flooded with his friends. My mother, Caleb's friends and I would sit in our living room recalling memories and stories. We did this for days. We laughed together, we cried together, we grieved together.

Several of his closest friends had special stories they wanted to share. Some were funny, some were odd and some were metaphysical. These friends offered to share their stories with us in private. We welcomed each story and my mother and I discuss them to this day. Do not be afraid to offer your story to a grieving family. Sharing our memories with one another is one of the best ways to keep our memories alive."

Is it appropriate for me to ask the family if I can participate in the funeral or memorial service?
Yes, by all means ask. They may not want you (or anyone outside the family) to participate, but most families welcome input from friends of the deceased. Personal stories illustrating your friend's humor or kindness are usually well received. If you are denied the privilege to read something at the service, perhaps there will be an opportunity if the family receives guests in their home following the funeral. Another way to convey your thoughts and feelings about your friend is to put them in a letter or card and send this to the family.

I want to place something in the casket—a memento of our friendship. Do I need to check with someone before I do this?
It is a good idea to check with the family before you place an object in with the deceased. The funeral director can also guide you. When Pam's friend, Eleanor died, she wanted her family to place in her hand a small golden goddess she had given her when she was alive. Pam knew this had great meaning to Eleanor, the family agreed and the funeral director was glad to comply.

I've been asked to participate in the memorial service. This is all so sudden and I haven't had a chance to prepare.

First of all, you are not expected to be a perfectly stoic performer. This is not a performance, it is meant to be a meaningful send off for your friend. If you are at a loss for words, you might want to select the lyrics from a song you both enjoyed as a way of conveying the depth of your relationship. Or you may simply want to say, "I have no words except, I will miss him. He was one of my best friends." If you feel you want to say more, we have provided a few appropriate readings to choose from. Additionally, there are books filled with suggestions. See our recommended resources section, and the eulogy form in the Appendix, for specific titles that may be helpful.

Pam read the following at a friend's funeral and prefaced it by saying, "As I read this, try to imagine these words being said by the departed..." (Feel free to fill in the name of your friend.)

> "Relatives and friends, I am about to leave:
> my last breath does not say "goodbye,"
> for my love for you is truly timeless,
> beyond the touch of bony death...
>
> I leave my thoughts, my laughter, and my dreams
> to you whom I have treasured
> beyond gold and precious gems.
> I give you what no thief can steal,
> the memories of our times together:
> the tender, love-filled moments,
> the successes we have shared,
> the hard times that brought us closer together
> and the roads we have walked side by side..."
> -Edward Hays, *Prayers for a Planetary Pilgrim*

The following, an excerpt from *The Prophet*, by Kahlil Gibran, was read by Pam for a friend who enjoyed singing and dancing:

"For what is it to die but to stand naked in the wind and to melt into the sun? And what is it to cease breathing, but to free the breath from its restless rides, that it may rise and expand and seek God unencumbered? Only when you drink from the river of silence shall you indeed sing. And when you have reached the mountain top, then you shall begin to climb. And when the earth shall claim your limbs, then shall you truly dance."

And here is a reading that anyone can use—and if your friend is a woman, feel free to change "he" to "she."

A Friend

What is a Friend? I'll tell you.
It is a person with whom you dare to be yourself.
Your soul can go naked with him.
He seems to ask you to put on nothing, only to be what you really are.
When you are with him, you do not have to be on your guard.
You can say what you think, so long as it is genuinely you.
He understands those contradictions in your nature that cause others
to misjudge you.
With him you breathe freely—you can avow your little vanities and envies and absurdities and in opening them up to him they are dissolved on the white ocean of his loyalty.
He understands. You can weep with him, laugh with him, pray with him—through and underneath it all he sees, knows and loves you.
A Friend, I repeat, is one with whom you dare to be yourself.
-Author unknown

When honoring a loved one, go with what feels intuitively right to you. What touches you deeply will likely touch others. When Brook was in her teens, she lost a friend in a car accident. At the service, the friend's father got up to speak. Barely able to get the words out between gasps and tears, he delivered a few minutes that moved everyone in the room. The deceased was a performer and he ended his talk with, "Always a performer, let's give him one more standing ovation for the time he gave us." Everyone in the room stood, clapping with all their might, tears streaming down their faces as they honored their friend. Typical? No. But it moved everyone more than any other spoken words could have.

Naturally, the best way to honor a friend is to speak from the heart—your heart. What you say doesn't have to be eloquent or full of fancy epitaphs. Simple, straightforward and heartfelt words are what the family is longing to hear. If you're feeling stuck as to where to begin, look to the form we have provided in the Appendix. This form is intended to give you a place to start and should help you cover the most important aspects of your friend's life and your relationship. Again, there is really no right or wrong way to eulogize a friend. You can sing a song, write a poem, dance a dance or read what someone else has written. Use your imagination and trust your instincts. If you are intuitively drawn to a particular reading or creative act, it may even be your friend who is gently nudging you, instructing you on how to celebrate his life.

Some Things You Can Do
Internalize Your Friend
The loss of a friend takes an enormous toll on the soul. You may feel like their loss has taken a part of you away. One of the best ways to honor your friendship is to take some aspect of your friend's life or the way he lived his life and incorporate this part of his personality into who you are.

Contributions
Did your friend love children, lost animals, parks, the theater? Find an appropriate way to contribute time or money to an organization that promotes one of those special values.

Helping His Parents
If your friend was the child of aging parents who cannot drive, or who may not be able to care for the grave site, assure them you will, with fresh flowers, weeding, etc. From time to time, take a photo of the grave site to show them.

Friend Support Group

Many support groups exist for those who have lost a partner or a child, but their are few that exist for the loss of a friend. One person that Pam knows, formed a support group with the deceased's friends. This is a wonderful way to keep a friend's memory alive, while working through grief. We have included the letter this woman used to begin her group in the Appendix.

Chapter Twelve
The Loss of a Parent

> *"...I learned to attend viewings even if I didn't know*
> *the deceased, to press the moist hands*
> *of the living, to look in their eyes and offer*
> *sympathy, as though I understood loss even then.*
> *I learned that whatever we say means nothing,*
> *What anyone will remember is that we came..."*
> *from the poem, "What I learned from My Mother" by Julia Kasdorf*

We expect to lose our parents—someday. We expect them to become frail and fragile and gradually "melt away" over time. And yet, few of us are really ready for our parent or parents to die, much less tragically or suddenly. We believe there is "always tomorrow" to say what needs to be said, to express what we feel. There is always tomorrow to express the anger, the pain, the love and the gratitude. Then we are cut short, mission aborted and we are left holding a bag full of feelings that may be heavier than we can bear. The unsaid gratitude becomes outrage. The unexpressed anger turns inward and we are depressed. The unspoken pain they caused us becomes a stone we carry in our hearts or perhaps guilt at the relief we feel in their passing. We waited for the right time, and when sudden death occurs, the right time is gone.

Many of us look to our parents for guidance and acceptance well into our adult lives. We rely on their opinions. We rely on them for our roots. When we lose a parent, a part of our history disappears. We can no longer ask opinions or hear stories of when we were younger. We lose a piece of our foundation. The following story details a girl's loss of her father and how that affected her throughout life.

"DADDY"
He was the center of my universe. He was my hero.
September 17, 1975

I was blissfully ignorant of what was to unfold. The phone rang. An employee of our riding stable. The horses had not been fed. Where's Frank? Where's Daddy?

Never would such a thing happen. Even as my mind raced to reach a sane and rational conclusion. I knew! Hopeless. Helpless. It was another 15 minutes before I fully understood, and felt the impact of these words. His car; parked at the church where he would meet a friend and run. Not jog. Run. There was something sinister about that car being parked there at this time. Still not fully grasping, understanding. It's locked and his shirt lay on the front seat. The car is never locked.

He's in trouble, passed out. I start to run down the trail. Halfheartedly. I knew that I couldn't help him alone and would need help. I tried to shout out for him. No strength. No use. Helpless. Hopeless. I weep.

Into my car and back towards the house to call. Who? The ranger. Find him. Help him. I pass Bonnie and my brother heading towards the church. My brother is pale and Bonnie is crying. And this I know is true: *My father's dead. How am I ever going to live!*

It will be many years before I pull that thought out to examine it.

Beat a tree: "Damn You For Dying!" And recover.

My good friend Naomi comes right away. She was my anchor then. To the barn to be with my horse and the woo-woo begins. Naomi's horse Greg has a nameplate on his stall door: "Casablanca, Naomi A" A moth lands on the first "a" in Naomi. It looks like: N*omi. Daddy always called Naomi, "Nomi." Signs are somehow important to me at this moment, although I have no conscious knowledge of their existence. This sign sets a tone that will come to be woven throughout the years.

Pickle is my best horse and my heart. He senses my overwhelming grief and lowers his head against my body. I embrace him and we stand like this forever. Such a magical moment to be comforted by my best friend in this way. I drink it in. Actually I let it out. Such unconditional love.

Later, as I walked away from his stall, something caught my attention. The bottom corner of my jacket had been chewed off! No wonder Pickle stood so patiently. No wonder he'd been so loving. It was the best kind of "step in the pants," as my father would say. Pickle brought me back to the joy that was/is my father. Ever the tease. Always the coyote. A part of me that lives.

This joy defined the shape and depth of my grief. The grief was huge, but it carried with it the best I knew of my father and myself. I went on, one step at a time.

Days later I'm folding laundry that's been in the basket for a while. In the middle of the clothes basket is my father's shirt. The one that he had worn on the last morning of his life. I pick it up carefully, tenderly, tearfully. A large moth falls out. Dead, if I remember correctly, but a moth just the same. A powerful sign. Daddy was all right. And I grieved.

Cigarettes. Marijuana. Alcohol. In excess, but somehow over the years I work my way through it, and I come out the other side alive. So Alive! and wanting to understand what motivated me, what dictated the choices I was making, had always seemed to make.

The wrong man; always the wrong man. And I found my way to a light. And she was Pam. She shined that light on me and I could see the beauty, and the strength, and the value of me. Me! She walked beside me as I explored the paths stretching out before me, and the ones that I had left behind. The choices I had made since my father died, and the ones I had made while he lived.

And now, 24 years since he died, more than half my lifetime later, the Spirit of my father is strong with me.

So say the ones that knew him in this life.
So say the ones that know him in the next.
So say I. I know him in both.

I feel the best he can be.
Beautiful.
Pure, with the perfection that only Spirit can inspire.

I am grateful for the sequence of events that has brought me to this place in time. I would not trade who I am or what I have experienced for the world. I was also grateful that my father died suddenly, without prior illness. He died in the middle of the land he loved, doing what he loved to do. I clung to this image whenever I needed to shift out of my grief. I read somewhere that when a person dies suddenly, it's because they've completed what they came here to do and have no reason for prolonged illness. I like this thought.

Years later a psychic told me that my father had actually stuck around longer in order to stay with me. That really made me feel special, at a time when I was terribly insecure. I needed so much. I have it.

by Rita Grenci

In addition to the loss of foundation and emotional challenges we face, there are other challenges. For one, roles may shift. If we have lost our last living parent we move from the middle generation position (you are a child and you have children) to the older generation position.

Additionally, if you lose one parent suddenly, like Rita, you may be left with the responsibility of caring for the surviving parent. Without warning or preparation, you must assume the role of caregiver. You become responsible for working with an attorney, the insurance company, perhaps a criminal trial in the courts.

If you and your parents were on the younger side (you in your twenties and they in their forties) at the time of death, you may have deep regrets over what you did and didn't get to do with them. If you and your parents were older (you in your forties and they over sixty) you may still have regrets, but it's more likely you have more memories to cherish.

"It is understandable that shock and denial follow sudden, unexpected death. There is a small corner of the mind of every distraught mourner that

hopes against hope for a reversal of reality—for the curtain to be pulled back and the dead parent to step forward, beaming, *It was all a big mistake!*"
Lois F. Akner, CSW, *How to Survive the Loss of a Parent: A Guide for Adults*

My mother died on December 23, 1990, just 30 days after collapsing from a burst aneurysm. She was a 61-year-old woman with *no* health problems whatsoever. She was very healthy, slim, followed a good diet and never suffered from any serious illnesses. According to doctors, she died of Adult Respiratory Distress Syndrome—which resulted from complications of two brain surgeries to repair multiple aneurysms that were found around her brain.

Apparently she was born with an AVM-Abnormal Vein Malformation, which she never knew about, neither did we. I am the oldest of three sisters, two of us were pregnant at the time. My father, who was 63 at the time, was devastated at the sudden loss of my mother and his companion whom had never left his side in 32 years of marriage.

It was the Sunday after Thanksgiving when she collapsed at 6:45 a.m. I lived two houses down from her. I had to call the paramedics, something I had never ever done before and that was very traumatic. I also had to ride with the paramedics and decide which hospital to take her to, without knowing how serious her condition was.

The last conversation I remember was the Monday before Thanksgiving when we were shopping for our family dinner. We spoke a lot about my baby, which she was so anxious to meet. Once she collapsed and after the surgeries, she was placed on morphine. I never had a normal conversation with her after that Thanksgiving dinner.

Even though it has been almost eight years since her death it is hard to say what stage I am in. My sisters and I have become even closer and have helped each other through the pain, although we are unable to speak a lot about it. Our children help us through it. Two of them were lucky enough to have been watched by her, one was a-year-and-a-half, the other just six-months-old. It is very difficult to go to the cemetery without breaking down, but the kids go with us and understand that she is buried there. We talk about her to the kids and keep her pictures to remind them about how wonderful she was. This has helped although I have yet to completely cry all the tears because I am terrified about not being able to stop. That deep pain one feels which touches the very core of your being is where I need to go because I know I will cross into a different stage. That is where I think I am now, ready to face the fear of feeling that pain and getting to a point where I can speak to my mother directly about things that happen to me or to ask for her advice.

I carry her with me every single day and with every action I take, I remember her wisdom and values as I teach my own child about how to be a good person who helps others.

What I have learned from the grieving experience and facing tragic death is that you never know when you will die. One must enjoy every day and enjoy family. Our family and children need us. It is important to keep my mother alive in her memories, I see a lot of her in me, I even see her expressions in me and that is good because I keep her legacy alive and I am passing it on to my son.

I went through a rough time when my father passed away three years later. It is scary to know that you are all grown up and are truly responsible for your actions. I am my mother now...I never realized what she meant when she said, "Just wait until you have your own family, you will understand why I am so strict and demanding of you." She was preparing me to take her place..."

Martha, California

Rachel, now a 30 year old divorced mother of three children tells her story...

"He didn't have to die. Some chemical imbalance that made him depressed contributed to my father's suicide. It was Christmas Eve and I was 14-years-old. Somehow I knew that Christmas Eve day, while I was busy baking cookies, that there was something terribly wrong. I had finished wrapping all the presents for my father when he gave mom a very hard, clinging hug. Then he disappeared from my life, forever. Self-inflicted, carbon monoxide poisoning from his car's exhaust.

I was a shy person to begin with and we had just moved. I was in a new school. I dealt with this tragedy by becoming an adult—at 14-years-old. Many of the kids were cruel and said things like, 'Do you know your father is going to hell because he committed suicide?' These comments disturbed me very much and I prayed for his soul every night.

I never had counseling for the loss. Instead, I coped by doing everything for dad—like shooting baskets in basketball. I became very needy in relationships as I grew older, and extremely afraid of losing someone. I still feel anxious when someone leaves the house, like they may never come back. I always make sure the last thing I say is 'I love you.'

The best healing for me happened six years after he died. I had a dream where he came to me and said, 'Thank you for your prayers, I'm with God now and at peace.' My mother told me she had a vision of the same thing on the same day! The dream and mom's vision had great meaning and healing for me."

"In the end, the way your father or mother died is not a complete statement about their lives. There is much more that remains to be remembered. To concentrate only on the manner of the end deprives not only your parents of their total identity, but you of a broader perspective."
Fiona Marshall, *Losing a Parent*

Some things you can do
Letter Writing
Write a letter to your parent expressing your true feelings and place it in the casket before burial or cremation. If the body was not recovered, you can burn the letter on a beach or some other outdoor place. As the smoke rises, imagine the words are being carried on the air to your parent.

Photographs

Find a photo of your parent that you have not yet framed. Take it to a photo store to be enlarged, have it framed and hang it in a special place.

Listening

Keep listening for advice and guidance from your parent. Your parent may have died, but she was a powerful influence in your life. If what you "hear" is negative, now is the time to turn DOWN the volume on negative influences and turn UP the volume on positive influences.

Seeking A Mentor

There may be someone else in your life that you can find who will help nurture and encourage you the way a good parent would. With the help of this surrogate parent, you may be able to get some of your unmet needs addressed.

Lessons Learned

Make a list of all you learned from your parent, good or bad. It can help to know that their life had meaning to you and that you received some very important life lessons from them. Even if your parent died an untimely death and was in your life for only a short time, you can surely find the meaning in your relationship. This can truly help you accept the loss and move on in your grief.

Chapter Thirteen
The Loss of a Child

"I've learned that I am much stronger than I ever gave myself credit for. I've learned patience, because grief does not go away just because you want it to. And I've learned that helping other people is sometimes the best help I can give myself."

Diana F.—Mother of a 17-year-old daughter who committed suicide

It has been said that there is no loss as devastating as the loss of a child. Sudden death is a mix-up of everything we know to be true in life. Losing a child to sudden death is a break in the natural law and order of life. The child we have spent our time loving and caring for and planning to watch well into adulthood, has been taken. It is a heartbreak like no other. Those who live through and survive such an ordeal without becoming bitter have the strongest, most loving souls of all people walking the planet.

In her book *Surviving Grief*, Doctor Catherine M. Sanders writes, "The reason parental grief is so different from other losses has to do with excess. Because loss of a child is such an unthinkable loss, everything is intensified, exaggerated and lengthened. Guilt and anger are almost always present in every significant loss, but these emotions are inordinate with grieving parents. Experts estimate that it takes anywhere from three to five years to reach renewal after a spouse dies, but parental grief might go on for ten to twenty years or maybe a lifetime. Our lives are severely altered when our child dies and there can be no replacement. Substitutes offer little respite. This is not to say that there is no hope for happiness. It is just that the shock and severity of this kind of loss leaves us feeling completely helpless and full of dark despair."

As Dr. Sanders points out in the previous excerpt, our emotions are intensified with the loss of a child. Let's look at these magnified emotions.

Extreme Emotions

There are so many dramatic changes and hardships to understand and overcome with the loss of a child. It has been said that after losing a child, we embark on a lifelong healing process. Understanding these unique challenges can help us to understand how to work through them.

Disorder

Disorder seems to be more prevalent after losing a child than any other loss. While we may face disorder in our physical and emotional lives, we also feel disorder within the world. When we have children, we expect them to outlive us. We build a future around our children. We build dreams and fantasies and goals. In short, we build a world. When a child is lost, these fantasies and dreams come crashing down without warning. Basic logic seems to have abandoned the world as we know it.

A Piece of Ourselves

Children are an extension of us. They carry many of our physical and personality traits forward into the world. We see ourselves in their eyes. Through our children, we envision a better future. When we lose a child we lose this extension, we lose this hope.

Guilt

Guilt runs strong in surviving parents. As a parent, we expect ourselves to be able to take care of our child. From birth, most parents promise their children they will protect them. When a child dies, we may feel a sense of personal failure. We may think we weren't "good enough" as parents. These thoughts are the mind's attempt to make sense of the unfathomable.

Anger

Although anger is present in most types of grieving, it is different when we've lost a child—it's often much more intense. Parents simply cannot passively accept this devastating loss—they must express their anger at someone. It might be God, it might be the doctors, it might be whoever was present—but the anger will come. Obsessive anger needs to be talked about with a professional. In order to function, it is imperative that parents funnel this anger into a healthy or creative outlet.

Stress

In her book, *The Worst Loss*, Barbara D. Rosof writes, "The death of a child is a loss like no other. *The Diagnostic and Statistical Manual of Mental Disorders*, psychiatry's diagnostic bible, does not overstate the case when it calls the death of a child a 'catastrophic stressor.' It robs parents of what they love most, isolates partners from each other, and deafens them so that they cannot hear the cries of their other children."

The stress experienced by a parent is unimaginable. It is important that each parent recognize and seek ways to deal with this stress. For women, who tend to find comfort and healing from discussion, joining a support group is a wise decision. The Compassionate Friends is a support group that deals specifically with child loss. They have over 500 chapters. See the Resource chapter to find out how to locate a chapter near you.

Men also need to find support. Some men find this in a support group setting and others prefer one-on-one counseling or handling their grief privately. Later in this chapter we take a detailed look at men's grief and the grief of couples.

Losing an Adult Child

Losing an adult child carries unique challenges. A parent has put so much time and energy into raising a child. You spend hours, days, even years lecturing children on how to be safe. Don't talk to strangers. Stay away from drugs and alcohol. Look both ways before crossing the street. After all this careful care and attention throughout their youth, you assume you are "out of the woods"—that now you will reap the rewards of watching your child develop into an adult. You wait for them to marry or follow a career or have children. When you lose a child at this life junction, although you are have many precious memories, you are robbed of the future experiences you have expected.

In the brochure titled, *The Death of an Adult Child*, The Compassionate Friends write, "If the adult child dies as the result of an accident or an illness, parents are often told (while being comforted by friends or family) that they should be grateful that their child lived as long as he or she did. Of course you are grateful to have had your child for 25, 30 or 40 years, but that does not mean your grief is lessened! Many parents have stated their relationship with the adult child had become one of friendship. They feel that they have not only lost their child, but a friend as well."

The following poem by Wendy Feiereisen details the emotions and trials of losing a child. It was written after the death of her 27-year-old son.

Three Weeks to the Day

PART ONE: Saturday
it is three weeks to the day—to the hour—to the minute
to that split second—when daylight-savings-time
became eternity

What day is that you ask?
the day the sun rose for the last time
the day my son rose for the last time

What hour you ask? It was around noon I am told
What minute? We can give or take a few of those
What second you ask? The second was that split segment
of the smallest minutae of measurement
when a life—my son's life—Caleb's life
spilled over that edge of earth time
into an all time—beyond time
(as we know it anyway.)

'Caleb is dead,' the doctor said
And I said no.
'Your son died,' he said yet again
And my scream came—loud—and raw—and uncontrollable
Grief such a small word—only five letters

such a soft, sad, quiet word
I thought I knew so much about it
how to shape it. Form it. Manage it.

Yet it thrashes through my brain waves
like a tide pounding, pounding—circling around and around
coiling, squirming like some screaming ugly snake.
Until its death rattle shakes and hisses me in the eye
striking so fast I'm not ready.
Are we ever?

I went home.
I anguished.
I languished
numb from shock.
I slept
exhausted
dreamless
unrefreshed

people answered my phone for me
people cooked for me
people understood for me

I became an animal—instinctual—senses heightened
muscles tensed—with an acute awareness of the very
air I breathed
      the wafts of incense from his room
      his footsteps up into the attic
      the clean, soapy smell from an untaken shower
      his bottle of cologne, still full
His ghost spirits moved through the house as he made his good-byes.
almost brushing against my shoulder with a last wispy hug.

and people answered the phone for me.
and people cooked for me.
and people understood for me.

My dearest friends cared for me
when I didn't care.

he felt no pain—he knew no fear
stung by a Yellow-jacket—he was unconscious in seven minutes
died in twenty—his friends around him—his best friend next to him
his dog swimming beside him—the sun beating down on him
as they poled across the marsh...   to get help

I was at home winding my Seth Thomas clock
to measure a time I couldn't even begin to imagine
Three weeks to the day that clock ticks heavily, slowly,
it's bell tolling every hour while every second
I try to understand, what isn't understandable
He was only twenty-seven, just half my age.

PART TWO: That Sunday
he lay there...softly sleeping...eyes closed...his lashes were so long
he felt cool like marble...smooth...confident...strong...immortal...

I sat cross-legged on the floor, close by
as we let him go, as we bid him God's speed.
He was in God's hands now.
my "mothering" done.

death
such a small word
only five letters...like grief.
Sad...soft...quiet...yet ironically...a great magnifier.
Life becomes reflected upon—
each minute detail remembered, captured
with a passion beyond passion
Time becomes this large space, within
which one moves in all directions at once.
The past becomes the present.
The future becomes the past.

A circling and drifting begins—
no earthly bearings pertinent now.
It's as if we try to go with...
we try to know all there is to know
we try to fix everything
we struggle for a sense of order, of balance
of weightlessness
and then gravity pulls our feet back to
shaky ground, and we crawl for a time

What is most important to remember is that you will need time, lots of time, to get back on your feet. Be patient with yourself. Ask for patience from those around you. Make sure you are moving forward, no matter how small the steps might be. At the end of this chapter you will find some specific ideas for working with your grief. Additionally, many of the exercises in Section Three will be helpful. The Resources section also contains many books with great thoughts and guidance for parents who have lost a child.

Suicide

"Gradually, I came to understand that while it may be possible to help someone whose fear is death, there are no guarantees for a person whose fear is life." – Carla Fine

According to a study released by the Center for Disease Control and the National Institute for Mental Health, suicide is the ninth leading cause of death in the U.S., with 31,204 deaths recorded in 1995. This approximates to around one death every seventeen minutes. There are more suicides than homicides each year in the United States. From 1952 to 1992, the incidence of suicide among teens and young adults tripled. Today, it is the third leading cause of death for teenagers aged 15-19 (after motor vehicle accidents and unintentional injury). Suicide is increasing, particularly for those under 14 and for those over 65. It is the third leading cause of death for people 15 to 24 years of age and is the sixth leading cause of death for children 5 to 14.

A 1991 U.S. Center for Disease Control survey of high school students showed that 34% of girls and 21% of boys have considered suicide, actually *during the last year* 16% of high-schoolers made a "specific plan," 8% "tried suicide".

Suicide is one of the most devastating types of loss. In her book *How To Go On Living When Someone You Love Dies*, Therese A Rando, Ph.D. writes, "This can contribute to a profound shattering of your self-esteem, with strong feelings of unworthiness, inadequacy and failure. Like homicide, this death was not inevitable. It was preventable. You must recognize that you are particularly victimized by this type of death, and are susceptible to intensified and conflicted bereavement reactions."

But we are not at fault for someone's suicide. In the end, in the final moment, they made the choice alone. In *No Time to Say Goodbye: Surviving the Suicide of a Love One*, Carla Fine writes, "Like most survivors, I was haunted by the infinite regrets that are woven into the fabric of suicide. I would replay the chronology of events leading up to Harry's death, searching for lost opportunities to reverse the inevitable outcome. Only as I began to accept the idea that my husband's choice to kill himself was his alone did the powerful grip of "what-ifs" of his suicide begin to loosen. Gradually, I came to understand that while it may be possible to help someone whose fear is death, there are no guarantees for a person whose fear is life."

Diana lost her seventeen-year-old daughter to suicide. She hung herself in the bathroom. Diana was kind enough to share the story of her grief. The following writings come from her journal.

"One year ago today, on a day quite similar to this in fact, I found out my 17-year-old daughter had committed suicide. The person who had to tell me this was my husband. He has never been the same since that day. I have never been the same since that day.

I have never felt pain like this in my life. I am an impatient person, to say the least, I do not like enduring something that shows no sign of going away anytime soon. I want this over and I want it over now. Immediately. But it doesn't stop.

Some days are better than others. Some days I can go through the day and feel halfway normal. Other days, I could very easily just crawl into a corner somewhere and just stop. Stop everything. Stop thinking and stop hurting and stop breathing.

I am at this point of trying to deal with the anger. I'm trying to deal with this anger at her, for quitting. For not thinking beyond that moment in time, and I've been there, that moment in time where it doesn't matter anymore. Where absolutely nothing in this world means a damn thing except what's causing your pain. And all you want is for that pain to go away, like I do right now. I know the moment intimately. I've been there a few times, I'm there now. But something inside me steps through that moment and won't let me end the pain that way. I have to live with it, I have to go and carry it and hope that over time it will be absorbed and become part of me that is just there.

The grief books give you stages. Yeah, you go through them. But more than likely, not in the order they are listed. This is not an exact science, I am becoming more intimately in tune with the effect of grief than I would care to be. And I can't stop it, I can't ignore it, it's there. It doesn't go away, it's there and all you can do is deal with it.

Some days 'dealing with it' has been laying on the bed and running through the entire channel selection on the remote for hours at a time, with no real coherent thought processes going on. Other times it has been a search and destroy run on a room in the house. Or standing outside staring straight up at the sky until my neck hurts, hoping for some kind of a sign, something to flash across the sky that will make sense of it all.

Pitching a fit and placing blame would be easy. It has been easy, that's why I've done it a few times. I blame me. I blame her father. I blame the schools. I blame the doctors. I blame the counselors. I blame _____ . Blame is easy. What's hard is getting past the blame and finally accepting the fact that, no matter what pushed her to do this, Anna took her own life. Anna killed herself. She did this, not me, not her father, not society. It was by her own hand and her choice.

I get through it, I struggle. I fall. I cry. I scream. I rant and rave. And I pace and pace and pace. But I am going through it. One day at a time.

Which is all that we can do. Some of us can quit. Some of us can't. I can't quit.

There are no rules. It's been a year today. I will be expected to start 'snapping out of this' and going back to the way I used to be. Sorry, it ain't happening. I will never be the same again. I'm going to be different from now on. That's part of the process. Like it or not. Hell, I don't like it. I don't like looking at bunnies and feeling pain instead of, 'Oh that's so cute, Anna would love that!' I don't like seeing special Barbie® dolls and knowing there's no reason to buy them anymore—especially the drag queen Barbie® I saw last night. She would've loved that one. I don't like knowing I will never have a grandchild of my own or a continuing relationship with the person she was becoming. I don't like laying awake at night remembering what she looked like laying in that coffin to make this a reality for me. I don't like knowing that for 28 days after coming home I couldn't get into the shower, because every time I did, I saw her hanging from the shower rod and I didn't even see her like that. Grief is a viscous thing and it does horrific things to your mind. After that you are never the same. Everything changes, brutal fact of life. All I can equate this with is an animal licking it's wounds. I'm wounded and I need time to heal—and I will heal—in my own time and in my own way.

The last few days have been the yelling at God stage. *What is expected of me? Why do I have to be so strong? How come other people get to go through life and never experience half of what I've gone through in my life?*

I need peace. Peace of mind, peace in my soul and peace in my heart. I have no illusions. Anna and I loved each other dearly, and when we were together it was special time. There were also some very bad times, but we can't predict the future and we can't go back and change what has happened. I know there are things I would most definitely do different if I could.

I held my Godson last night. I watched him be born, what an emotional experience that was. It's funny, in the last few months there have been five new babies born into my immediate circle of friends. People expect this to be painful for me, but it's not really. I never thought I could be optimistic again. Especially right now, but I am. My child is gone but with each new baby that comes into this world, there is a new hope. One new chance for things to go right.

It's a long and slow process. Sometimes for every two steps forward, you drop back three. But other times you get to take two more steps forward without falling back. You just have to keep putting one foot in front of the other and keep going. And that's exactly what I'm doing, one step and one day at a time."

Common Reactions to Suicide

Shock, guilt, grief, anger, depression and denial work overtime when someone commits suicide. Suicide is seen as a *preventable* death in the minds of many people. With this being the case many survivors feel intense guilt and anger since they were unable to prevent it. When the one who has died is your child, the emotions intensify further. The Compassionate Friends write, "The suicide of one's child raises painful questions, doubts and fears. The knowledge that your love was not enough to save your child and the fear that others will judge you to be an unfit parent may raise powerful feelings of failure. Realize that as a parent you gave your child your humanness — your positives and negatives — and that what your child did with them was primarily your child's decision."

Questions and Suicide

"Why?" is the question that survivors of suicide ask over and over again. "Why would he (or she) take his life?" The "need to know" feelings are intensified when suicide occurs. The Mental Health Association in Waukesha County Wisconsin, published a pamphlet titled *Grief After Suicide*, which states: "Why would anyone willingly hasten or cause his or her own death? Mental health professionals who have been searching for years for an answer to that question generally agree that people who took their own lives felt trapped by what they saw as a hopeless situation. Whatever the reality, whatever the emotional support provided, they felt isolated and cut off from life, friendships, etc. Even if no physical illness was present, suicide victims felt intense pain, anguish and hopelessness. John Hewett, author of *After Suicide*, says, 'He or she probably wasn't choosing death as much as choosing to end this unbearable pain.'"

While you will never know the complete thought processes of the person who took his or her own life, know that you are not alone in your questioning. Many support groups, both in-person and via the Internet, can help you explore your questions and feelings. Please see the Resource Chapter for support ideas.

Religion and Suicide

There are many mixed emotions, thoughts and feelings on suicide and religion. For those affiliated with churches that take a harsh view of suicide, this can be an especially difficult time. In Eva Shaw's book, *What to Do When A Loved One Dies*, she writes: "While suicide is mentioned throughout the Bible's Old Testament, there is no opinion, condemnation or condoning. Saint Augustine said it was a grievous sin and the Catholic church and a few Protestant denominations have, at times, taken a harsh view of suicide. All major religions have abolished the philosophy that suicide is a cardinal sin, however, you may have to forgive [or ignore] a few people who make comments about the religious aspect of suicide."

The Stigma of Suicide

The Compassionate Friends offer the following on the topic of suicide, "Cultural and religious interpretations of an earlier day are responsible for the stigma associated with suicide. It is important that you confront the word *suicide*, difficult as it may be. Keeping the cause of death a secret will deprive you of the joy of speaking about your child and may isolate you from family and friends who want to support you. Rather than being concerned about the stigma surrounding suicide, concentrate on your own healing and survival. Many parents prefer to use the phrase "completed suicide" rather than the harsh "committed suicide" when speaking about their child."

The people around us may also have a hard time understanding and accepting suicide. Therese A. Rando, PhD, writes, "The normal need to know why the death occurred will be intensified in suicide." You will need to work hard at answering the questions in your own mind, so that when you are ready, you can talk to others about your child comfortably.

If you have lost someone from suicide, get more information. The Internet has many valuable resources and online support forums; additionally, many books are devoted to the topic. If you are comfortable in a support group setting, there are many for suicide survivors. Check the Resource Chapter or call your local church, hospital or college for ideas on local groups. You will need to come to a point where you can remember your lost loved one realistically—both the positives and the negatives.

Tattered Kaddish
by Adrienne Rich

Taurean reaper of the wild apple field
messenger from earthmire gleaming
transcripts of fog
in the nineteenth year and the eleventh month
speak your tattered Kaddish for all suicides:

Praise to life though it crumbled in like a tunnel
on ones we knew and loved

Praise to life though its windows blew shut
on the breathing-room of ones we knew and loved

Praise to life though ones we knew and loved
loved it badly, too well, and not enough
Praise to life though it tightened like a knot
on the hearts of ones we thought we knew loved us

Praise to life giving room and reason
to ones we knew and loved who felt unpraisable

Praise to them, how they loved it, when they could.

Your Relationship with your Partner

The most intense stress to a relationship is the loss of a child. Studies have shown that married couples experience extreme stress during the three-year-period that follows the loss of a child.

Tonya lost her five-year-old son when he got in the crossfire of a robbery. She explains what she went through with her husband. "We were both so drained. It was like staring at each other through a thick fog—we kept trying to reach out to each other, knowing we needed each other, but we couldn't reach. He saw my pain and I saw his, and yet there was no energy to console each other."

Tonya's experience is a common one. A couple that previously worked as a team is left unable to function or help each other. The grieving process of couples is further complicated by history, gender differences and expectations.

In his book, *When Goodbye is Forever: Learning to Live Again After the Loss of a Child*, John Bramblett shares his experiences after the death of his son. One story exemplifies the differences within a couple. In this story, he and his wife were at a Rotary party. While discussing unusual events surrounding his son's death with a small group of people, he noticed his wife staring at him through the sliding glass door. He writes, "I knew what she was thinking; she knew what I was talking about. I wanted to communicate my experience; it was part of my way of coping. She felt that talking about those striking episodes in our family's life cheapened them. Neither of us was wrong; our approaches were just different."

Another complication is blame. If one parent was present when the death occurred, that parent may blame himself or the other parent may blame him. Blame creates guilt, conflict, anger and resentment. It is destructive and serves no purpose—yet it's a natural human emotion. One way we can combat blame-thinking is by putting ourselves in the other person's shoes. For example, if you are the one blaming your spouse—imagine how that makes your partner feel. If you are the one blaming yourself, imagine hearing a similar story from a friend. What advice would you give him or her?

Grieving styles:
The differences between men and women

Grieving within a couple is complicated further by gender differences. Men and women are taught to handle their feelings differently. Because of this, a woman may feel she is not being "heard or understood," when really her spouse is coping with grief the best he knows how. Likewise, a husband may feel he's not being heard because he is being pressured to talk or share uncomfortable feelings, when actually the woman is coping the best way she knows how.

Understanding the difference of men and women's grief is paramount to working through grief in a partnership. Here we will explore the common differences between men and women in the grieving process. By understanding the differences, we can become more open to other styles of grieving. Keep in mind that this section is written based on the majority of men and women, but there can be a great deal of crossover. These are general patterns that are not written in stone.

Terry Matine and Kenneth J. Doka offer the following summary in *Living With Grief After Sudden Loss*, "Masculine grief tends to be private, dominated by thinking rather than feeling, and action-oriented. While most masculine grievers are men, many women adopt this pattern of coping as well. Although traditional therapies have encouraged grievers to openly share their emotional distress and to recall painful events, masculine grievers may respond best to private, problem-solving approaches that respect and encourage emotional mastery."

Martin and Doka offer this outline as the usual masculine grief pattern. Reading this outline can help men identify their patterns and help those close to them create ways to work through the grief process.

- Feelings are limited or toned down
- Thinking precedes and often dominates feeling
- The focus is on problem-solving rather than expression of feelings
- The outward expression of feelings often involves anger and/or guilt
- Internal adjustments to the loss are usually expressed through activity
- Intense feelings may be experienced privately; there is a general reluctance to discuss these with others

▪ Intense grief is usually repressed immediately after the loss, often during post-death rituals

Let's explore some of the specific differences in the ways men and women grieve.

Problem Solving

One of the main communication barriers is what men and women seek to get out of a conversation. Women seek someone to talk and explore with, whereas men often look to "solve the problem." Men will commonly put "solving and thinking" before "feeling and expressing." When faced with grief, a man may want to figure out how to support his family and how to be the anchor before exploring his feelings. Remember that many men believe they are responsible for taking care of the family. This belief makes it hard to show emotion when they feel they need to be providers. This is complicated further in many men by guilt. As the "protector" of the home, a man may feel guilty or that he has failed when his child dies. "I should have been able to protect him," is a thought that runs through the minds of many men.

Women are more apt to see relationships as the central point in their lives. Often, women's relationships and emotional ties to children and spouse come before any other need. When a child dies and the relationship is permanently severed, women often become introspective. Women worry less about the "outside world," and the logistics of "getting by," and more about life within the four walls of home.

Articulating Feelings

In her book, *The Worst Loss*, Barbara A. Rosof writes, "Men have learned to suppress feelings, not express them. When your wife asks what you are feeling, and you answer 'I don't know,' it is probably an honest answer. The ability to know what you feel and to know how to put your feelings into words are acquired skills; you learn them only if you are encouraged to do so. If, on the contrary, when you were growing up feelings were a hindrance or a sign of weakness ("big boys don't cry") then you are less likely to pay attention to yours." In men's circles, it is uncommon to express and articulate feelings. When men are pressured to show feelings, everyone can become easily frustrated. Women get frustrated because they feel "closed off," and men feel frustrated because they can't find the words to express themselves in the way a woman wants. These are times to remember that each person expresses themself in unique ways. There is no right way. There is no wrong way.

Women are much more likely to clearly express their thoughts and emotions. Women spend much of their time discussing emotions with other women. Articulating feelings usually comes naturally and easily, and it can be hard for a woman to understand why men can't do the same. Patience and recognition of our differences is vital.

Support

Society has long led men to believe that they are leaders and should be self-reliant. Men want to be able to take care of themselves and their own needs. Women are often led to believe that they need others and are used to talking amongst other women. Men, on the other hand, are not provided with many opportunities to share their emotions safely. When grief strikes, women are more likely to seek a support group, whereas men are more apt to seek time alone. Recognize that you may each define "support" differently and be open to each other's definitions.

Guidelines for Grieving Men and their Partners

Ask Specific Questions

Men often aren't as familiar with their feelings and emotions as women. Questions like, "How are you feeling?" and "How are you doing?" are likely to be answered with, "I'm all right," or "Fine." It's not that men are avoiding answering the questions, they are simply answering them as they have in the past. Try more specific questions for more specific answers. Questions like, "What was the hardest part of the funeral for you?" "What do you think John would want us to do today?" will usually open up more conversation.

Allow Time

It may take a while for men to articulate how they feel. Keep in mind that most men have not had as many opportunities to articulate their feelings in a safe environment as women have. If a woman asks a question she needs to allow some time for the man to form his response. It could take a couple minutes (or maybe even ten) but patience is key.

Start an All Male Support Group

Since men often grieve differently it can be valuable to start a support group that consists only of men. In the book *Men and Grief* (see Resources) there is a comprehensive section on how to start an all male support group.

Find a Physical Outlet

A punching bag, running, racquetball—anything physical can help release penned up emotion. When Brook's brother died, her mother wanted many things from the house thrown out. It had been years since they had completely cleaned the "very-lived-in" home. Brook's husband Andy ordered a big dumpster to be brought in by a semi. Andy and about ten other male friends of Caleb's, threw "everything" into the dumpster. They broke glass. They broke doors. They vented. They cleaned. They purged. And in the end the dumpster was full of no longer needed clutter. The attic was clean, the basement organized and somehow their souls lightened. They had begun to let go. They had made order out of collected chaos. They had started the process of selected memory.

Give Men Space

Men don't like to "burden" others with their troubles. They may feel that grief is "their own problem" and that they should work through it on their own. Men may cope better by taking some time to "work through" their grief in a private setting. Since we all grieve differently and find different things helpful, it's best to be supportive of this need.

Guidelines for Grieving Couples

Read This Chapter Together
It's important that you both understand grief and how it affects a couple. Read and discuss this chapter together. Use it as a springboard for questions such as, "Do you experience that?" or "Would you like to try that?"

Find Additional Support
One mistake that many couples make in a marriage is the expectation of having all their needs met by one person—their partner. This is unrealistic and puts too much pressure on a partner. Our needs are so diverse, it takes a diverse group of people to meet them. The same is true with grief. We need more than one person to help us through—we need diversity.

Discuss issues away from home. The home environment will be charged with emotions and memories. To help overcome complicated emotions and distractions, make time to talk and share away from home. Go out for dinner, focus on one another and talk through joys, problems, pains and life.

Consider Letter Writing
Therapist Tom Golden, LCSW, offers this advice in his column, "One way to give men more time is to write to them, rather than talk to them. By writing a note it gives the man the freedom to read it more than once, to take it with him...and [more] importantly to respond in his own time. Another benefit is that writing takes the non-verbal communication and the "tone of voice" out of the equation. I know a couple that has a terrible time talking about their grief but when they start writing notes to each other they gain a greater understanding. Give it a try." (Tom Golden maintains an excellent web site, which has many articles on men and grief. *Tom Golden: Crisis, Grief & Healing.* See the Resources chapter for more information and the web address.)

Listen, Listen, Listen
For men, the job of "just listening" can be incredibly challenging. Men hate to see others in pain—they think that they should be able to prevent

or "solve" the pain of their wife or loved ones. But it's important to remember that women need someone who will just listen. Practice listening at every opportunity you have. For women, listening involves paying close attention to non-verbal communication such as body language as well.

Convey Your Needs
Miscommunication is the number one problem in any relationship—from work relationships to friendships to marriage. Don't let miscommunication further complicate your grieving process. Don't expect your partner to know what you need—tell him specifically. Likewise, don't assume that you know what your partner needs—ask him specifically.

Compromise
Barbara D. Rosof offers this advice to couples, "In many areas of your life together, such as socializing, family activities, holiday observances, one of you will be more ready to reengage than the other. If your partner wants to do something and you feel unready, you may need to push yourself. There is a balance to be struck in your efforts. Your child and your loss will always be with you. But giving up your life with your partner and the pleasures you have had together will not lessen your loss. Your balance has to do with holding onto your child, yet finding a way to live your life for yourself and with your partner. Your balance will not be arrived at quickly. Expect false starts and uncertainty. You need your partner's patience and your own."

At some point, in order to effectively move forward, you will need to nudge one another and learn the art of compromise.

Stay Connected
Even though you are wrapped in your unique grief, do not give up your connection as a couple. Make time to spend with each other. Don't shut each other out or you will be strangers when you get to the other side of grief. Schedule at least 30 minutes a day to sit together. Try and talk to each other about your feelings and the challenges of the day. If you can't talk about that, try talking about memories. If talking is too difficult right

now, just hold hands or hold each other. This daily communication, whether physical or verbal, let's each partner know that the other is committed to working through the tragedy—together.

Single Parents

The loss of a child carries unique challenges for the single parent. If the deceased was the only child, a single parent may find themselves living alone and the silence unbearable. There is no partner with which to share and work through the grieving process.

Perhaps the only challenge more difficult than the loss of a child, is facing that loss alone. Yet that is the prospect faced by many single parents. For single parents, it is especially important to find a support network—preferably an in-person grief recovery group or a psychotherapist. Finding other parents that have survived the loss of their child, will be a vital component in getting back on your feet. Also, it is common for the single parent to have a "longer haul" on the road of grief. What some people recover from in months, may take years for the single parent. Be especially sensitive to your needs and emotions and seek the help of a professional or support group.

Some Things You Can Do After the Loss of a Child

Singing Lessons

In *Singing Lessons* author Judy Collins writes about her personal journey of recovery after her son, Clark's suicide..."On the anniversary of Clark's death, I woke from a dream at midnight. In my dream I had been trying to persuade Clark not to die—striving to convince him that he didn't have to die, he didn't have to end his life. My son smiled and looked at me with love in his eyes. 'Mother...' he said, 'death is not an ending.' Today, I don't have to stay in depression. I know I have tools:

- I read a spiritual book
- I call a friend who has a kind word, a lift in her voice.
- I think about the good things in my life—often writing them down.
  There is so much in my life for which to be grateful.
- I smile with my husband, my friends, my mother and my sister.
- In the moment of silence, there is the sound of God bringing me strength—bringing me healing."

Develop a Living Memorial

Many parents find comfort in developing a memorial, informational pamphlet or organization in their child's name. In our interviews we have found parents who have published information on drunk driving, drug use, suicide, gangs, etc. and distributed them in their local community and sent them to newspapers around the country. Other parents have developed or founded organizations that are now national in scope. Other parents have found peace in starting a scholarship fund in their child's name and awarding the scholarship to a child who wants to pursue an interest similar to their child. Brook's family started an annual water-ski tournament in his honor. Caleb was a nationally recognized water skier who enjoyed tournament skiing. Each year, they hold a tournament at the lake at which Caleb loved to ski, and award cash prizes and plaques.

International Star Registry

We discovered this group and thought the idea was precious. "Honor your loved one by giving them the stars! What a beautiful way to memorialize your child by naming a star after him or her! Since 1979, the International Star Registry has been bringing these dreams to earth by offering a unique and magical opportunity to name a star. Plus, when you purchase your star through MISS, a portion of the proceeds will be donated directly to the combined efforts of MISS and the Arizona SIDS Alliance." The star kit includes a certificate, a telescope coordinated for locating the named star, a large sky chart with the star circled for easy identification, an astronomy booklet and a memorial letter. The price ranges from $57-106 including shipping and handling. For more information write to MISS/Star Registry, 8448 W Aster Dr., Peoria, AZ 85381 or visit the site online at http:// www.misschildren.org/family/starreg.html

Donations

In her book *A Handbook for the Living as Someone Dies*, Elizabeth A. Johnson suggests, "It may be very therapeutic and rewarding for you to donate your child's toys and other belongings to a children's home or to the children's wing at a hospital or hospice. In this way, the energy of your child's possessions is passed onto other children. A part of him continues to brighten the lives of others."

Memory Books

In *How to Support Someone Who is Grieving*, June Cerza Kolf writes, "Souvenirs, memorabilia and even some clothing can certainly be kept. In fact, putting old photographs in albums can be a task that is very rewarding at this time. It helps the bereaved recall happy memories." See the Exercises chapter for ideas on how to create a memory book.

Chapter Fourteen
The Loss of a Partner

*"Trying to put my pain behind brought me to many dead ends... Sometimes I
wondered if I was losing my mind. The old rules did not apply anymore.
I felt as if I had been dropped by parachute into a different country
where I had no map and everyone spoke a foreign language."*
Cathleen L. Curry, *When Your Spouse Dies*

The loss of a partner or spouse is devastating on many fronts. Our partner
is often our confidant and best friend. We have both our emotional and
physical highs and lows with this partner—day in and day out. To have
this "half" taken away leaves us feeling incomplete, confused and
shortchanged.

This is often intensified by the length of time we have spent with our
partner. If we have been with our partner for many years, we may find that
our partner completes our thoughts and is a compliment to our actions.
We are left feeling as if we have lost half of our self in addition to our
partner.

Added stressors arise at the life changes that often accompany the loss
of a partner. We may have a significant financial change to endure, we
may need to move, we may need to comfort our children and have few
people to comfort us.

Loss of Identity

Our partner makes up a significant portion of our identity. Through and
with our partner, we interpret the world, daily events and the ups and
downs of life. When we lose this partner unexpectedly, we lose many of
the foundations of our identity. We are left to rebuild at a time when we
are both emotionally and physically depleted. This rebuilding process will

take time. Our friends and children may encourage us to move forward before we are ready. This is only to be expected, since those who care for us hate to see us in pain. Many people feel that by "getting back into life" our pain will be alleviated. These are good intentions, but this route does not work in reality.

As we grieve, we will need to rebuild our foundation one brick at a time. In his book *Loss*, John Bowlby writes, "Because it is necessary to discard old patterns of thinking, feeling and acting before new ones can be fashioned, it is almost inevitable that a bereaved person should at times despair that anything can be salvaged and, as a result, fall into depression and apathy. Nevertheless, if all goes well, this phase may soon begin to alternate with a phase during which the bereaved starts to examine the new situation and to consider ways of meeting it. This redefinition of self and situation is as painful as it is crucial, if only because it means relinquishing all hope that the lost person can be recovered and the old situation re-established. Yet until redefinition is achieved no plans for the future can be made." At first, nothing will feel comfortable. Each day will bring new realizations and troubles. But in time, you'll find yourself engaging in a memory or hobby or thought that you enjoy. It may be only a minute of "peace," but it's peace nonetheless. This becomes your first brick. Seek out these sources of peace and record them in a journal. Notice what you like and what you don't. Form new opinions. Pursue a new interest. You may not be able to move quickly on these things. You may want to take a "getaway," but not have the emotional energy. That's fine. Order a few travel brochures on the Internet and page through them. A step is a step—no matter how small.

In the exercises chapter, you'll find a "Redefining Ourselves" exercise that can help you in this process.

Circles of Friends

While living as part of a couple, there is a tendency to make friends as a couple. Many widows experience a troubling problem after the death of a partner. Frequently, many friends that the couple has known are lost, when the couple dissolves into a single person. There are many reasons for this. One is that it is awkward to relate with other couples as a single person—especially when these other couples knew you as part of a duo.

Memories also play a large part in the loss of friendships. When we are with other couples we have shared with, we remember times passed. The other couples may be uncomfortable discussing or remembering these events. As we explored earlier, we are not a society equipped to deal with loss. It's unfortunate that this means one loss will often lead to other losses, due to others' resultant discomfort with death.

The loss of a partner is often a unique loss. It is rare that others in our immediate circle have likewise experienced the sudden death of a partner. Although our friends experience the loss with us, they do not have the firsthand knowledge of what it is like to live through this kind of death. We resurface, torn and viewing the world through different eyes. We return to these friendships a different person. It is this difference in viewpoint that accounts for many dissolving friendships.

Another reason that friendships fade, is that our loss reminds others that tragic loss can happen to anyone, to people they know—and maybe even to themselves. These explanations offer little comfort or justification for the actions of friends. However, there are a few things to remember. First, don't assume friendships won't work out. Give each friendship a chance. Secondly, it is unfortunate that you will incur other losses besides the death of your partner, but know this leaves room for growth. When you are ready, focus on making new friends. The AARP publishes a great brochure for those who have been out of the friend-making loop for a while. See our resources section for ordering information. Lastly, do seek out a support group of people in like circumstances. Create a group of close contacts who are at different points on the grief path. Use them as your mentors. Share your concerns. It may be that you are too depleted to actually attend an in-person support group. If this is the case, see our Internet resources in Part Three. There are many groups for widows and widowers that offer online chat.

Lingering Memories and Images

Many widows and widowers report seeing images of their loved one and feeling their presence. You may have dreams where your partner is still living. According to studies, about one-third to one-half of widows and widowers have these experiences. Realize the images are normal and needn't disturb you. You may feel your partner's presence with you constantly, like that of a guardian angel.

Many widows and widowers find it helpful to internalize an image of the deceased. In a 1974 report of Boston Widows by I.O. Glick, he found that "Often the widow's progress toward recovery was facilitated by inner conversations with her husband's presence." When we continue to talk and communicate with our loved one, we open ourselves to their presence—whether real or imaginary is irrelevant—but we open ourselves to their guidance. Learning to talk, and listen, to our loved one can be immensely comforting as we progress through our grief work.

MARILYN'S STORY

"We planted tulips and daffodils in the woods by our beautiful new house, our dream home, the place where all the kids and grand kids would come, the place where we would grow old together. We had lived there for five months when Gary died suddenly of a brain aneurysm and my world became a dark, terrifying, lonely place, where just days before it had been full of joy and wishes come true. No words can fully describe the shock and horror of sudden death with its untimely issues, especially when your loved one has never been sick. He'd served with the Marine Corps in Viet Nam and came back without a scratch. *How could he be dead now?*

A case of the flu....that's what we thought the night before he "officially" died; the night before the transplant arrangements were made and life support removed; the night before my heart felt the unbearable crush of a tremendous stone of grief. We had both been married before, divorced and finally (we thought) got it right. Seven years was all the time we had together, but we had no idea that death would come so soon for one of us. We always said we could deal with anything as long as we had each other. We'd discussed death: my son, Dan, had served in the Army Signal Corps during the Persian Gulf War; I was a Hospice volunteer; and my friend, Kathy had died suddenly two weeks before, followed by my Hospice patient one week prior to my husband's death. I said a eulogy at Kathy's funeral, encouraged by Gary, who was so proud of my seminary studies. I never dreamed that I would be doing the same thing for Gary in the same chapel two weeks later...three weeks before Christmas. What I could not have known was that my grandmother and another dear friend would both also die within months of Gary.

The support groups....yes; I went to them all. I even eventually facilitated one myself. I cried and ranted with the others, yet I felt that because of the unexpected nature of Gary's death, it was different for me; different for those of us who did not have a chance to make final plans, to get things in order, to say good-bye. I was mad at God. I felt that the loss of four people I dearly loved all at once was a cruel joke and I thought I was losing my mind. But, worst of all, I lost my faith and so, felt truly abandoned, adrift, punished, terrified. I had dedicated my life to serving God, yet I was in hell. Things got worse. People expected me to 'get over it.' I awoke in the middle of every night and was haunted by a replay of the events of the night Gary fell in the bathroom and the emergency people couldn't find the house; how I frantically ran up the road looking for them and how I had to leave Gary lying there, alone on the bathroom floor. I tortured myself with 'what-if's,' feeling like a failure, as if I could have saved him. The doctors told me that his aneurysm was so massive that even if it had happened in the hospital, they would not have been able to save him. Yet, I continued to have the repetitive thoughts replaying every event leading up to the removal of life support; the night terrors; the panic attacks; the chest pain; the disorientation; the absolute abandonment. I sank deeper and deeper into a clinical depression. I couldn't work, I couldn't pray, I couldn't do anything. I felt like I was an absolute failure and that I was dying. That I was next. Then the blizzard came. I was lost in a surreal world and I was certain I had lost my mind.

I asked my therapist, 'How did you ever make it through everything after your wife died suddenly?' He said, 'I went crazy.' Those three words probably helped me more than anything. If my psychiatrist went crazy when his wife died unexpectedly, and he was still alive and functioning, then maybe there was hope for me. I went to see him every week; I tried different medications; I looked for information on sudden death in books, but only found a sentence or two on the subject. I continued to attend support groups. Why is death such a taboo in America, I thought. It's as if the available literature was focused on "neat and tidy" death....the kind people prepare for, but that's not what happened to me.

Finally, after seven months, I was able to move Gary's shoes from the floor where he had put them. That act of moving the shoes made me realize he was really dead and my depression worsened and at around the same time, my son's Gulf War illness worsened and he had to be hospitalized repeatedly. I screamed in my car. I screamed until my throat and neck were aching. I cried and cried and cried. How is it possible to cry that much? The flowers we had planted bloomed beautifully the following Spring, as if nothing at all had happened. The world was still doing what it always did. How could that be when my whole world was changed forever? I wanted to die, but I had to be there for my son, who was, and has been so ill, and desperately needed me.

Therapy continued and after eleven months, I was able to return to work, yet I was not really 'emotionally present,' I was so alone. Comments were made: 'things must be better now, since a year has passed.' People treated me as if death were catching. They didn't know what to say, so they said nothing. They had no idea that I was still in hell and that I felt like a freak. I covered it up. Switched to drinking coffee; couldn't drink tea any more because Gary had made my tea every morning and placed it beside the bed, a small loving act, a kindness that I missed so very much. Months dragged on; then years; I finally was able to pack up Gary's clothes and give them away, but even now, after five and one-half years, I still find things of his in unexpected places and I cry. The dream house is sold, his car is sold, his books have been given to the library, clothes and mementos have been given to his friends and family, and Gary's ashes lie in Virginia's Quantico Cemetery and I have the flag on my closet shelf.

Depression still follows me, but looking back I can see that I have come a long way since the awful day when my world disintegrated. Gary's organs have helped others to have another chance at life. That was what he wanted. I dreamed about him on our anniversary last year. He kissed me and had a bottle of champagne in his hand. I think he wanted to tell me that he loves me and that he wants me to make a life for myself. Now, I know that's possible, at least a day at a time. I believe I can make it now, but it's been a long journey to hell and back again. Where I am now can be summed up in a poem I wrote:

PATHFINDER

You learn to take a little bit
extra on the in-breath
just in case you come up short
when heartbreak comes.

You learn to lean a little
less than most, just enough
to catch yourself and keep a balance
should you start to fall toward the abyss.

You learn to love a little
more intensely should life
send grief to poke you in the eye
and a golden moment pass unseen.

You learn to speak the language
of the heart more clearly
to the ones you love just because
there's so many ways the night can come
and stop you in your tracks,

so many ways the boot
can crush the rose."

Marilyn Houston—Springfield, Virginia

"For two years —I was just as crazy as you can be and still be at large. I
didn't have any really normal minutes during those two years. It wasn't
just grief. It was total confusion. I was nutty, and that's the truth. How did
I come out of it? I don't know, because I didn't know when I was in it that
I was in it." **Helen Hayes, actress, after the death of her husband.**

JOAN'S STORY

Joan was a thirty-two-year-old, divorced and remarried woman when her ex-husband, the father of her two children, was killed in a gruesome, alcohol-related auto accident. Thirteen years later, her eyes still well with tears as she relives the sudden impact his death had on her life and those of her children.

"We were married almost 18 years, but Tom and I were divorced at the time of his death. Even though he had a drinking problem, we had managed a friendship after the divorce, mostly for the sake of our two children. We had even spent a Christmas together. But, before New Years he was drinking again and each time was getting worse. I was remarried at the time although that relationship was rocky as well. Tom had called me earlier on the night he was killed. My son was supposed to go with him that night to the movies and I didn't allow him to go—Tom sounded drunk. Anyway, I got a phone call or two from him at a bar asking me to meet him which I refused to do. I also got a call from the bartender, or maybe it was a friend at the bar asking me to come and get him.

I began praying very hard because I knew what kind of battle Tom had been fighting with alcohol and I remember praying to Jesus to take him if he was going to be so tortured in this life—especially if he was going to be unable to conquer his alcoholism. I knew that my children couldn't take much more of his behavior. It had been so hard dealing with their father's disease.

I knew Tom was intoxicated. My husband of two years was asleep next to me at the time, so I suggested to the person at the bar that he call Tom a cab. I don't remember what the response was. It was probably three or four hours after that—by then my husband had left for work and it wasn't time for my kids to leave for school; they were still asleep. I got a call from the police department saying, 'This is Sergeant Smith, I'm calling to let you know that Tom McKenzie was killed in an auto accident. I apologize. Normally we would have come to the house to tell you, but we couldn't find the house.'

It felt like my insides had dropped to the floor. What crossed my mind was that I had prayed for this just a few hours before. How would I tell his children! I knew what their reaction would be and I began to feel enormous guilt. So, I not only felt guilty for not picking him up but for praying that he be released from his life of torture. I don't know if it's strange, but I immediately thought, 'Who would walk my daughter down the aisle when she got married?' My thoughts went in all different directions.

Although I was in disbelief, I picked up the phone to call my mother. I said, 'Are you sitting down...Mom, a police officer just told me that Tom died in a car accident last night.' I kept thinking, I have to talk to Tom—I didn't know what I was going to tell him. I felt crazy. I wanted to ask him 'Is this real?' Are you really dead?" And the guilt.

I was angry—why are they telling me this over the phone? Couldn't they have told me in person. I was angry with the police department.

Jenny was 13 and my son Paul was 16 at that time. I remember agonizing over what I could say and was grateful they were still asleep. Jenny was the first to awake. I wasn't ready to talk to her, I needed to calm myself first. But there she was. I decided to put my own grief somewhere else because I had to be there for my kids. I knew they'd be devastated. I jumped from hysterical to concentrating on Jenny and Paul. When I told her, she cried out in disbelief. I begged her not to wake her brother, but we had to. We went together to tell him. To this day, I'm not sure exactly how he meant it, but he jumped out of bed, pulled on a shirt and said, "Damn it, I knew it! I should have gone to the movies with him." He was already feeling guilty.

I immediately thought, I must call the school and tell them my children won't be coming in and I had to call my work.

The policeman knew we were divorced, but wanted to know if he should call family members or did I want to. I asked him to call Tom's brother so they could give the news to his mother.

My kids were emotionally a mess. We spent the hour trying to calm each other. An hour later Tom's brother called to reassure me that I would be part of any arrangements they would make. Even though we were divorced, I wouldn't be left out.

I could only focus on my children. At the time, my son's best friend had lost his own father and sister in tragic accidents and I remember my son only wanting to be with him. I knew it was the right thing to do. He needed to be with someone who could understand the experience of sudden loss.

Without my children's input, Tom's family decided to have him cremated. This was hard on Jenny and Paul, I think. Anyway, even though it was a closed casket the kids insisted on seeing their father before the cremation. I guess I'm glad they did. It helped make it more real.

I think back now and I'm glad we had made some amends before he died."

Learning to do Things Alone

Suppose you were dependent on your partner to travel with you, to drive the car, to make the plane reservations, to pack your bags—now is the time to seek out a network of others to help you. As you move through the first months of acute grief, it's best not to take too many new steps. Instead, focus on finding a support group to help you, so that you can work on your grief.

In time, it will be helpful to learn to do these things alone. Some people say it builds character to travel to new places and face what comes on your own. Others would prefer to travel with a friend. Both offer opportunities for growth.

Some people depended on their significant other to *do* for them—others depended on the significant other to *be* with them—and some both. Some needed their partner for a sense of belonging in the world. Whatever you can do at this time to loosen your dependency-hold on your deceased loved one, can only be beneficial in the long run. But remember, do this at your own pace—no one else's. The most compassionate message you can give yourself is to drop the expectation that recovery will be an easy, logical process.

For most it is only with time and enormous personal or spiritual introspection, coupled with the wisdom gained, that the true meaning of the relationship will emerge. There will never be an answer as to why the one you loved died—but, perhaps you can answer for yourself why they "needed" to be in your life and the significance of their life—and death—to your own journey on this planet.

Funeral Arrangements

MaryAnn, thirty-seven-years-old and a mother of two young children laments, "I knew my husband very well. We talked about lots of things, especially our plans for the future. We never talked about what we wanted as far as funeral arrangements were concerned. Who does at our age? When it came time to make decisions, I did the best I could. I will always wonder if I did the right thing, if I chose what he would have wanted."

This scenario is more common than not. One can only do the best they know how under very stressful conditions. If you are able to make even one choice on behalf of the deceased, you are among the small few. Give yourself some credit.

What can you do when your significant other's family wants their wishes honored over yours and what you believe to have been the wishes of your loved one? In the absence of a will or other document that clearly states what the deceased would have wanted, you must remember that if you were legally married at the time of death, you have the right to do as you wish.

In other cases where you are living together under no formal arrangements, it is more difficult to assert your rights. Sometimes a professional mediator can help with these kinds of conflicts. Mediation offers people the opportunity to resolve their disputes with the help of a neutral person trained in mediation skills, domestic violence issues, financial issues and other topics. The mediator is not a judge or an arbitrator who imposes a decision on people, but is trained to assist people in negotiating their own resolutions to their problems or concerns.

Although mediators may come from a variety of professional backgrounds including: attorneys, psychologists, social workers, marriage or family counselors, clergy people, accountants and financial specialists, they have received specialized training to become mediators.

The Academy of Family Mediators was established in 1981 as a non-profit educational membership association and is the largest family mediation organization in existence.Their members are mediators working in a variety of settings including private practice, courts, schools and government in the United States and internationally. You can find mediators listed in the phone book under mediators or family counseling, or you can contact the American Counsel of Family Mediators for a referral. Alternately, a clergy person or a family therapist can be helpful in discussions of this nature.

When One Parent is doing the Job of Two

If a mother or father has died, one parent becomes the key decision maker and responsible person for the children. He/She will be in charge of decisions on college, finances, rules, curfews, limits and all other responsibilities. Both parent and child will need time to adapt to these new roles.

The newly single parent should consider all outside help that is available. There are many organizations and resources for single parents (see Brook Noel's book *The Single Parent Resource* for a comprehensive listing). Immediately work on seeking out support and information. Find a confidant who is a single parent that you can use as a mentor.

Involving children in restructuring the home is one idea that many parents have found helpful. This works best with children that are ten and older. A month or two after the services, explain to them that with one less family member, your family will need to use teamwork and cooperation. Offer ideas on how you think the family could run smoothly. Brainstorm ideas beforehand. Try things like chore distribution, helping with dinner, doing something together as a family on one day each weekend, etc. It may seem hard to be talking of functionality so soon after losing someone, but although someone's life has stopped, our lives don't.

Children need a stable base in order to thrive. Part of creating a stable base is consistency, boundaries and limit setting. Often, we are so emotionally depleted that maintaining consistency and boundaries is challenging at best. Keep things as regular as you are able. This will help children find the room needed to grieve.

Be careful, not to spend so much time focused on the children that you forget your own grief. You still have many of your own issues to work through. Make time for this. You may choose to join one of the many support groups listed in Chapter Nineteen, or you may find that just a night out by yourself each week offers the needed space to explore your grief. It's true that you must take care of yourself before you can take care of your children. Terri Ross said it best in *The Single Parent Resource*, "Just like with airplane oxygen masks—'Put yours on and then help the child next to you.' You have to get back on your feet before you can truly be of help to your child."

For Parents Who Have Surviving Children

In her book *The Bereaved Parent*, Harriet Sarnoff Schiff touches on one of the hardest issues, that of grieving children. "…a recurrent theme appears to be that the living children received precious little by way of comfort from their parents."

Surviving children often feel their parents have abandoned them. A parent's grief is strong and often they cannot emotionally cope with the grief of their surviving children as well. This happens with many forms of loss, but when the loss is a child's sibling, the intensity is increased. In the chapter, Losing A Sibling, we offer valuable insights into how surviving children feel.

When you have lost one child and still have surviving children there are several things to be aware of. In the first weeks of grieving, it is important to have alternate contacts for these children. Emotionally, you will need to use any energy for yourself to make it through each day. Ask a close friend to help you with your other children. Consider having that friend stay at the house. If your children are four and under, consider having them stay with a relative whose company they enjoy. Older children will be unnerved by a change in surroundings.

While you are engaged in acute grief, which will take at least a year, and for the loss of a child usually much longer, it's important to remember the perspective of your other children. Children are trying to cope with the loss of a sibling, while also coping with a strange distance from their parents. It's important that surviving children understand that you are facing grief, and your behavior does not mean your love or feelings toward them have changed.

Children experience the loss of a sibling on two levels. They lose their kindredship and also the relationship they had with their parents becomes altered drastically. Their feelings can be compounded when parents begin to idealize the deceased. This often occurs, since by idealizing someone, we think we can make the memory stronger. In the book, *When a Friend Dies*, Marilyn E. Gootman writes, "Sometimes people are afraid to say anything bad about someone who has died. They turn the dead person into a saint. Every person in this world has strong points and weak points, even those who have died. Loving someone means being honest and accepting the whole person, both the good and the bad, even if the person is dead."

A common scenario after losing a child is an attempt to "make it right." Some parents will start an organization, fundraiser or other memorial in the child's name. It is an admirable goal to keep the child's memory alive for generations to come. However, it is all too common for these memorials to become all-consuming. The parent spends so much time wrapped in the details of preserving his child's memory that he forgets to enjoy the children that are living!

Likewise, parents may constantly talk about the child who has died. Other children may quickly feel inferior, ignored or unimportant if their parents focus so heavily on the other child. It is common to talk about the deceased frequently throughout the first six months to a year, but after that there should be a point of letting go. While we can, of course, discuss emotions with friends or a counselor, within the family the letting go process has to take place if the current family unit is to remain healthy and intact. This doesn't mean that we forget. It means we begin to look toward the future and not dwell on the past. We bring balance into the home. We keep the memories of the past alive while creating new memories.

When helping your children cope with grief, it's important to remember the dynamics of a sibling relationship. Siblings typically have a love-hate relationship until well into adulthood. While still kids, it's not uncommon for them to be best friends one minute and worst enemies the next. This double-sided relationship often complicates the grief process. The living sibling may wish he had been nicer, more forgiving or less jealous. Blame and guilt can reign strong for surviving children. The Compassionate Friends offer the following in their brochure *Caring for Surviving Children* (see the resources section for how to obtain this brochure): "Remember, grief will exaggerate the positive and negative feelings between your children; encourage them to discuss these feelings. Children often feel guilty and/or responsible for their sibling's death. Reassure them that fighting and negative feelings between brothers and sisters are common and do not cause death."

One question many grieving families ask is, "How do we act around one another *during* the grieving process?" As we explored earlier in the book, everything we thought to be certain changes when we experience tragic loss. Even the dynamics of our relationships change. There are no hard and fast rules to make life appear normal again, but there are guidelines that can help your family get through this process in a healthy way.

First, it is a good idea to show your grief to your children, don't hide it. Many times parents are under the illusion that they should remain completely controlled and collected. This isn't healthy. Kids will not know how to deal with their own grief without an example. If you show little or no grief, the children may feel their emotions are inappropriate. Do not be afraid to show emotion with your surviving children. Silence is harder for children to take than emotion. It also shows children that it is okay to face grief head on—it need not be suppressed.

Lastly, don't avoid talking about what happened or mentioning past events that involved the deceased. The best way to keep a memory alive is to tell the stories about the deceased's life. Children often won't know whether or not it's okay to discuss the deceased. Take the initiative and set the example. Don't avoid saying the relative's name. Even if it's difficult, talking does lead toward healing.

Will I Ever Love Again?

"Will I ever love again?" is a common question. "Why do it again? Why should I risk losing another love?" Committed love can provide numerous opportunities for growth as we struggle to stretch ourselves to bring our best to bear in relationships. The experience of sudden loss of love, when used to our benefit, can provide a basis for growing and expanding us as human beings in ways we never thought we were capable.

Some widows look forward to a new relationship but are unsure of how to initiate it. Others feel "guilty" at the thought of a new partner. Is there a right time, a guideline? In an article titled "Starting Over," that appeared in *People* magazine, author and psychologist Froma Walsh shared that the signs of readiness are subtle. You're not thinking about your partner all the time and you no longer dream of them or picture them when you're with another person. "There is no such thing as totally getting over a loss, but over time you will have those pains less and less often. When you can appreciate the unique qualities of a new partner and not mold that person to fit an old image, then you know you're ready to love again."

Sexual feelings will also resurface. For some, this will happen sooner than others. In the AARP brochure, *On Being Alone*, they offer the following insight, "When you lose your spouse, you lose your sexual partner. It is a painful fact of widowhood. Although sexual feelings are common after being widowed and should not make you feel guilty, there can be a conflict between societal taboos and your personal needs. You need to sort out those conflicts and do what you feel most comfortable doing. If you are considering taking a new sexual partner, you may want to think about what you are really looking for: sex, intimacy, companionship, admiration or cuddling. Knowing what you want can help you know how to go about getting it."

Seeking Purpose

Finding purpose in the relationship can be effective in understanding the death. You're in pain, nothing makes sense and you may feel totally alone. You're in crisis! So how can you be expected to believe that nothing happens in your life that is not ultimately beneficial, that you may have been pulled by some mysterious force into a relationship meant to serve your personal or spiritual growth. Perhaps you are meant to know that the pain of separation by death serves some end, some purpose. To make things harder, all this questing of meaning comes in the midst of excruciating and unrelenting confusion. Trusting there is some ultimate benefit to be found takes an innate trust in the process of healing, at a time when your trust in life itself may have been broken or destroyed. However, if you allow for it, the loss of your loved one can represent a significant marker point in your continuing, eternal process of growth.

"Why did the relationship need to begin?" can seem like an odd question to ask oneself at a time like this, but the answer can help put the death of your loved one into a meaningful framework. In an attempt to give an easy answer you might say, "Wasn't it just love and a sexual passion coupled with a desire to have a family and a partner in life that drew me to my lover or spouse?" But, ask again. Why might it have been "necessary" on a spiritual level to begin the relationship? Perhaps it grew out of a pressing psychological need, or maybe a spiritual exigency, or maybe, if you believe in the possibility of past lives or reincarnation, it began in response to some karmic requirement. A step toward healing the wounds your loss has created can be taken regardless of which understanding you choose. If you look closely and objectively at yourself, as you were in the relationship when it first began, you might be able to see the urgency, feel the compelling need or sense the undercurrent of "something else" pulling you together. You may have all along wondered "Why him?" —maybe from the minute you said, "I do." No matter which of these "pulls" it may have been, what matters is that you try to see that your relationship (including its ending) was meant to serve a specific purpose in your journey toward becoming a more whole person.

Some Things You Can Do

As you move on with your life, remember this: The love you have for your deceased partner can always have a special place in your heart, even if/when you have another love relationship and/or remarry. Buy a special box for your momentos and revisit this box on special days if you want to.

Create a Special Place

If no body was recovered, you may want to create a "burial place" and a memorial of some kind (perhaps donating a park bench or tree plantings, etc. or burying a box containing photos or other personal items at a location you can visit).

Donate

Donate time, money or special items to a charity that was important to your deceased partner.

Incorporate Traits

Incorporate some special trait or behavior of your deceased partner into your own life so that every time you exhibit that trait or behavior, you will be honoring the loved one's memory.

Place an Ad

Place an "In Memory Of" ad in your local paper, in remembrance of your deceased partner and have it signify the closing of one phase of your life and the beginning of another. The ad can contain a favorite poem, song lyrics, special graphics or thoughts about your deceased partner. You can choose any date that was meaningful to both of you.

Chapter Fifteen
The Loss of a Sibling

"My big brother was so good to me.
When we were kids, he always let me go first.
The night he died, he looked up at me,
Smiled his little crooked smile, and said,
'Sis, this time let me go first.'"

Connie Danson, eulogy for her brother, Frank Darnell

The loss of a sibling carries many unique challenges. First and foremost, when we lose our sibling, we lose one of the people who knows us most intimately. This person grew up as we grew. We laughed together, schemed together, cried together, fought with each other, hated each other and loved each other. It is one of the only relationships that experiences, and endures, such a full spectrum of emotions day after day.

In *The Worst Loss*, Barbara D. Rosof writes of siblings: "They are playmates, confidants, competitors; they may also be protectors, tormentors or have special responsibilities. Siblings know each other more intimately than anyone else. Siblings know, as no one else in the world does, what it is like to grow up in your particular family. Relationships with a brother or sister help children know who they are and how they fit in the family. The bonds between siblings are woven into the fabric of each one's life."

When we lose a sibling, we lose a piece of ourselves, a piece of our family, and a reflection of ourselves.

Being Overlooked in the Grieving Process
One of the hardest parts of sibling loss is being overlooked in the grieving process. A person can find evidence of this by opening the many books on

grieving in a bookstore. Pages upon pages are devoted to parents and spouses. However, the loss of a sibling is not listed as often—and when it is, the coverage is often short. For the resource section of this book, we had a hard time finding anything geared specifically to sibling loss. One young adult who lost his sister wondered why everyone always asked, "Well how are your parents taking it?" and never asked how *he* was taking it. An article in the *Journal News* titled, "Forgotten Mourners" offered the views of many surviving siblings. One person quoted in the article said, "...I was so mad. It was as if everyone thinks, *Oh my gosh, losing a child, that's the worst thing in the world,* and they don't even consider there are siblings." It is true that losing a sibling is as traumatic as losing a child in many ways.

Double the Loss

In addition to losing a sibling, the surviving brothers or sisters often lose a piece of their parents. Parents become wrapped in their grief. For years to come, they may have difficulty relating like before with the surviving children. Many of these surviving siblings don't feel they can go to their parents. "My father had enough on his mind," said one man we interviewed, who sadly watched his relationship with his father deteriorate. One thirty-five-year-old woman named Lee said this in the *Journal News* article, "I don't think society understands what sibling grief is all about. It's a misunderstood grief because it's a double-edged sword. You have your own pain and your parents' pain."

A support group or person will help you to move through these pains. Be careful when selecting your group and make sure they understand the difficulties specific to sibling loss.

Identity through a sibling

Siblings identify each other. We become "Joe's sister" or "Frank's brother." It's common for a sibling to also explain themselves in relationship to their deceased sibling, or a parent i.e. "I act more like my mother and my brother has my father's traits." When we lose our sibling this identity is taken from us.

Additionally our birth order is altered. Mothers Against Drunk Driving offer the following in their brochure, **WE HURT TOO.** "When a brother or sister dies, you now experience a gap in the birth order. If the oldest sibling was killed, the second oldest is now the oldest. If there were just the two of you, you are now an 'only child'. It is difficult to know whether or not you should try to assume a new role, but you are painfully aware of the void left by your sibling's death."

In time we most likely will fill part of our sibling's role if it feels comfortable to us. "Time," is the key word. Many will expect us to be strong for our parents, which is fine, but at some point we need to make room to experience our own grief and readjustment.

We fought so much

Sibling rivalry is a natural part of growing up. In some families it's exemplified and in others it's practically nonexistent. You may have fought with your sibling, said terrible things or thought terrible thoughts. No matter how crazy, outrageous or hateful these things seem to you—be assured, this is *natural*. Inside our guilt, we magnify these bad times—we narrow in on our regrets; there is no need to do this. One way siblings learn about one another and their place in the world is through these rivalries. For each rivalry you focus on, remember a wonderful shared moment, no matter how small or how simple.

No one understands

If you have moved on to a family of your own, the loss of a sibling can create difficult issues in your current family. Many times, when we move and marry, our siblings are not that involved in our "new" family. When we lose a sibling at this junction, it can be hard to find the support we need. Our "new" family will often be sad for our loss, but they may have a hard time understanding the impact. They may be anxious to keep the family unit intact and have a hard time watching you experience your grief. Support groups will be especially helpful if this is your situation—especially if you live far away from other parents, siblings or friends who knew the deceased.

When we lose a sibling we are left with few places to release emotion. We find it difficult to share emotion with our parents as they are consumed with their own grief. We don't want to share our emotions with our spouse as they may not have known our sibling as intimately and they may not understand. Our emotions are valid and we need to share them somewhere. A trusted friend, pastor or support group can help in these cases.

"Jim and I were like most brothers and sisters. On some days we were best friends and on others we were enemies. With Jim being five years older, at times I was a tag-a-long and at others, a welcomed friend. There is something about a sibling relationship that is different than any other—a special bond. Jim and I knew each other inside and out. We could show each other our darkest parts and our brightest—and never fear that we would turn away from one another.

Jim and I explored the world together. We were adventurers. From early on, we sought rhyme and reason together. We built forts and ponds trying to be "brave explorers." We held bake sales and lemonade stands trying to raise money for new games. In many ways, he was my life preserver.

I remember when he left for college and I was just starting high school. I was so lonely. I wondered how I'd make it without him. The pain was intense—but nothing like the pain that would come two years later.

I was sleeping that night when the call came. I heard my mother begin screaming as I struggled out of bed. She held the phone receiver in her hand, her face white. My dad stood rigid next to her. David, Jim's roommate, had called with the news of Jim's death. Half way across the country, my brother had been returning from his job at the video store when the cars collided.

I knew immediately what had happened. I said nothing. I simply turned around, walked back into my room and hid under my covers. I wanted it all to go away. I wanted to wake up from the nightmare.

The service was incredibly difficult. Jim's body was so mangled my mother would not let me see him. I still wish I would have gotten to see him. Somehow, I think it would have helped.

The blackness that covered my world was thick. My friends were all choosing colleges, getting drivers licenses, going to prom—excited about finishing their junior year and entering their senior year. They all seemed so young and naïve. I had seen truths of the world that they, hopefully, wouldn't know for many, many years.

I moved through those last two years of high school like a robot. It wasn't until I left for college and got away from many of the places where Jim and I had shared memories, that I was able to begin rebuilding. The process was slow. I sought out a local pastor at college. At first we talked once a week and now it's once a month. Sharing and caring with another has been immensely helpful in working through my grief.

I graduate this year and am excited for that—though I still am saddened greatly by the fact that Jim and I won't get to experience the rest of our lives together. Sometimes I feel shortchanged, but I try not to get caught up in self-pity. Life's too short.

I talk to Jim a lot now. I feel he is with me and he can somehow hear me. This thought is comforting for me. I'll always miss him, but now I can smile at his memory and appreciate the wonderful gifts he gave me while he was alive." – Terri, Idaho

October
by Brook Noel
excerpted from *Shadows of a Vagabond*

I stand within this room
blanked and stripped of your essence,
wishing you might turn around
call my name
say it's a joke
praying for something
to take it all back
to rewind to yesterday
when you were still here.

You walked on water,
we dreamt inside stars
trading childhood dreams
and day into night—

you held my hand
and now I hold yours.
searching for a way
to erase what I witness
to erase what I see.

And inside October's fall light
you let go
while all of us
try so desperately
to hang on.

Brushing your pictures with
hands that once held yours.
Rock – paper — scissors –
learning to snap...
those days we were too young
to realize how we had so little
while having it all.

There are no words
to frame your soul
to capture this gold
as we helplessly watch
these days slip away
searching for your face, a sign
a world still with you.

I want to revisit the past.
Take you back, take me back,
replay the scene a bit differently.

We look for reasons in forests
where none exist.
We look for answers
while eagles drift by.

Only questions rest on wings.

And though I can't understand
what has happened here—
I tuck our pictures
between your palms.

You have always held me
and I want you to still.
My brother, my father, my friend
I know you will

I know you will.

Love,
"Your Little Sister"

Some Things You Can Do
Forgiveness
If your parents were unavailable to you when you experienced your grief
or didn't know how to help you through it, it's important to forgive them.
When we hold onto angry feelings we don't leave the room needed to
heal. One effective way to forgive is to write a letter. Explore all your
feelings on paper. Write out your anger, your fears and your hopes. When
you finish, put the paper in a drawer. Periodically over the next month,
pull it out and read it. Feel the pain that you experienced. After a month,
add a note of forgiveness to your parents. Then burn the letter and let your
feelings of anger rise with the smoke.

Talking
Talk to your sibling like you always did. No matter what your relationship
with your sibling—good or bad—you are bound to be tied by the closeness
of growing up together in a family. Talk to your sibling and internalize his

spirit. When you have a question or doubt, find a quiet place and think about your sibling and what advice he might have given you.

Memory Album

Preserve your sibling's memory through a special album of pictures. Albums are fun to put together because they help us focus on the good times. Looking through the album over the years can be a heartwarming experience.

Grief Session

Take a weekend getaway to explore your grief. Often we don't want to share our strong emotions with our parents. If we are married, we may feel like we are putting too much on the shoulders of our spouse or children by sharing with them. A weekend where you need only worry about yourself, and not day-to-day demands can be especially cleansing. Take a journal and this book and work on some of the exercises. Take long walks outside and talk to your sibling. See page 267 for one sibling's creative way to get support.

Part Three
Pathways through Grief

Chapter Sixteen
Pathways through Grief:
Questions and Answers

"You will not grow if you sit in a beautiful flower garden, but you will grow if you are sick, if you are in pain, if you experience losses, and if you do not put your head in the sand, but take the pain and learn to accept it, not as a curse or punishment, but as a gift to you with a very, very specific purpose."
Elizabeth Kübler-Ross

As we've stated before, the world becomes confusing and unfamiliar as we move through the process of grieving. It's likely that you'll have many questions throughout the stages. Throughout this book, we've attempted to answer many of your questions in previous chapters. In this chapter we will cover additional frequently asked questions we have heard from those facing grief.

I know my parent's experienced loss in their lives, but they handled it better.

Our thoughts, feelings and ideas of what grief and the grieving process should look like are formed when we are children by observing our parents and other adults. How they handled loss is how we most likely believe we should. But can we "do" our grief differently if we want to? Can we devise our own pathways? Is there room or energy for creativity at a time like this? Some will find comfort and stability by handling loss the way family and community have always done, while others will find more comfort by creating a unique passage. You are your own best guide through this maze. Have faith in your ability to handle grief in your own way.

Remember, when life feels out of control, and it's bound to now, the one thing you do have control over is *how* you will grieve.

Does anything good ever come of all this?

In the very beginning you will find it extremely difficult to accept that any good could emerge from your tremendous loss. However, as difficult as it is to move through the stages of grief, it is possible to shift from feeling grief as "something that happens to you" to "grieving is something you do to heal." You are the one person who can change the pain to possibility, the loss to some creative expression. After a while you may want to start a charity, scholarship or foundation to honor the deceased. You may be inspired to write a book (as we have done), create a painting or sculpture, or write a song.

The wrenching and ripping apart that the sudden death of a loved one creates can leave one with an open wound subject to infection. The "infection" can then manifest itself as self-abuse (liquor, promiscuity, pills, etc.) or it can manifest itself, by choice, as growth.

For some, the bereavement process can bring a new appreciation for life, for their relationships, and for the world around them. Many report a feeling of being more strongly connected to the rest of humanity.

By choosing growth and creativity as a result of this major life transition, you may even find new friends. This is especially true if you seek out support groups consisting of people who have a mutual need. You can share your struggles at trying to create a meaningful new life, and at the same time facilitate some useful understanding of the recovery process. By choosing growth, you may begin to see your relationship with the Universe in a different way. You may begin to see God (or however you choose to name that energy in your life) in the small acts of love from those we least expect, in our communities and families, and maybe even from a stranger as Maggie did...

MAGGIE'S STORY

"My husband died suddenly while playing baseball—a heart attack. He was young. We were young. When I found myself feeling dysfunctional during the early stages of grief, I barely had the energy to cook meals for my two young children. So, off we went to McDonalds. As we were eating our hamburgers and french fries, I noticed a woman sitting at a table with her own two young children. I also noticed she wasn't wearing a wedding ring. I was new in the community and most of my friends had abandoned me because they were "our" friends. After announcing to my children that I would be right back, I approached the woman, introduced myself, told her I was recovering from the death of my husband and asked her if she knew of any support groups or therapists I might turn to for help. I simply took the chance she might know what I could do. In a few minutes of conversation she told me that she was also widowed and invited us to sit at her table. She then asked if I would come back to her house for a glass of wine where she gave me the name of her therapist. This total stranger became one of my best friends, offering me love and support over many months of pain and readjustment."

Andrea LaSonde Melrose describes this unexpected movement of human spirit in the book, *Nine Visions*: "We stumble blindly on our way, often running from a responsibility we are afraid to take on, from a burden we don't think we can carry. We thrash and flail, certain that we are drowning, panicked, as if unreasoning activity were going to help us. Somehow, into that darkness, comes a moment of peace when a friend gives us a hug, a stranger reaches out a hand...and we realize that we have been standing on a rock all along; supported, stable, safe. However we see that gesture, as God working through the human beings around us or simply as the generosity of the human spirit coming through the day-to-day masks we all wear, the gift is infinitely precious."

You can chose to allow the spirit (creative force, God, higher power) to move into your life, providing an opportunity to look at previously challenging and fearful situations in a new way, with the ultimate outcome of a new sense of self awareness. By choosing growth you are saying to yourself, and those in your life, that as painful as this transitional experience is, "I am going to survive and be better for it."

I am a single, working mother. When am I supposed to find time to grieve?

If you have to hold down a job, try scheduling grief sessions for yourself. For example, if you work during the day and then prepare dinner, try having the kids in bed (or in their rooms) by eight o'clock and then set aside an hour or so for your grieving. If the loss was one that has left your children grieving, devote some time to hearing their stories, thoughts and feelings each evening. To help your children even more, identify a program in your community that works with grieving children—or start a support group through your local school, church or youth center. This will offer them another outlet for their grief and help to take the pressure off you to handle it.

I feel like I'm falling apart, not just emotionally, but physically. Sometimes I feel like I'm going to die next. What's going on? What can I do?

There are many dimensions of the physical and emotional self to consider as you wind through the pathway of grief. Psychological, spiritual, nutritional and social dimensions all play an important role as you struggle to find balance.

A loved one has died, suddenly, and it is a shock to the entire system because your thoughts and perceptions affect every cell and hormone in your body. One of the most neglected areas of health is the emotional component and its effect on physical well-being.

If you are unaware of the toll this shock can have on your body, you are not likely to take care of yourself when you need to most. Some people overindulge with nicotine, drugs, alcohol, sleep or food.

If you are to prevent the ill effects of the loss on your physical body, you must pay close attention to the messages you are giving yourself. Are you giving yourself "die" messages because you wish it had been you that died instead of your loved one? Are you giving yourself "I don't deserve to live" messages because you believe there was something more you could have done to save them?

Your emotions are powerful. In her newsletter, *Health Wisdom for Women*, Dr. Christiane Northrup writes, "The brain and immune system communicate in two ways: By means of hormones that the brain regulates; and through protein molecules, called neuropeptides (or neurotransmitters) and receptors, which send messages back and forth. These same molecules are not only in your brain, but also in your stomach, your muscles, your glands, your bone marrow, your skin and all of your other organs and tissues. Since the network expands to every organ in the body, it means that every thought you think and emotion you feel is communicated to every cell in your body."

It is not always possible to use "willpower" to avoid the tendency of overindulging. Many times we need a support group or therapist to assist in the process. Before going "over the edge," seek help. The resources section of this book contains many ideas that can assist you in finding a professional group or organization to act as a support network.

I actually saw my loved one die. I was there! Now I feel anxious all the time...what's happening?

If you witnessed the tragic death and find yourself running the "movie" of the tragedy over and over in your mind, you may be storing "fight-or-flight" responses in your body resulting in major or minor anxiety. Dr. Northrup explains it this way, "The Fight-or-Flight Response is your body's way of handling acute stress by using stored glucose and fat so your muscles have the energy they need to get you out of harm's way. But you cannot function in this mode forever....As your anxiety builds, all of your immune cells start running around in circles, preparing your body to fight....but, because there is nothing to actually fight against, the cortisol stays in your system. This is when your emotions become 'toxic.' If this Fight-or-Flight Response continues for a long time, you will deplete your adrenal glands, your hormones will become imbalanced and you can set yourself up for a number of illnesses..."

You may need professional help and guidance to work through this anxiety. If you want to try a few ideas on your own, begin with the calming exercise in the Exercises chapter. You may find several of the herbal remedies in the next chapter helpful as well.

Would the use of a medium be helpful in resolving some of my unanswered questions?

Perhaps the difficult questions that plague us after a sudden death can be put to some rest with the help of what's known as a medium. A medium is defined as someone who can communicate with the dead. Visiting a medium can be a very powerful experience, it can also be an expensive one. A meeting with George Anderson, considered the "world's greatest living medium" and author of many books including, *George Anderson's Lessons from the Light: Extraordinary Messages of Comfort and Hope from the Other Side* can cost hundreds of dollars an hour.

If you choose to consult with a medium, make sure the person comes highly recommended by a friend or family member. Also make sure the medium does not ask any leading questions that might give information away, before the meeting. Trust your intuition—if you feel the person is disreputable, they most likely are. Not all mediums will make successful contact, and you may or may not come away feeling settled. A successful meeting that one of Pam's clients had is described below:

Experience with psychic medium George Anderson, written by Dolores Anselmo whose only child, Nicholas, took his life at age 14

"Nothing can ever erase from my mind the horror of that night when I returned home from work to find my fourteen-year old, only child, Nicholas, hanging with his Boy Scout rope from the staircase railing leading to our apartment in a private home. The unbelievable had happened and my life would never be the same!

He was an extremely bright, handsome, caring and sensitive young man with a troubled dark side who four months before had refused to continue therapy. In my disbelief and numbness I reached out for help by joining support groups, praying for God's strength to work through the pain and loss, and to pull my life together again. There were so many unanswered questions and fortunately the opportunity for insight, answers and peace came three years later when I went for a reading with the noted psychic, George Anderson.

During my reading, Nicholas' spirit came through and George was able to convey exactly what happened at the time of Nicholas' death. His thoughts, despair and personality traits came through. If there was any doubt in my mind that Nicholas' spirit had been contacted, it was dispelled when George told me my favorite Uncle Joe (who had died four years before Nicholas) was there to help Nicholas with his transition to the other side. I had felt this but never voiced this thought to anyone! He also said our beloved toy poodle, Bandit, was with Nicholas to comfort him (Bandit died 2 ½ years after Nicholas).

There was no way George could have known these and many other facts unless true contact had been made. As the reading continued, a feeling of peace and security came over me with the new found knowledge that Nicholas was safe in God's care…"

Brook had the pleasure of attending a talk by John Edwards, author of *One Last Time*. John had many experiences that made him aware of his abilities as a medium from an early age. He tried to suppress these abilities and lead a more "normal" life. Yet as time went on, he was drawn back to work as a medium. Brook asked John, how one could tell if they were receiving a message from a loved one or just engaged in wishful thinking. He answered that if you were thinking about the deceased when the image came, it was probably your mind at work. However, if you were doing something completely unrelated—washing the car, watching television, mowing the lawn—and a voice, message or words come to you, it is very likely the deceased communicating.

I'm afraid the bereavement process will cause me to get over the loss and I'll forget my loved one. I don't want to forget him!
Grief is not something we 'get over' or heal from as if it were an illness. It is a journey to a new stage of life. The goal is not forgetting or resolving. The goal is to reconcile yourself to your loss and discover some kind of spiritual meaning. You will always have a relationship with the person who died, but the relationship is different. Your quest is to discover that relationship.

I inadvertently caused the death—how do I forgive myself and go on?
Perhaps you were driving the car, flying the airplane or steering the boat. Perhaps you bought the cruise tickets, chose the restaurant or suggested the trip. What do you do then? How can you go on with the knowledge that you may have, in some way (big or small) been inadvertently to blame? How do you go on? The answer is, by putting the emphasis on the word, "inadvertently." Inadvertently means unintended, unintentional. Say these words to yourself or write them down 100 times, "I DID NOT INTENTIONALLY KILL OR CAUSE THE DEATH OF _____" (fill in the person's name).

If you are having trouble forgiving yourself, try helping someone in need. There is no better cure for regaining your self-esteem. You are valuable. Your life has meaning. Turn the energy you are using in self-condemnation outward to help someone, or some organization that needs your valuable gifts.

Is it really possible to transform my grief and pain into creative energy?
Yes, as a matter of fact, it is recommended that you find a way to transform your grief and pain into creative energy. The book you are holding is an example of that transformation of energy. Olympic medallist, Ekaterina Gordeeva, used this energy the first time she went back on the ice after her husband and skating partner's sudden death. Her choreography on ice was an extremely moving and powerful example of grief turned into creative expression.

In the Prologue to *My Sergei*, Ekaterine Gordeeva wrote, "For me, a new life is coming, a different life from that which I knew. I felt it for the first time when I was back in Moscow, two weeks after my beloved Sergei's funeral. In my grief, I feared I had lost myself. To find myself again I did the only thing I could think of, the thing I knew best, the thing I'd been trained to do since I was four years old. I skated. I went onto the ice, which was always so dear to Sergei and me, and there, in the faces of young skaters training with their coaches, I recognized their bright dreams and hopes for the future. The new life is coming, I thought."

The book also reveals that, "As Ekaterina and her coach, Marina worked on the choreography for the 'Tribute to Sergei,' Marina helped her visualize the ice dance by saying, "Imagine that you're skating with Sergei for the last time...Now you've lost him, you're missing him, you're looking for him and can't find him. You get on your knees and ask God why it happened. Your legs feel broken, as if they have no strength. You cannot move. Everything inside you feels broken, too. You must ask God for some help. You must tell God you understand that life goes on, now you have to skate. You must thank Him for giving you Sergei for half your life, the most beautiful time in your life. This is about how all people can get up from their knees in the face of adversity, can go forward, and can have the strength to persevere. You can find someone to live for. You can have a life of your own now."

You don't need to be an Olympic ice dancer to express yourself creatively. It may be writing a small collection of poetry. You may want to write or compose a song. Creating a simple photo collage may be helpful. You may choose to write a book or start an organization. Allow yourself to discover a creative outlet that suits you.

Grief has an absolutely transformative power. When we lose someone, we lose what they gave us, whether it's economic security, love or guidance. Taking these functions upon ourselves, or finding new ways to achieve what we have lost, can be an enriching experience. Think of one special way that person had of *being*. What we most appreciated is what we yearn and grieve for—and by making that quality stronger in ourselves, we keep the spirit of our loved one alive.

Can I expect my religion to offer me the answers and support I need right now?

Rev. Stephen Goldstein, a clergy person of the United Methodist Church shared his thoughts with us, "All too often religious professionals rely on the glib or trite religious language in the face of death or human pain, with a pat sensibility that does little to show a genuine concern for the grieving person. Our simple human availability is initially demanded in such pastoral encounters, not coded objective 'answers.' When with someone, I try to voice the questions I sense they are asking. I ask why?, etc. *with them* and communicate my own question. It is not the time for solutions or problem solving. The key is *being* with someone and expressing my own human limitations, that I have the same questions. I am certain that this is how to be available to the 'presence of God,' or the 'spirit,' or whatever your tradition 'calls' the transcendent. God is available at such times, especially when we are vulnerable enough in our care and genuine concern for the other for that presence to 'breathe' through us, perhaps even with a physical touch during prayer when we seek the love of the transcendent other.

When looking carefully and examining through the questions with someone grieving after a sudden death or any death, it is important to hear and listen and not assume what is being expressed by the other. Sometimes it's guilt, fear, anger or even relief and usually a combination of these normal emotions, but to be the 'church,' 'the gospel' or the presence of God in such situations, it is of primary importance to pay attention beyond our own expectations. If we can be vulnerable enough to feel the other's experience by revisiting our own experience, we may create the opportunity for the presence of healing. Or as Henri Nouwen gave expression to this role—becoming a "wounded healer." It's not so much naming the other's feeling, but being one—open to, and in, the spirit. It is not naming the other how they feel, but being one with the person through the spirit. Offering one's own personal experience in an intuitive way may most adequately define that presence. The closure ceremonies such as funerals and memorials is the time to verbalize the 'historic language' of the faith. This brings the person into community with loved ones and the greater community of which we may be a committed part.

Of course this can only be really effectual when such community is part of the person's life. To expect religion or a religious leader to come to the rescue, is both unrealistic and unfaithful.

If a pastor only offers written prayers or pat scriptural expressions such as 'there are many mansions in my fathers house,' to avoid sharing honest experience, without listening to the persons raw grief, this will surely avoid and block any significant "spiritual" expression. Religion then becomes a barrier to the presence of God and grace.

If the pastor or religious professional is only disingenuously available you will of course know it and will have to go elsewhere in your community for care and a real presence. It is of course important to already be in community, specifically religious or not, to have such availability in a time of crises. That is part of being a spiritually mature person to begin with. That a particular clergy or professional are uncomfortable dealing with someone's pain and loss is a different issue. If one is a mature follower of a religion, then either the teachings themselves have been translated to be available to you in your life so that they can be a means of grace to you as a genuine expression of your experience."

NOTE: We have included a form in the appendix to help you communicate with the officiant at your loved one's funeral or memorial service.

Shouldn't I be strong enough to "tough it out" by myself?

Don't expect to get through this time alone. You need all the support you can get. Your need for support may be wearing on your family and friends and you may be getting the mistaken idea that after a while you should tough it out on your own. We can only recover from our loss if we are in an atmosphere where honesty and loving acceptance are encouraged and where our burdens are shared. Seek out or develop a support group where you can share your pain, process any lingering guilt and see hope for the future.

One of the best ways to "see" your personal growth is to join a support group that will assure you of "how far you've come." In a group we see others who are back where we once were in the journey, or ahead of us in their healing, some who are ready to begin new relationships and others who are at the very beginning of the process. Wherever they are you will find many common threads as you share your experiences together.

Healing from the trauma of sudden loss in isolation is extremely difficult and may even be hazardous to your health. When you're having a problem, isn't it a comfort to talk to someone who has "been there, done that?" There is something comforting about being with others who understand the painful process and lifestyle alterations you are experiencing. Lots of heads nodding in agreement while you talk of your suffering as well as your accomplishments in the face of it all, can be very healing indeed. According to research one of the benefits that a group can offer is a boost to the immune system!   In helping others, you will find yourself moving a little more quickly in the healing process. Groups, large and small, professionally operated or member run, can provide not only understanding and support, but also an exchange of useful, pragmatic information.

ELLEN'S STORY

Ellen was at the beginning stage of readjustment to the unexpected loss of her husband of 38 years. She felt she had no friends in the community. Her sense of isolation was enormous and overwhelming to the point where she felt she needed medication for the anxiety she was experiencing. She was also dealing for the first time with financial and estate matters she knew very little about. This was creating even more anxiety for her. She attended a support group where she found immediate acceptance and validation. She was literally lifted to a higher, more positive place after attending just two meetings. Ellen is now attending the group regularly and is feeling much less "crazy" and more in control of the process. With the group's support, she asked her attorney and accountant to slow down a bit and explain things more clearly. She put off making too many decisions and found out from a group member where she could get more information about real estate issues, and allowed the group to give her feedback on her financial concerns.

So much change has happened in my life since the loss. How do I cope?
Suddenly your life has changed, for some more than others, but it can be less overwhelming if you are willing to confront the meaning of each change. Following are some guidelines for doing so.

- Confront your feelings. Denial can prolong the adjustment period and can prevent healthy adjustment.
- Maintain relationships. Isolation can have the same effect as denial.
- Give yourself time. No one can adjust to change overnight.
- Look for positive aspects in the change. It will take time, but you may find yourself beginning to open to new possibilities that may not have been there before.
- Keep your change in perspective. Look at the big picture. What may seem drastic now may seem less important when considered in a "lifetime" perspective.

"Each of us has the most amazing, magical facility to change our experience instantly simply by altering our perception."   Yogi Amrit Desai

I feel like my life is over, that everything has been put on hold—forever.
The first step toward positive change is to recognize that the life of the person you cared about is over and that yours is not! To do this you must recondition your thoughts and your words. Many people hold on to the thought that he or she is coming back. They find themselves waiting or putting life on hold. This kind of waiting, or holding back, uses a lot of energy that could be funneled into other pursuits. You must consciously be aware of pulling your thoughts back from the past to the present moment so you can maximize your energy to create a positive, forward-looking present.

Important Things to Remember on the Pathway

- Remember, if someone says something like, "It's time now to get on with your life," you have the right to say, "In my time and God's time, not in your time."

- If you want to wear black you can. You can also wear any other color you want during the time you are grieving.

- If you need isolation for a while that is okay. You will be with people when you are ready.

- Find a safe time and place to "go crazy" if you want to. Go yell in the woods, throw rocks at trees, swear at the TV or wear the deceased's clothes to bed.

- Be kind to yourself. Perfection is not necessary; there is no arriving, only going. There is no need to judge where you are in your journey. It is enough that you are traveling.

- Make a commitment to your future. Commitment enables you to bypass all your fears, mental escapes and justifications, so that you can face whatever you are experiencing in the moment.

- Get out of your own way. The main block to healing from loss is the thought that we shouldn't be where we are, that we should already be further along in our growth than we perceive ourselves to be. Let these expectations go.

- Affirm yourself. Who you were and who you will be are insignificant compared to who you are.

- Your life has not been a waste. Every individual in your life reveals a part of you that you need to encounter and serves as a medium through which you can see yourself, grow in awareness and come closer to God within. Live every experience and every event you encounter as a learning opportunity, rather than as a threat of failure.

- Fear is not always a bad thing. If you allow yourself to experience fear fully, without trying to push it away, an inner shift takes place that initiates transformation.

There is no experience that exists in this life that does not have the power to lead you to greater knowledge and growth. Major loss can only become a vehicle for creating a renewed life when we stop thinking of it as punishment and start to see it as process. This process begins with the death of a relationship, proceeds through a period of grief and mourning, in which the death is recognized and accepted, and ends with a rebirth.

Chapter Seventeen
Self-Help and Therapy

"What is needed is an impossible situation where one has to renounce one's own will and one's own wit and do nothing but wait and trust the impersonal power of growth and development. When you are up against a wall, be still and put down roots like a tree, until clarity comes from deeper sources to see over the wall."

- Dr. Carl Jung

Survivors can feel isolated and may experience a loss of identity. Some may experience not only the clearly defined stages in counselors' handbooks but also a lingering sadness. You may be aching for the deceased. Many people consult a pastoral counselor or grief therapist, but there are other sources—poetry, music, volunteer work, support groups, group therapy, self-help books and a variety of useful professional therapies which can frequently provide solace in unexpected ways. We have explored some of these in this chapter. One therapy or self-help avenue may work better for you than another. We all have unique needs and what will work best for you depends on your background and your belief system.

I've heard a lot about self-help.
What kind of self-help should I try?

Journaling and Letter Writing
One of the most powerful tools for recovery is writing down your real thoughts and feelings in a journal—no editing or judgment. Writing a letter to the deceased can also be comforting. Some of your initial feelings

will be quite strong or angry. Don't let this deter your efforts. You need to get those feelings out. After a while, your writing will turn softer as the emotional charge lessens. You have a unique and meaningful story to tell—the story of the beginning, middle and ending of a relationship. Telling your story, writing it in a journal, creating poems, hearing other's stories...these are some ways we heal. No one has to read what you wrote for this exercise to work, although you may want to read portions of your journal to your support group members. One woman I spoke with said, "What worked best for me was to keep a daily gratitude journal so I could see that my life was full of more than just grief and loss. It helped me feel more balance and gave me a perspective that was empowering."

In her book, *The Fruitful Darkness*, Joan Halifax reflects on our collective as well as personal stories when she writes "stories are our protectors, like our immune system, defending against attacks of debilitating alienation...They are the connective tissue between culture and nature, self and other, life and death, that sew the worlds together, and in telling, the soul quickens and comes alive."

In his classic book, *Reaching Out*, Henri Nouwen writes that though our own story "can be hard to tell, full of disappointments and frustrations, deviations and stagnations...it is the only story we have and there will be no hope for the future when the past remains unconfessed, unreceived and misunderstood."

Don't put any expectations or limitations on your writing—simply write. If you find it hard to get started, set a timer for five minutes and write anything that comes to mind. Don't stop. The writing may not make sense or be coherent, but it will help you get used to placing words on paper. Don't worry about spelling, grammar or style—just get the words out. Try doing a five minute writing exercise each morning when you awake or at night before going to bed.

For those of you who would appreciate guidance from the Bible in your journaling, there is a wonderful Internet site at GreifShare. The area is called "On Your Own: Daily Help and Encouragement." The area guides you to sections of the Bible that are relevant to the feelings, emotions and questions a person deals with during grief. The site offers 13 weeks of personal devotions. Each week contains five daily Bible studies and suggestions for further reading. Each day also has an "In Your Life" area, which asks you questions to help you identify where you are in your journey from mourning to joy. You can access this tool at http://www.griefshare.com

Take the time to find a way to tell your story. Listen to your story. Listen to the stories of others.

Self-Help Books

Reading entire books will probably be very difficult in the beginning. However, there are some wonderful books on grieving that can be helpful. Do not plan to read an entire self-help book from cover to cover. Simply find what you need most in the index or table of contents and read a page or two at a time. In time you will be able to read more. A list of books is provided in the resources section of this book.

Frequently Asked Questions about Self-Help and Therapy

I know I need group support but what kind of group is best for me? How do I know which one is right?

A support or therapy group can be the ideal place for you to inexpensively explore your feelings. Your previous circle of mutual friends may no longer be available to you and a support group will be valuable in helping you re-establish your place in the world. Let's explore the basic group types.

A *professionally led support group* is organized and facilitated by a psychotherapist, pastoral counselor, psychologist, social worker or other mental health professional. You should feel supported and nurtured without judgment in this type of group. A fee may be charged since it is run by professionals.

A *peer led support group* is just that—led by someone who has experienced sudden death of a loved one and has decided to help others. Usually it is someone who is at least a year or two into the grieving process. There is normally no fee, or perhaps a donation will be requested of you.

A *professionally led therapy group* requires you to be in private counseling with the professional running the group and is an adjunct to your therapy work. You may also feel supported and nurtured in this group, but the therapist may challenge you on some of the beliefs you have that get in the way of your healing.

Many organizations form groups. Hospitals and religious organizations sometimes sponsor these groups. Therapists and social workers also form groups. Finding the right group for you will be easier if you pay attention to your intuition during and after the first meeting. At a time when we aren't sure of our ability to make decisions, trust your gut feelings to guide you. And don't give up, keep trying until you find the right fit.

Try the following exercise. The first time you go to a support or therapy group, take a pencil and paper with you. Either during or immediately after, jot down words that describe how you are feeling. Pay close attention to your feelings. Now do this again the second time you go, and once more on the third. Are you still feeling the same as you did the first time and second time? If your experience is mostly positive, continue with the group. If you notice you have written mostly about anxiety, fear, stress or shame, then stop going. Keep looking until you find a group that gives you positive feelings. Remember, a group is meant to be part of your extended support system. Take into account however, that you will not feel uplifted each time you go because the grieving process takes time and is full of its own ups and downs.

The stories of loss we have heard are as diverse as fingerprints—each one slightly different from the next. When we gather with those who attend and begin sharing, the connections, one to another, are astounding. Regardless of where we are in the process of grieving, or how we lost our loved one, we become supportive, relating and recognizing of each other's pain almost immediately. This sense of community and acceptance is vitally important to our spiritual and emotional healing.

There are some questions you will want to ask the person who is in charge.

- Is there a fee?
- How often do you meet?
- Is there an attendance requirement?
- Is it mandatory to share or speak at the group?

- How many people are there in the group? (If the group is larger than 10, you may not get your needs met as readily. There is only so much time for each person.)
- Is the group for men/women only? A group consisting of women only will help women develop supportive female relationships; and a group of all men will help men safely express their feelings.

Allow the group the opportunity to "give" to you. Work on believing you have earned the right to receive. Don't be afraid to talk about or express your feelings. After all, that's why you came. You will not receive the support you came for if you hold back. Think about friends in your life and realize that it was with time that the level and depth of their friendship was revealed—the same is true in a group experience.

Maybe I'm spending too much time alone. Is this bad for me?
Solitude is as important as a group experience. In solitude comes the opportunity (if we are not afraid) to slow down, to reflect, to gain a deeper inner vision of our responsibilities, our needs and ourselves. However, if we spend too much time alone, we risk believing the inner voices that beat up on us, so you may do better if you attend a weekly support group in conjunction with your alone time. A group offers the opportunity to check out what we "learned" in solitude, and to find out if what we've been telling ourselves is true.

Everyone is saying I should find group support, but I can't seem to find anything in my area.
Some of the ways these groups are listed or advertised are:
bereavement group
bereavement support
newly widowed
young and widowed
parents of murdered children
suicide support
If you can't find a group in your area, you may want to start one. Talk to your local library. Many libraries have a community room they will let you use. Talk to a minister, priest or rabbi in your community—find out if they

would be willing to organize a group and have you be the contact person. You don't have to go the course of loss alone! Many existing groups offer starter materials for forming a group. Contact national headquarters in the resources section for these offerings. Also keep in mind that the Internet has opened up worlds of support. The great thing about the Internet is that you can "sign on" whenever you need support. See the Internet resources in chapter nineteen for ideas.

I'm a man and it seems like all this self-help and group support stuff is for women. I'm afraid I won't find the help I need.
Men grieve differently from women. They are often silent, solitary mourners who immerse themselves in activity and private, symbolic rituals. They have a tendency to approach grief in a cognitive way and may be judged as cold and uncaring. They feel profoundly, but often cannot express the depth of their loss—even to intimates.

Men have a tendency to "tough it out" rather than seek support. But when they do find support, they most often find a strong bond with the other men and a safe place to express feelings. Ken expressed great relief when he spoke with tears in his eyes, "And I thought I was the only guy in New York whose heart was being ripped out every time I looked at my wife and saw my daughter in her face." There is no "manly" way to grieve, the experts say. There are many ways to cope with loss that have more to do with personality than gender. However, there is a stereotype for a man who loses his wife for instance—two or three months of sadness, then "suck it up" and get on with living.

There are eight widows for every widower among the 13 million widowed people in the United States. Little wonder men who lose their wives feel adrift. Society expects men to "walk tall" through their grief, yet offers little male-related support.

Jim Conway, a minister and author of *Men in Mid-Life Crisis*, believes in group therapy. Jim joined four grief groups after the death of his wife. Conway likens grief groups to Alcoholics Anonymous. "You don't have to explain what it means when you say, 'I am grieving.' I need to go and sit and listen and cry. I needed to know I'm normal. By the time a year was over, I knew I needed to move on when my primary purpose turned from being helped to helping others."

The Internet can come in handy here as well. We found several pages for grief sponsored by men. Read through the Internet Resources section of the last chapter for ideas. You may also want to review our section on Men and Grief in the Losing A Child chapter.

I'm considering attending a support group once a week. Will going to a group help me cope even when I'm not there?

When you commit to a bereavement support or therapy group you "take the members with you" when you go into difficult situations. You are never really alone. Sometimes if you ask, members will go with you not just in spirit, but also in the flesh. For example, Maureen had to go to the city hall to pick up her son's death certificate and she expressed her anxiety and fear to the group. After she admitted she was scared that she might break down in a public place, Shelly, another group member, volunteered to accompany and drive her if she wanted.

My friends and family all say I need the support of others who have gone through this, but I don't feel ready to talk about this face-to-face. Are there any alternatives?

Fortunately, there are. The Internet has opened up many avenues to exchange and share information. One of the most popular features of the Internet are chat rooms. While many chat rooms have no designated topic or are unmoderated, there are many that offer grief support, specifically. The Internet Resources section of chapter nineteen lists several such groups. You can listen or read other's stories and share as you choose. You can also remain anonymous. Another advantage is that you can seek help when you need it. If you are feeling low in the middle of the night you can simply "sign on" to your computer and find someone to comfort you.

Some Therapies that Can Be Useful

Therapists and specialists in grief counseling agree that bereavement (especially in cases of sudden loss) closely parallels traumatic stress reaction. Based on this fact, here are some therapies you may want to seek out:

Bioenergetics: This mind/body therapy can be quite useful in treating emotional problems. According to Dr. Alexander Lowen who developed the process, it can help heal trauma and release emotion. Various releasing exercises are used, coupled with breath work. Consult a trained professional.

Biofeedback: If you are under distress and are suffering stress-related physical problems, this technique may provide some relief. This therapy uses electronic sensors which are attached to various parts of the body to measure such variables as heart rate, blood pressure, and skin temperature. Biofeedback training teaches one to produce a desired response by reproducing thought patterns or actions that triggered the displays. The person is told to relax, to picture pleasant scenes, and at the same time to concentrate on the audio or visual displays. These indicate how much, if any, physical change is resulting from the person's moods or thoughts.

Craniosacral Therapy: This non-invasive form of body work has been proven effective for anxiety, depression, headaches and other problems. This type of therapy uses the craniosacral rhythm to relax and calm.

Feldenkrais Therapy: This therapy incorporates a method of movement that combines awareness with attention. Feldenkrais therapists teach the individual to discover what makes them feel comfortable. Mental or emotional problems that involve letting go (as is the case in the later stages of grieving the loss of a loved one) can be helped by Feldenkrais.

Psychotherapy: This type of therapy can help in altering an individual's interpersonal environment, relationships, or life situation. This kind of therapy, practiced by a qualified therapist, involves verbal communication (as in psychoanalysis, nondirective psychotherapy, reeducation, or hypnosis) and is intended to have the effect of alleviating symptoms of mental or emotional disturbance .

Spiritual Counseling: For some, looking to a "higher power" or God and believing there is something beyond your skin that sustains you, can offer profound hope. A spiritual counselor (or a pastoral counselor) can help guide you to a deeper, more hope-filled understanding of your loss.

Hypnotherapy: This therapy can be useful in helping the survivor relax and can help with the symptoms of post traumatic stress. It is administered by a professional, using a relaxed, focused state of awareness. Hypnosis can help change the physiological and psychological reactions to trauma.

Eye Movement Desensitization and Reprocessing (EMDR): EMDR is proving to be effective with any one of a wide variety of problems, including traumatic grief/bereavement. EMDR is used within the context of an effective treatment plan, though the procedure is extremely powerful and efficient in uncovering and resolving trauma-induced anxiety.

Magnet Therapy: Used therapeutically to reduce pain and discomfort and to increase blood flow and enhance relaxation. It is important to purchase magnets from reputable companies (i.e. Nikken, Tectonic). Check with your health professional before beginning magnet therapy.

Thought Field Therapy (TFT): This is a brief treatment approach that has been found to be extremely promising in treating traumatic stress associated with grief and bereavement. TFT includes "psychological reversal," a procedure that helps clients reverse their disinclination of reaching a certain clinical goal. It also includes, "perturbations," the sensation of traumatic stress experienced not only cognitively, but also kinesthetically, emotionally, neurologically and biologically.

Visual/Kinesthetic Disassociation (V/KD): Like EMDR and TFT, V/KD is very brief, powerful and apparently successful in reducing subjective distress, yet without requiring grieving clients to describe their traumatizing experience. At its best, V/KD achieves success but without the unwanted time requirements and emotional distress.

Traumatic Incident Reduction (TIR): TIR appears to be very promising for enabling clients to make significant progress in only a few sessions. In contrast to the treatment approaches listed above, TIR depends upon the client retelling his or her story over and over until the client finds an "end point." In this approach, the therapist helps the grieving person by bearing witness to the person's accounting, but nothing else. This witnessing has been found to be extremely powerful in helping those who have lost a loved one through murder.

(Portions of this list were adapted from *Living with Grief After Sudden Loss*, edited by Kenneth J. Doka, Ph.D., Hospice Foundation of America and from *Nature's Prozac* by Judith Sachs, Prentice Hall)

Rubenfeld Synergy Method: Often in the case of a traumatic event, the body will react to shock and create a tension that holds the emotion of the trauma in the muscles and tissues. This body/mind/spirit form of psychotherapy incorporates gentle touch with gestalt therapy and Eriksonian hypnotherapy. This touch gently supports the client as muscles relax and the emotions of the trauma are released. At the same time, the talking allows the client to say goodbye to their loved one in a new way, deal with the issues of loss in their own life and gain the strength and permission to move ahead with their own life in time. (*Healing Journeys* edited by Vicki Mechner contains a number of stories of individuals and their experiences with Rubenfeld Synergy)

Project Nature Connect (and other nature related therapies): Nature in its vastness and omnipresence has frequently been a tool for healing and inspiration. In today's culture our lives are often cut off from nature and its cycles. Taking time to consciously connect with nature puts the individual back in touch with the cycles of life and death, in touch with a container (nature itself) that is vast enough to contain the "awe-fullness" and awfulness of the trauma. There is a life force in nature that nourishes one. Project Nature Connect offers a web site (www.ecopsych.com) where an individual can learn about these activities, an on-line group that discusses supportive experiences in nature, and mini online courses where an individual can do experiments in nature and share in a group.

Aromatherapy is an alternative treatment that uses scent to alter our moods and mind states. This healing art uses Essential oils—which are oils extracted from specific plant materials. In her book, *The Fragrant Mind*, author Valerie Ann Worwood writes, "Science is catching up with what aromatherapists have been saying for years: aromas can improve performance and capacity to remember, they can make you alert, or relaxed and change your mood. Aromatherapy uses natural aromas which have, of course, been used for similar purposes throughout the centuries. The reason aroma has such a direct action on the brain is that aroma molecules connect with receptor cells in the cilia extending from the two olfaction bulbs, which are themselves actual extensions of, and part of, the brain. Olfaction is thus the most direct interface between the brain and the outside world. Through our sense of smell, aroma molecules set off a cascade of reactions involving proteins, enzymes, cell depolarization and second messengers—all leading to an electrical impulse being sent to the brain. The part of the brain most directly involved is the limbic system, evolutionarily the oldest part of the brain, and home of our emotions."

For many of the listed emotions and states we have provided the name of several beneficial Essential oils. The easiest way to use these oils is to place 3-4 drops in a small container of water. Suspend the container over a small candle. The heat will release the oils into the air. You can order this heating mechanism and oils from many different companies. Incense cones, diffusers and aroma lamps also work well. One reputable supplier is The Essential Oil Company. You can print their catalog on the Internet or call and order one via mail. Their Internet address is http://www.essentialoil.com or write to 1719 S.E. Umatilla St., Portland, OR 97202; or call (800) 729-5912.

Alternative Solutions to Specific Symptoms: herbs, therapies and other techniques

In this section we will explore some alternative solutions including herbs, therapies and other techniques. Some people report great success with the use of herbal remedies, others report mild improvement and others report little difference. Since these ideas are all natural, they are worth trying should you find yourself suffering from any of these symptoms. Always consult your doctor before taking any herbal medication or starting any alternative therapy.

Sadness

It may not always work, but try renting a comedy. The Marx Brothers or the Three Stooges are so completely ridiculous they are bound to give you a laugh or two. Medical researcher, Judith Sachs also recommends sighing. She says, "It's therapeutic to sigh, so do it as much and as often as you want. There's a quality to sadness that makes you feel stuck inside your feelings, so by taking a deep breath and letting it out with a long sighing sound, you can expel some of the stale air and toxic carbon dioxide that help to make you feel miserable."

There's always exercise if you can get yourself out to do it. A brisk walk raises the blood pressure and releases endorphins, which are natural opiates in the brain!

Essential oils to try: Bergamot, Lemon, Neroli, Rose, Ylang Ylang, Mimosa

Feeling Depleted

The work of grief can leave one feeling extremely depleted. If this is the case with you, it is recommended you try Siberian ginseng or an oat-based tincture called avena sativa. There is also a homeopathic remedy called Phosphoricum acidum that might help (check with your health food store).

Essential oils to try: Rosemary, Peppermint, Eucalyptus Citridra, Petitgrain, Litsa Cubeba

Depression

Consider the herb, St. John's Wort as an alternative to prozac or other medications. It is well documented that this herb can help alleviate mild to moderate depression in about 2-3 weeks. The usual dose for adults is 3 tablets a day (900 mg). The only known side effect to date is sensitivity to sunlight in some people.

There is also a wonderful homeopathic remedy called, Natrum Muriaticum, which works well on depression that results from intense grief or the the loss of a loved one. According to the National Center for Homeopathy, there are no side effects to homeopathic remedies, and they are not habit forming.

SAM-e is a natural substance that has been used in Europe since the 1970s to treat depression and is now available for the first time in the US as an over-the-counter supplement. According to an article in *Prevention* magazine, "In clinical studies 400 to 1600 milligrams of SAM-e a day were as effective at reducing depression as prescription antidepressants. But here's what's special about SAM-e: It causes far fewer side effects than prescription antidepressants routinely do. And you get results within 4 to 10 days." The only caution we have is that SAM-e has not been used that long in the United States, so research within the US is slim. Consult a doctor before taking this supplement.

Vitamin supplements can also aid in depression. A good B-Complex, Vitamin C and Selenium supplement have proven to be beneficial according to the editors of *Prevention* magazine.

Essential oils to try: Mandarin, Bergamot, Ylang Ylang, Rose Otto, Geranium, Lemon, Chamomile Roman, Frankincense, Jasmine, Sandalwood

Inability to Cry

Some people are annoyed by their inability to cry when they are grieving. Homeopathic remedies have proven to be helpful such as, Natrum mur, Nux vomica, Pulsatilla and Ignatia. Check with your health food store or homeopathic physician.

Essential oils to try: Patchouli, Cypress, Linden Blossom

Fatigue

The stress of grief can sap your energy. You may find yourself in a constant state of fatigue. There are some herbal remedies that can help: black cohosh, ginseng and yellow dock are just a few. You might also try a tea made with ½ teaspoon of cayenne, cinnamon, or ginger powder.

Many vitamins can also help fatigue. NADH is one alternative that looks promising at 10 mg. per day. An article in *Let's Live* magazine reported, "The substance, nicotinamide adenine dinucleotide (NADH), had shown promise in the treatment of CFS. McCumbee joined 25 other patients who were given 10 mg of NAFH or an inert placebo for four weeks. Then after a four-week 'washout' period, when no one took supplements, the NADH and placebos were switched, so everyone had an opportunity to take NADH.

'I knew right away when I started taking the NADH,' McCumbee says. 'My thinking and energy improved, and my aches and pains went away.'"

The article listed other nutrients that can help fight fatigue. These included Alpha Lipoic Acid, Carnitine and CoQ10.

A good B-Complex vitamin will also help with energy. In Prevention's book, *Healing with Vitamins*, additional suggestions of an Antioxidant-complex, Magnesium and Vitamin C supplement are made.

Fatigue may also be the result of the medication you are taking (either over the counter or prescription). Speak with your doctor or pharmacist about side effects that could be causing you to feel tired.

Essential oils to try: Grapefruit, Helichrysum, Clary Sage, Peppermint, Eucalyptus Citridora, Cardamom, Basil

Guilt

Some holistic practitioners suggest that a homeopathic remedy is best for guilt. Guilt is also something you should discuss with your counselor or therapist as well. But if you want to try the homeopathic approach, try a Bach flower remedy such as Pine and Hyssop. Follow directions on the bottle.

Essential oils to try: Myrrh, Ginger, Rose Maroc, Cinnamon, Marjoram

Headaches

The stress of grief and loss can certainly bring on headaches. Headaches can also be a symptom of something more serious, so check with a doctor. Relaxation techniques such as meditation and guided imagery can help. Chiropractic visits and massages can also be beneficial. In *Nature's Prozac,* Judith Sachs says this about Chinese herbs: "...for headaches that are accompanied by cold hands and feet, loss of appetite, nausea, tension in neck and shoulders, and/or migraine: *wu ju yu tang* (Euodia decoction), made from euodia, ginseng, Chinese jujube, and fresh ginger. If your headache or migraine is accompanied by pain, nausea, congestion in the chest or solar plexus, and profuse perspiration, you might try *gui jir ren sheng tang* (cinnamon and ginseng decoction): cinnamon, licorice, atractylis ovata, ginseng, and dried ginger. Take one of these decoctions morning and evening over three to six months on an empty stomach (these should give short-term as well as long-term relief)."

In *Healing with Vitamins,* Prevention Magazine editors recommend 3000 milligrams of Magnesium, taken as three divided doses and 400 milligrams of Riboflavin.

In the book *Prescription for Nutritional Healing* (a wonderful book for thorough nutrient and herbal suggestions and guidance) authors James F. Balch, M.D. and Phyllis A. Balch, C.N.C. write, "The following herbs may relieve headache pain: brigham, burdock root, fenugreek, feverfew, goldenseal, lavender, lobelia, marshmallow, mint, rosemary, skullcap and thyme. Caution: Do not use feverfew during pregnancy. Do not take goldenseal internally on a daily basis for more than one week at a time, do not use during pregnancy, and use it with caution if you are allergic to ragweed. Do not take lobeilia internally on an ongoing basis."

Essential oils to try: From a vile of Peppermint oil, put a drop on your finger. Rub between your two pointer fingers and then massage into temples or the back of the neck, depending where the headache is located.

Distraction

Stress is a major factor in distraction and is usually an emotional reaction to overload. There is no question that the sudden death of a loved one is overload! Try concentrating on just one thing at a time (refer to "If you're forgetting things" below). Herbal teas with cowslip, ladyslipper, lobelia or California poppy consumed three times a day can be helpful. Just taking the time out to sip the tea is in itself a way to handle the overload.

Essential oils to try: Ginger, Basil, Rosemary, Cypress, Black Pepper, Grapefruit, Lemon

Forgetfulness

Write everything down! Not just the important things—everything (i.e. take a shower, eat lunch, put stamps on mail, keys are on the dresser). Put sticky notes everywhere. Carry a small spiral-bound notebook with you wherever you go. Leave an additional one open on the kitchen counter. Mark tasks off as you complete them.

According to some sources, wintergreen lifesavers can enhance memory and clarify thinking. Wintergreen has been known to stimulate the cerebral cortex in the brain, the area responsible for memory.

Herbs such as Gingko biloba and Gotu kola have also been shown to increase mental alertness.

Essential oils to try: Ginger, Cardamom, Grapefruit, Corainder, Thyme, Pimento Berry, Rosemary

Lack of Concentration

Lists can help and so can some alternative approaches. The Bach flower remedy is Indian Pink, which should help you feel focused under stress. Some homeopathic remedies are Silica, Belladonna, Calcarea and Ignatia.

Essential oils to try: Basil, Cedarwood, Lemongrass, Litsea Cubeba, Cardamom, Eucalyptus

Stomach Discomfort

The stomach is sometimes the barometer for what we're feeling. If you have a history of ulcers and are feeling stomach pain, consult your physician right away. For mild discomfort, you may find relief in using the following herbs: chamomile, peppermint, ginger or wild yam have been known to ease stomach spasms and aid in digestion.

In Andrew Chevallier's book, *The Encyclopedia of Medicinal Plants*, he suggests mixing three parts relaxing herb to one part carminative herb and making an infusion. Drink up to five cups a day. Relaxing herbs include: German chamomile, lemon balm and cramp bark. Carminative herbs include: Anise, fennel, mint and angelica.

Essential oils to try: Lemon, Anise, Fennel

Anxiety

For most, anxiety is a residue of fear and so addressing any fears you have should be discussed with a therapist. However, there are some alternatives you can try: Aromatherapy using Geranium, Bergamot or Ylang-ylang or herbal supplements such as Siberian ginseng, and St. John's Wort have proved quite helpful to others experiencing anxiety.

Another therapy known to help with anxiety is massage therapy with essential oils like Jasmine, Neroli, or Rose. If massage therapy is not for you, then placing these oils in a diffuser will also be effective.

Insomnia

The stress of sudden loss will probably interfere with your sleep patterns. Lack of a good night's sleep over a period of time can result in many of the problems mentioned above. One of the best natural solutions is to take a small dose (1 mg.) of melatonin about one hour before bedtime. (Older persons made need more—a good book on the topic is *The Melatonin Miracle.*) It should make you drowsy. Don't take melatonin during the day as it works best after nightfall and don't give this to children. Some foods that are rich in melatonin include bananas, tomatoes and rice.

Some herbs that may help you get a good night's sleep are valerian root, Jamaica dogwood, California poppy, hops, kava kava, skullcap and passionflower. Try to not to rely on one particular herb but to rotate among several.

Essential oils to try: Chamomile German, Chamomile Roman, Clary Sage, Ormenis Flower, Neroli

Note: Before taking melatonin, educate yourself on any possible ineractions with other medications.

For more information on homeopathy, contact the following organizations:

National Center for Homeopathy
801 North Fairfax St, Suite 306
Alexandria, VA 22314
(703) 548-7790

Homeopathic Academy of Naturopathic Physicians
12132 SE Foster Place
Portland, OR 97266
(503) 761-3298
Email: hanp@igc.apc.org

We know there is no quick fix or cure for the upset and shock sudden death causes one's body, mind and spirit. Some of the therapies we've mentioned above can help. We wish we could do more. Sometimes the best we can do for each other is listen. In the case of self-help therapies, you also need to listen to yourself. Allow your intuition to guide you to what you need. If you have any questions, don't hesitate to ask a trained professional for an opinion.

Chapter Eighteen
Grief Recovery Exercises

"If you bring forth what is within you,
What you bring forth will save you."
—*Gospel of St. Thomas*

As we move through the processes of grief it's important to *do* and not just *think*. By actively engaging in rituals and exercises we allow ourselves to release our emotions. The exercises in this chapter can be done over and over as you move through the grieving process. In her book, *Part of Me Died, Too*, Virginia Lyn Fry writes, "We never get a choice about who will die in our lives. But we do get to choose what to do with our memories. By using our memories to make poetry, drawings, and stories, we create a truth we can live with. By turning our feelings...into something we can touch, explore, and treasure, we transform our grief so that it brings us new understanding, new strength." These exercises will help you transform your feelings into creation.

Not every exercise will be right for you. Read them through and see how you feel toward the exercise. If it sparks your interest or feels like an exercise appropriate to your stage of grief, try to work it through. If you read through an exercise and it makes you uncomfortable, don't discard it immediately. Identify what makes you uncomfortable. Often uncomfortable feelings arise from our sensitivities and fears—it could be one of these exercises that would be the most valuable to you.

Lastly, these exercises are tools for your grief work; they are not a substitute for support groups or other help. They will help you identify and release your feelings; but a support group of peers with similar experience is also important during the grief period. Our Resource section lists many support groups—some of which meet in person and others that you can "chat" with via the Internet or through letter writing.

Anger Exercise

You may find it useful to turn your anger into a loud prayer or shouting match with God for example.

Dear God! The pain is horrible. I am angry with myself. I am angry with my spouse. I am angry with you ! I know you can handle my anger because I see you as loving me no matter what. But why can't you make it stop! Make the pain go away! How much do you expect me to take?

Pounding your fists on a bed or sofa while shouting this "prayer" is one way of moving painful, stuck energy through your body. You might notice a sense of relief when you're done. You may even feel like you've been blessed in some way. You may want to do this exercise with your therapist or trusted friend if you don't feel safe doing this alone.

If the sound of your own screaming and yelling is too scary for you, you might begin by writing a short note to the deceased. Each of the following was at a point in the process where all they could feel was anger and where they were temporarily unable to feel *anything* at all *but* their anger:

Dear Allison: I am hurt and angered by your abandonment of the kids and me. Regards, Rob

Chris: All I want to do is rage at you and cry. Brenda

Dear Tom: If I could get my hands on you right now, I'd kill you for leaving me. Love, Annie

Dear Artie: Friends don't desert friends, man. You really messed me up.

Of course, you can write more if you want to. What's important is to find an outlet or exercise that helps you release your anger. In chapter three we discussed other outlets for anger and the emotion in more detail.

Thank You Exercise

As you continue to grow and heal you will eventually discover at least something (no matter how seemingly insignificant) for which you can express gratitude. If the expression is not available to you now, it is probably a temporary condition.

After you have honored your anger, and when you are ready, you might want to try this Thank You Exercise. Compared to all other acts, personal and spiritual growth is greatest through the expression of gratitude. No matter how difficult at first, expressing appreciation for the life that is gone can help make some meaning in the face of tragedy. Acknowledging, in writing, what was empowering and uplifting about your relationship to the deceased, will help you keep sacred what you had together—to retain what was valuable and to let go of the false belief that they are incapable of inspiring you (now that they are dead).

Why pick up a pen and write a note—why not just think about it? The act of writing, choosing the type of pen and paper, the color of the ink, moving the pen across the paper, seeing the words—all make what you are saying more real—more concrete. You will notice your energy shift—from confusion about what to write, anger at having to sort through your life for the first time (or the thousandth time), tears as you recognize what you have lost and ultimately a sense of relief at having given yourself the chance to express the unsaid.

Date and save your notes in a special place or put them in your journal. You may want to destroy the note. Remember, this is about expressing feelings that need to be expressed. Rereading it again, however, after several months or years is sometimes useful, so you may want to save it for future reference. It is also useful to write another note after some time has passed. Each time you write, you will gain new insights. If you have young children you may even want to read it to them when they are older.

Here is an example:

Dear Jim, Thanks for the holding. You were good at holding when I needed to be held—when I was having trouble learning to trust—you helped me to know that I was capable of loving.

You held me when I was sad. I had so much sadness then. Thank you for the many times you were able to say, "Everything will be all right." Thank you for coming into this lifetime. This time I received the lesson I was so long denying that I needed to learn. What did I learn? I learned that it is unwise to marry someone to give you what you didn't get from your parents as a child. It is important to nurture and love yourself.

Thank you for being a good father to our son—you were the kind of father I would have wanted for myself. Thank you for the 10 years of our marriage—for 10 years I felt loved. Thanks for being with me at the birth of our son and for supporting us so I could stay home with him when he was a baby—yes, MOST OF ALL, thank you for our son for without you, he would not have been born.

Love, Joan

Although she sobbed on and off for the better part of an hour after writing this, she admitted to experiencing a sense of relief and to feeling better about herself than she had in some time. She affirmed why she had chosen the man she did and felt great comfort in this.

The Search for Meaning
(to be done 1-2 years after the loss)

How can one expect to make meaning of a suddenly ended life, an aborted relationship, a disrupted lifestyle and the painful losses that go along with it? These are profound questions, which are not easily addressed. There are no flip responses or boilerplate answers. However, what can be offered as a pathway to healing, are possibilities and new perspectives you may not have investigated. You are welcome to "try on" these possibilities knowing they will either fit your understanding of how the Universe works and give you some peace of mind and stillness of heart, or conversely create even more questions for you. In any case, the exploration into why your relationship with the deceased needed to begin and to end may well be worth the energy invested.

Could the relationship have ended just when a particular phase of change and growth was completed for you? Could it be that you are now being catapulted into a greater phase of growth—that in spite of your tremendous loss and disrupted life, that a new you, full of vital life force and creativity is ready to emerge (or has already emerged)?

When a significant other dies suddenly, it is not unusual to have a sense that one was rejected or abandoned in some way. When you are feeling the searing pain and anger of abandonment, it is even more difficult to consider that your pain may be transformed into something meaningful or that the end of the relationship through death can be in any way beneficial to your growth. It can be. Especially if you were dependent on the other person for good feelings about yourself. Now is the time to look within and to affirm yourself as a person of value. It is also the time to remember and replay the positive messages you heard from your significant other before they died. Everyone has heard at least one life affirming, positive message from his or her deceased loved one worth repeating to oneself. Allow those former positive messages, coupled with your own, to lift and inspire you.

Look at your life in totality to this point. Think about your life before you met the deceased. Think about your life with this person when they were alive. What lessons did you learn? What cycle was occurring? What purpose could this person have been "sent" into your life for? We believe that every opportunity, no matter how painful, offers growth if we are strong enough to meet the challenge. What life lesson could this person have taught you? What growth might their time in your life have encouraged? What might their death encourage? What characteristics could this experience unveil within you? These are tough questions and there is no need to answer them right away. In fact, this exercise is best a year or so down the road when you've had a bit more time to assimilate and reflect. When you are ready, though, we believe you will find it valuable. Spend some time with these questions. Write about them in your journal. See what surfaces—and how what surfaces—might be the beginning of a new phase of life for you.

Learning through Loss

Patricia lost her fourteen-year-old son, Doug, to a self-inflicted gunshot wound. She offers ten affirmations of life that she learned from her grieving process:

1. "I let my feelings flow; they are my life's blood; they will not kill me; they will heal me. (By the way, a punching bag is a good way to move from rage to tears.)
2. I follow my lead. I only need to know and then honor the next step.
3. I can trust the Universe to support me and it will in ways seen and unseen.
4. Help is there—I need only let it in at times, to ask others and to trust that people want to help in these ways:
   Physically—mow my lawn, scrub my deck (where my son died)
   Metaphysically—pray for me, hold me in the light
   Psychologically—send me your memories of Doug, poems that mean something to you
5. I will confront my demons. Anxieties are not stoppers or signs to give up, they are just a new place to step slowly and to be creative.
6. Gratitude—every situation has a gift and a limit. I won't deny the limits and the pain and I will let myself see the gifts and the goodness as well.
7. Be there as a friend—the greatest gift I can give to someone is to accept him or her fully as they are.
8. Life is a journey, not a destination. I will live each day fully for its gifts of grief and gladness.
9. Grief comes in waves. Each carries me forward to the next step. An ocean never becomes stagnant water.
10. I will pray, meditate and stay in touch with the spirit in whatever way works for me."

Patricia's final note: "Upon completion of this… a fresh wave of grief hit as spring and Easter arrived. I found myself needing to read what I had written over and over to remember the lessons I had so painfully learned.

Which brings me to an old affirmation of mine...*I will tell a friend what I see as my truth so that someday when I forget, my friend can tell it back to me.* So dear reader, help me remember when times get tough."

Patricia chose to use the power of lessons learned in facing her grief. This practice is both healing and empowering. Try it for yourself. Purchase a small and beautiful bound book at a stationary store. In this book, record the lessons you learn moving through the grief process. It can be a great reminder of the steps you are taking and a wonderful way to become more aware of purpose and meaning. – Contributed by Patricia Ellen

What my Loved One has Left Me...

When someone dies suddenly, it is not unusual to have a sense that one was rejected or abandoned in some way. When you are feeling the searing pain and anger of abandonment, it is even more difficult to consider that your pain may be transformed into something meaningful or that the end of the relationship through death can be in any way beneficial to your growth. It can be. Especially if you were dependent on the other person for good feelings about yourself. Now is the time to look within and to affirm yourself as a person of value. It is also the time to remember and replay the positive messages you heard from your significant other before they died. Everyone has heard at least one life affirming, positive message from their deceased loved one worth repeating to oneself. List those messages in your journal or write them in letter form (i.e. Dear ___, these are the life affirming messages I bequeath to you. Love _____).

Allow these positive messages to lift and inspire you.

Screaming Exercise

Sometimes the only thing left to do is SCREAM! Emotions may well up inside you and they need a place to go. It can be a release and a relief to scream as loud as you can and to say whatever comes to mind. It will be a challenge to find an appropriate place to do this exercise. You may have to travel some distance to find a wide open space where no one can hear you. Here is an example of how Pam and her sister Marilyn solved the problem:

> "A few months after my sister's husband died suddenly and I was still reeling from George's death, we decided to go to Canada to attend a workshop. In our free time we drove across vast empty spaces with miles of road and no one around. We found ourselves in the car one afternoon in the middle of a Canadian "no man's land" highway screaming 'Why did you die!,' 'I hate you for dying,' 'This death stuff really sucks!' and a host of other expletives. We laughed at how ridiculous we sounded and we cried because we needed to. We decided it was safest if the one who wasn't crying drove the car because it's hard to see the road with tears in your eyes!"

Our intense emotions need to have an outlet, otherwise they can make us sick. A very potent outlet for our grief is to go to a private location (your parked car can serve this purpose very well) and SCREAM and RANT as loudly as you can. By giving ourselves permission to do this, we validate ourselves and our healing process. Do not stifle this need to give voice to your pain. It is your right as a human being to express your deepest feelings in this way if you choose to do so.

Define Your Priorities

After losing a loved one the world often seems to have spun out of control and we are left trying to make sense of our place within it. Thinking about what is important to you and exploring ways you can make a difference can be very helpful. The following exercise asks you to identify your priorities. Keep in mind that there are no right or wrong answers.

- What three things matter most to you?
- What do you value most spiritually?
- What do you value most emotionally?
- What possessions do you value most?
- What people are most important to you? (List them by name.)
- What do you feel you need to accomplish to make your life worthwhile?
- When you die, how would you like to be remembered?
- What are two things you could do *each and every day*, to make every day special?
- What in your life are you most grateful for?

After answering these questions in a journal, write a page on what you discovered about yourself. Answer these questions in your entry:

- What are the most important elements of life for me? (Often you'll discover a common thread in your answers.)
- Based on what I've learned, how would I describe a fulfilling life for me?
- What steps can I take now to move toward that fulfilling life? What steps can I take later?

Coping with Guilt

If you are suffering from the "if onlys" or the "I should haves," and you are left with a deep feeling of regret that you couldn't do more to help your loved one or prevent the death, try the following exercise:

Write at least a one page letter to the individual who died. Tell them whatever you want but remember to include the following:

- the facts of what happened
- how you feel about what happened
- how their death has affected your life

Now, turn the page over and imagine the deceased responding to your letter. Asking questions of the deceased will make this exercise extremely valuable. So write down such questions as, "How do you feel about what happened?" and "Will you please forgive me for _____?" "Have I been punished enough for my part (real or imagined) in all this and is there anything else I can do to show you how sorry I am?" "How can I show you how much I have suffered?" Then close your eyes and answer each question as if they were speaking through you.

If you find this is a difficult exercise to do on your own you may want to ask a therapist or trusted friend to sit quietly with you. If you are being "told" by your inner voice to hurt yourself in any way, seek professional help immediately.

Poetry

Poetry creates a bridge of feelings between the material world and the world of creativity and spirit. Visiting and/or joining a poetry group can have an extraordinary effect on the way we heal our grief. Poets, by definition, get to the raw feelings behind the masks we all wear. When we are wearing the mask of grief, we may feel that others cannot possibly know the pain we are experiencing, yet we must still continue living day to day in spite of our tremendous loss. As a result, we may feel out of touch with friends who have not experienced such a loss. We may feel that the strength of our feelings is unacceptable to others. Feelings are the dynamic force behind poetry groups. Within these groups you will find a welcome and sensitive home for the expression of your grief through the written and spoken word.

Search the World Wide Web for "Artists Salons" and/or "Poetry" in your state; also check your local paper for poetry readings. Attend the readings and ask participants about other local events in your area.

You can also write poetry on your own. Many books exist that can fuel creativity and offer guidance. Check the writing/reference section at your local bookstore. It can be extremely cleansing to spend a morning, once a week, at a cafe or park writing poetry in a beautiful journal. Don't worry about form—just creatively put down words to express yourself. Write poetry.

In the book, *The Poet's Companion: a guide to the pleasures of writing poetry*, author's Kim Addonizio and Dorianne Laux have a specific section on death and grief. They offer 10 suggestions for working with this subject. "Write a poem about a ritual that accompanies a death. It might be about a traditional funeral, a wake, or some more private or individual observance. If you find an occasion for joy of beauty in the midst of mourning, include it." Another suggestion is, "If you own some object that used to belong to someone who is no longer alive, describe it in detail, along with your memories or images about how that person used it. You might also talk about how it is used in the present."

The Gratitude Journal

Sarah Ban Breathnach in her best-selling book, *Simple Abundance: A Daybook of Comfort and Joy,* advocates the use of a gratitude journal. She sites this as "a tool that could change the quality of your life beyond belief." We completely agree. This is how Sarah explains the gratitude journal:

> "I have a beautiful blank book and each night before I go to bed, I write down five things that I can be grateful about that day. Some days my list will be filled with amazing things, most days just simple joys. 'Mikey got lost in a fierce storm but I found him shivering, wet but unharmed. I listened to Puccini while cleaning and remembered how much I love opera.'
>
> Other days—rough ones—I might think that I don't have five things to be grateful for, so I'll write down my basics: my health, my husband and daughter, their health, my animals, my home, my friends and the comfortable bed that I'm about to get into, as well as the fact that the day's over. That's okay. Real life isn't always going to be perfect or go our way, but the recurring acknowledgment of what is *working* in our lives can help us not only survive but surmount our difficulties."

Recognizing the positives in our lives is especially important when we are engulfed in dark times. We often focus so heavily on our loss and what isn't going right, we can't see any of the good things. For the first few months, it will be extremly difficult to find the positives, but after that time period, we need to begin looking again—no matter how simple these positives might be. Your list might include something as basic as "I was able to get out of bed today." What's important is that we be open to the fact that there are positives. By recognizing them, we attract more positives to our life.

Purchase your own special notebook to use as a gratitude journal and keep it by your bed. Each night, before turning out the light, search your day for five positive happenings.

Calming

Stress, anxiety, sadness, depression—these emotions can leave us knotted inside. Practicing breathing exercises can help us to relax and unwind our wound emotions. The following exercises will help calm you during trying times.

Place one hand on your abdomen. As you inhale, you want to feel the movement in your abdomen, not in your chest. Inhale for the count of ten, then exhale for the count of 10. Repeat this ten to fifteen times for deeper relaxation.

To relax your whole body, lay down in a quiet place. Breathe deeply, slowly inhaling and exhaling. Beginning with your left leg, clench your muscles as tightly as you can for the count of three. Then relax them. Do the same to the right leg, left arm and right arm. Then move up your body tightening your pelvis, then stomach, then chest, then shoulders, then neck and lastly facial muscles. When you have completed this exercise you should feel extremely calm and peaceful. Visualize an ocean beach or other calming scene to deepen the relaxed feelings.

Visualization

Creative visualization can be a wonderful way to calm our minds and bodies. When our bodies are relaxed, we can play calming, healing and encouraging "movies" on the screens of our mind. These movies or imaginings can promote healing, forgiveness and peace.

Visualization may take a while to get used to. The first time you try it you may feel you aren't "getting anywhere." Give yourself some time. Like any exercise, visualization takes practice. Also, you may want to do your visualizations while laying on the floor or sitting in a chair. If you do them in bed, you could very likely fall asleep, since the process is extremely relaxing.

To begin, follow the whole body relaxation that is written about in the calming exercise. When your body is relaxed and you do not feel any excess tension, begin your visualization.

As you do the exercises, thoughts and images may come to you that would be valuable to record. For this reason, it's a good idea to keep a visualization journal nearby.

Following are some visualization ideas. Choose one that feels comfortable to you or create one of your own. Feeding these positive messages into your mind will help reduce anxiety and depression—and help you to feel more joy and peace in life.

- Visualize yourself using your grief in a creative way. Notice what you are doing, who is around you, how you feel and what you see.
- If you feel guilt for the death, imagine blowing all the guilt within you into a balloon. See the guilt move out of your body, up through your lungs and into the balloon. See the balloon getting larger and larger until it contains all of your guilt. Hold on to the string of the balloon tightly, feeling all your guilt one last time. Then let it go. Watch the balloon carry the guilt away from you. You can use this same visualization with any other emotion that you want to get rid of—hatred, anger, jealousy or revenge to name a few.
- If you want to communicate with the deceased or want to feel their presence, visualize them sitting in familiar surroundings. Go to them with your question or concern and let an exchange take place.

- Visualize yourself one or two years from now. Visualize the person you will have become and the positive changes you will have made. What comes to mind? Who is around you? What is your life like on a day-to-day basis? What do you believe in?

Rituals

Rituals are an part important of life. Through rituals we are able to observe, remember and structure our beliefs and feelings. In her book, *Surviving Grief*, Dr. Catherine M. Sanders writes, "In the past, rites of passage for every shift point in life were marked by rituals, which commanded a respected place in our culture. Large extended families came together to honor the person being celebrated. During chaotic times of change and transition, these rituals provided important direction and spiritual strength."

Funeral services are an example of a ritual. They give us guidance and direction that allows us to come together and celebrate life with those who share our loss.

Creating your own ritual may seem like a difficult task, but it doesn't have to be. To begin, ask yourself what you are trying to remember or celebrate. For many, a ritual on the anniversary date of the death is valuable. Others find they'd like to create a ritual for the birthday of the deceased. If the deceased was a spouse, the wedding anniversary may be a good time for a ritual. There are no limits on rituals. You can have one each season of the year, or one annually or every other year. Think about the purpose of your ritual as you decide on frequency. For most who are grieving, the ritual period becomes a time of breaking away from the day-to-day demands so we can experience our grief fully and focus on the memories we hold of our loved one.

Next, decide if you want the ritual to be just for yourself or if you want to share it with others. You may find that having a group of friends engage in the ritual is helpful. Others like this time to explore their emotions by themselves.

Where you should conduct your ritual is the next question to answer. There may be a special place that you associate with the deceased. You may want to stay close to home or you may wish to travel overseas. Again, keep your purpose in mind as you choose your location.

Here are a few rituals that those who we've known have conducted and found comforting. Feel free to conform these to rituals that suit your needs or to use them as a springboard for other ideas.

Karen was living in France, when her mother died suddenly at the age of 50, leaving her father alone in the United States. Each year, Karen returns home for a week over the anniversary of her mother's death. She and her father use this time to recall their memories and visit the grave site.

Jessica, Monica, Laura and Allie were close college friends, all living together. When Laura was killed suddenly in a car accident, the other three young women were torn apart. Each year, on the anniversary of the death, the three women get together and take a cruise. They recall their fun college days together. It has been five years since these women graduated and they still continue with this ritual.

David wanted to be alone on his deceased son's birthday. He rented a small cabin in the mountains and took nothing with him but spare clothes. He walked in the mountains, absorbed the beautiful scenery and "talked" to his son.

Cassandra, a single mother, was lost after the sudden death of her daughter. On the anniversary of her death, she asked her ex-husband to watch her other children. She took the weekend to write, cry, watch movies and look through old photos.

Which of the above ideas sounds comforting to you? Make a few notes of what would be comforting in your time of need. Take some quiet time to sit and think about what might help you to heal. Then commit to a ritual. Mark the dates off on your calendar.

Memory Books

Creating a memory book is a wonderful keepsake of our loved one. When Brook's brother died, she collected articles, photos and other memorabilia to put in a keepsake album. Using different papers, stencils, markers and stickers she created special pages to "frame" her memories.

Album making has become popular in recent years. Many scrapbooking stores now exist that offer classes on how to archive our memories creatively. Through collage, rubber stamping, paper decorations and other means, we can make a beautiful book to serve as a remembrance.

In addition to stores that can serve as creative outlets, many magazines and books offer guidance. Even if you don't consider yourself creative, there are tools to help you get started. Check the craft section of your local bookstore for books on scrapbooking. A large newsstand or craft store may carry magazines such as *Memory Makers* and *Somerset Studio*, which offer ideas.

There are also consultants for companies like D.O.T.S. and Creative Memories that sell supplies and can help you choose supplies and offer creative guidance. Check your yellow pages for these companies. Current is another great source of materials. They can be accessed on the Internet at http://www.current.com

Here are a few basic tips for building your memory book.

- Choose a good album to hold your memories. Creative Memories and D.O.T.S. both offer wonderful albums. Also make sure to use acid-free papers and supplies whenever possible. When papers are acid-free, they will not damage your photographs over time.
- Collect all the materials that you think you would like to include. The possibilities are endless—postcards, words clipped from magazines, photos, special poems—anything that you like can be included.
- Sort the items you have gathered until you see a natural progression take form. You may want to move through the book chronologically or another theme may occur to you.

- Gather stencils, stickers, stamps and papers to use as decorations. Craft and scrapbooking stores are obvious suppliers. Additionally, office supply stores and stores like K-Mart, Wal-Mart and Target often have good selection at reasonable prices.

- Choose the materials you would like to use for a given page. Lay them out and move them around until you are comfortable with the design. If you have problems coming up with ideas for layout, consult one of the aforementioned magazines.

- Take your time. There is no need to try and rush through the process of creating a memory book. Many people find joy in the "putzing" and creating. It may be a book that you continually add to throughout your lifetime.

Chapter Nineteen
Resources and Support

In the following pages you will find a collection of resources to help you on your pathway of grief. Some of these are organizations that offer support groups that meet face-to-face. Others offer groups that meet on-line. Still other organizations offer newsletters, free brochures or magazines and many offer a combination of these services.

Some of these resources are available only via the Internet. Those resources are marked Internet Resource in parenthesis.

Supportive Publications

after loss
after loss provides a monthly newsletter on grief recovery. For more information write or call: 79301 Country Club Dr., Suite 1001, Bermuda Dunes, CA 92201; (800) 423-8811

Bereavement Publishing
Bereavement Publishing cares for the bereaved by providing resources. Bereavement Magazine functions as a "support group in print." They also offer a "Grief in the Workplace" program to help corporate America understand the needs of grieving employees. The group offers a magazine, 15 booklets, books, gift baskets and products, teaching tapes and a catalog.

For more information write to Bereavement Publishing, 5125 N. Union Blvd., Suite 4, Colorado Springs, CO 80918.

Concern for Dying

After experiencing sudden loss, it is common for people to want to get their own affairs in order. The Concern for Dying organization provides resources that can help. *The Living Will* and *Durable Power of Attorney* are two documents that they will supply free upon request. Contact information: 250 West 57th Street, New York, NY 10107 or by calling (212) 246-6962.

One Caring Place

One Caring Place publishes many pamphlets dealing with difficult emotions like grief, anger and loss. Brief and to the point, these caring publications offer wonderful support. You can contact them for a complete list of their publications by calling toll-free (800) 325-2511 or by writing to One Caring Place, Abbey Press, St. Meinrad, IN 47577.

The Centering Corporation

The Centering Corporation supports grieving people and those who care for and love them. They provide supportive resources for families, individuals, professional caregivers and friends. The organization was founded in 1978 and offers a free Creative Care Package Catalog. The catalog features over 200 books to support those experiencing grief or loss. You can request the catalog by calling (402) 553-1200 or by faxing (402) 553-0507 or by writing to 1531 N. Saddle Creek Road, Omaha, NE 68104.

Support for Loss of a Partner

American Association of Retired Persons – Widowed Persons Service

"The AARP Widowed Persons Service (WPS) is a community-based program in which trained, widowed volunteers reach out to the newly widowed. Established in 1973 and based on the 'Widow to Widow' research of Dr. Phyllis Silverman, WPS is a self help program offering one-to-one support, group work, public education, a telephone and referral service, and an outlet for rebuilding life as a single person. To locate the closest AARP Widowed Persons Service program in your community, call **1-800-424-3410** or e-mail griefandloss@aarp.org Additionally the AARP offers many helpful brochures including, *On Being Alone—A Guide for Widowed Persons, Final Details, Reflections and Suggestions on Making New Friends and When an Employee Loses a Loved One*. Their web site also contains comprehensive information, links and resources for dealing with grief. You can visit their web site at http://www.aarp.org They also hold online grief support chats three days per week on America Online. Visit their website for further details. You can write to them at 601 East Washington Street NW, Washington, DC 20049.

Death & Dying (Internet Resource)

This site offers comprehensive support for widows and widowers. They have a monthly newsletter that is delivered via e-mail and a moderated chat room. They also have message boards. Check out their offerings at http://www.death-dying.com

National Association of Military Widows

This group provides referral services for the newly widowed, sponsors social events and support groups, and lobbies for legislation beneficial to military widows. Contact them at 4023 – 25th Road North, Arlington VA 22207 or call (703) 527-4565.

Society of Military Widows (SMW)

This group serves the interests of women whose husbands died on active duty military service or during retirement from the armed forces. They can be contacted by e-mail at or writie to 5535 Hempstead Way, Springfield VA 22151 or call (703) 750-1342 ext 3007.

THEOS (They Help Each Other Spiritually) International

THEOS International has groups in both the United States and Canada that support widows and widowers. They also publish a magazine, book and organizational materials. For more information write or call: 1301 Clark Bldg., 717 Liberty Ave., Pittsburgh, PA 15222; (412) 471-7779.

The Beginning Experience

They offer international support programs for divorced, widowed and separated adults and their children enabling them to work through the grief of a lost marriage. They can be contacted at 305 Michigan Avenue, Detroit, MI 48226 or by calling (313) 965-5110.

To Live Again

This mutual help organization is for widowed men and women who support one another through the grief cycle. Cotact them at P.O. Box 415, Springfield, PA 15222 or call (412) 471-7779.

WidowNet (Internet Resource)

This is the most comprehensive site we've found for those who are widowed. WidowNet is an informative and self-help resource created for, and by, widows and widowers. "Topics covered include grief, bereavement, recovery, and other information helpful to people, of all ages, religious backgrounds and sexual orientations, who have suffered the death of a spouse or life partner." You can access the site at http://www.fortnet.org/WidowNet/. They also have an IRC Chat. The group is most active on Tuesday, Thursdays and Fridays after 8:00pm. To learn more about the group visit

http://www.fortnet.org/WidowNet/online/irc.htm

Support for Grieving Children

Camp "Good Grief"

Camp "Good Grief" is a summer camp program which offers grief education workshops and provides support and understanding for youth ages 12-16 who have experienced the death of a sibling, parent, grandparent or close friend. The camp is held in New York. For more information visit the web site at http://www.campgoodgrief.com or write to The Good Grief Epxerience, Inc., 24 St. Bernard St., Saranac Lake, NY 12983.

KIDSAID (Internet Resource)

KIDSAID is an extension of GriefNet, a comprehensive Internet community that has provided support to over 3 million people in the last year. The KIDSAID area provides a safe environment for kids and their parents to find information and ask questions. To learn more about KIDSAID, visit GriefNet at http://www.griefnet.org

Motherless Daughters, Inc.

This national organization was founded in 1995 and now has 46 affiliated groups. They provide support, community and resources to women and girls who have experienced early mother loss. Information and referals, national conferences, a newsletter, phone support and pen pals are available. Contact Motherless Daughter, Inc at Box 663 Prince St Station, New York, NY 10012 or call (212) 614-8047 or visit them online at http://www.dfwnet.com.md

Teen Age Grief, Inc.

Teen Age Grief, Inc is a non-profit organization that provides expertise in providing grief support to bereaved teens. Their goal is to make grief support available to all teens from all walks of life in an environment that is accessible, safe and non-judgmental. Contact Teen Age Grief, Inc. at P.O. Box 220034, Newhall, CA 91322-0034 or call (805) 253-1932 or visit their web site at http://www.smartlink.net/~tag/index.html

RAINBOWS

RAINBOWS provides curriculum and training for establishing peer support groups for children, adolescents and adults who are grieving a death, divorce or other painful transition in their family. Contact this group at 1111 Tower Road, Shaumburg, IL, 60522 or call (800) 266 3206.

The Dougy Center for Grieving Children

This group, founded in 1982, offers two outlets—one for the region of Portland, Oregon and another that is national in scope. Through the National Center for Grieving Children & Families, this group offers support and training locally, nationally and internationally to individuals and organizations seeking to assist children and teens in grief. The mission of the Dougy Center for Grieving Children is to provide to families in Portland and the surrounding regions, loving support in a safe place where children, teens and their families, grieving a death, can share their experiences as they move through their healing process. You can learn more about these programs by contacting The Dougy Center for Grieving Children, P.O. Box 86852, Portland OR 97286 or call (503) 775-5683 or fax (503) 777-3097 or visit their web site at http://www.dougy.com

Support for the Loss of a Child

Aiding a Mother and Father Experiencing Neonatal Death (AMEND)
This organization strives to offer support and encouragement to parents grieving the loss of an infant through miscarriage, stillbirth or neonatal death. To learn more, write to 1559 Ville Rosa, Hazelwood, MO 63042 or call (314) 291-0892.

Alive Alone
Alive Alone is an organization for the education and charitable purposes to benefit bereaved parents, whose only child or all children are deceased, by providing a self-help network and publications to promote communication and healing, to assist in resolving their grief, and a means to reinvest their lives for a positive future. The group offers a newsletter subscription and special events. Contact information: website: http://www.bright.net/~alivalon/ e-mail: alivalon@bright.net, Address: Alive Alone, 11115 Dull Robinson Road, Van Wert, OH 45891.

Bereaved Parents of the USA
This national organization was founded in 1995 to aid and support bereaved parents and their families who are struggling to survive their grief after the death of a child. Information and referrals, a newsletter, phone support, conferences and meetings are available. They also offer assistance in starting a support group. You may contact them at P.O. Box 95, Park Forest, IL 60466 or by calling (708) 748-7672.

Center for Loss in Multiple Birth (CLIMB)

This International network was founded in 1987 to support parents who have experienced the death of one or more of their twins or higher multiples during pregnancy, birth, infancy or childhood. They offer a newsletter, information on specialized topics, pen pals, phone support, materials for twin clubs and loss support groups. Contact them by e-mail at or by writing to P.O. Box 1064, Pamer, AK 99645.

Committee to Halt Useless College Killings (CHUCK)

This national network was founded in 1979 to support families who have lost a child to hazing or alcohol in fraternity, sorority or other college groups. They educate on the dangers of these practices and offer information, referals and phone support. Contact CHUCK at PO Box 188, Sayville, NY 11782 or call (516) 567-1130.

Hannah's Prayer

This International support group was formed to help those facing infertility, stillbirth and infant loss. They hold a Christian focus. You can contact them at: P.O. Box 5016, Auburn CA, 95604 or by calling (916) 444-4216.

Invincible Summer (Internet Resource)

Offers online e-mail support for those who have lost children. For more information e-mail jimncarol@earthlink.net

Meeting of Hearts (Internet Resource)

Two parents who lost their son tragically at the age of 20 founded this web site to offer others support. The site is beautifully done and offers a message board and valuable information. They also have a chat room. You can visit it at http://www.meetingofhearts.com/

Mothers in Sympathy and Support (MISS)

"The mission of Mothers in Sympathy & Support is to allow a safe haven for parents to share their grief after the death of a child. It is our hope that within these pages you discover courage, faith, friendship and love: The *courage* to speak out about your child and the love you have, regardless of the age or cause of death; The *faith* and reassurance that one day, we will all be reunited with our children—this time for eternity; *Friendships* with other families experiencing this tragedy; and finally, it is our hope that you discover the enormity and depth of the *love* you have for your child. A love that transcends time and distance; heaven and earth; life and death. MISS provides support to parents enduring the tragedy of stillbirth, neonatal death and infant death from any cause including SIDS, congenital anomalies, trisomy 13. Grief education for parents and professionals is our main focus. We must realize that the grief journey lasts a lifetime. Our child has changed our lives forever. Come with us and get lost in our pages...find healing, honesty, hope and a rediscovery of yourself." Visit this valuable web site on the Internet at http://www.misschildren.org/

Mommies Enduring Neonatal Death (MEND)
MEND is a nonprofit corporation whose purpose is to reach out to those who have lost a child due to miscarriage, stillbirth or early infrant death and offer a way to share experiences and information through meetings, a bi-monthly newsletter and Internet web site. You may contact them at P.O. Box 1007, Coppell, TX 75019 or call (888) 695-MEND or e-mail bek4@ix.netcom.com

Mothers Against Drunk Driving
Mothers Against Drunk Driving is a non-profit grass roots organization with more than 600 chapters nationwide. "MADD is not a crusade against alcohol consumption. Our focus is to look for effective solutions to the drunk driving and underage drinking problems, while supporting those who have already   experienced the pain of these senseless crimes." MADD offers support groups and resources. You can search for a chapter near you on their web site at http://www.madd.org or by e-mail at Info@madd.org or contact their national office at P.O. Box 541688, Dallas, TX 75354-1688

National SIDS Resource Center
The National Sudden Infant Death Syndrome Resource Center (NSRC) provides informational services and technical assistance on sudden infant death syndrome (SIDS)and related topics. Their goal is to promote an understanding of SIDS and provide comfort to those affected by SIDS

through information sharing. NSRC's products and services include information sheets and other publications such as *What is SIDS, Sudden Infant Death Syndrome: Some Facts You Should Know,* and *Facts About Apnea and Other Apparent Life-Threatening Events*; Annotated bibliographies on SIDS and related topics from NSRC's databases, such as *Infant Positioning and Sudden Infant Death Syndrome, Smoking and Sudden Infant Death Syndrome, Children's Grief,* and *SIDS and Epidemiology*; Reference and referral services related to SIDS research, bereavement and public awareness about SIDS. To contact NSRC call, write, or e-mail: National Sudden Infant Death Syndrome Resource Center, 2070 Chain Bridge Road, Suite 450,Vienna, VA 22182, Phone: (703) 821-8955, Fax: (703) 821-2098, E-mail: sids@circsol.com Many of their informational sheets can be read online at: http://www.circsol.com/sids/

Parents of Murdered Children, Inc. (POMC)

Charlotte and Bob Hullinger in Cincinnati, Ohio founded POMC in 1978, after the murder of their daughter. What began as a small group, is now a national organization with over 300 chapters and contact people throughout the United States and abroad. The group provides the "ongoing emotional support needed to help parents and other survivors facilitate the reconstruction of a 'new life' and to promote a healthy resolution. Not only does POMC help survivors deal with their acute grief, but with the criminal justice system as well." The staff of the national headquarters of POMC will assist you, and if possible link you to others in your vicinity who have survived a loved one's homicide. In addition the staff can provide individual assistance and support. Should there be no chapter of POMC near you, they can aid you in starting one, if you wish. POMC also trains professionals in the fields of law enforcement, mental health, social work, community services, law, criminal justice, medicine, education and other fields that wish to learn more about survivors of homicide and the aftermath of murder. You may contact the National Headquarters at 100 East, Eighth Street, B-41, Cincinnati, OH 45202 or call (513) 721-5683 or fax (513) 345-4489 or e-mail NatlPOMC@aol.com or visit their web site at http://www.metroguide.com/~world/pomc/info.html

PenParents

Pen-Parents officially began its journey in April of 1988 in San Diego, California. Founder Maribeth Wilder Doerr, a bereaved parent, envisioned the need for a "pen-pal" network to help those who didn't feel comfortable with support group meetings or for those who lived in areas where traditional groups weren't available. The small kitchen-table operation has grown to over 800 members. This group serves as a support network of grieving parents who have experienced pregnancy loss or the death of a child(ren) through adulthood. They provide an opportunity for bereaved parents to talk about their child(ren) through a pen-pal type service by networking them with others in similar situations. You may write, e-mail, fax or visit their website at , Email: penparents @penparents.org, Mailing Address: Pen-Parents, Inc., P.O. Box 8738, Reno, NV 89507-8738, Telephone: 702-826-7332, Fax: 702-829-0866.

Pregnancy and Infant Loss Center

The Pregnancy and Infant Loss Center offers referrals for bereaved families experiencing miscarriage, stillbirth and infant death. Contact them at: 1421 E. Wayzata Blvd., #30, Wayzata, MN 55391 or call (612) 473-9372.

Save Our Sons and Daughters (SOSAD)

SOSAD offers crisis intervention and a violence prevention program that provides support and advocacy for survivors of homicide or other traumatic loss. They offer weekly bereavement groups, professional grief counseling and training, education on peace movement to youth, advocacy, public education, a monthly newsletter, conferences, rallies and assistance in starting support groups. Contact SOSAD at 2441 W. Gran Blvd, Detroit MI 48208 or call (313) 361-5200.

SHARE: Pregnancy & Infant Loss Support, Inc.

This group offers support to those who have lost a child during pregnancy or infancy. Their extensive web site offers a chat room and many valuable reading areas. Additionally they offer a free newsletter. You can visit their web site at http://www.nationalshareoffice.com/ or you may contact them at: National SHARE Office, St. Joseph Health Center, 300 First Capitol Drive, St. Charles, Missouri 63301-2893, Phone: (800) 821-6819 or (636) 947-6164. All of SHARE's information packets, correspondence and support is free of charge for bereaved parents. They also publish a bi-monthly newsletter that is available to bereaved parents, free of charge for the first year.

SIDS Network: A World of Information and Support (Internet Resource)

This web site details Sudden Infant Death and Other Infant Death. Go to http://sids-network.org/ for an incredibly comprehensive and valuable web site. At last look, the site contained over 1000 files with information on, or related to SIDS. This is a very well done place for anyone seeking support or information about SIDS.

SIDS Alliance

The SIDS Alliance was established in 1987 in an effort to unite parents and friends of SIDS victims with medical, business and civic groups concerned about the health of America's babies. You can locate an alliance near you by visiting their web site at http://www.sidsalliance.org/family/ or by contacting their national office at (800) 221-7437 or write to Sudden Infant Death Syndrome Alliance, 1314 Bedford Avenue, Suite 210, Baltimore, MD 21208.

The Canadian Foundation for the Study of Infant Deaths - The SIDS Foundation

The Canadian Foundation for the Study of Infant Deaths is a federally registered charitable organization, which was incorporated in 1973 to respond to the needs of families experiencing a sudden and unexpected infant death. They offer some valuable brochures including: *Information about Sudden Infant Death Syndrome, When Your Baby has Died of Sudden Infant Death Syndrome, Having Another Child After a SIDS Death, Facts You Should Know About SIDS* and others. You may contact the resource by writing to 586 Eglinton Avenue East, Suite 308, Toronto, Ontario, Canada M4P 1P2 or by calling (416) 488-3260 or by faxing (416) 488-3864 or visit their web site at http://www.sidscanada.org/sids.html or e-mail sidscanada@inforamp.net

The Compassionate Friends

The mission of The Compassionate Friends is to assist families in the positive resolution of grief following the death of a child and to provide information to help others be supportive. There are 575 Compassionate Friends chapters. You can locate the one nearest you online at friends.org/states.htm or for a chapter's contact number and meeting information call the National Office at (630) 990-0010 or fax (630) 990-0246. TCF also offers many helpful brochures. You can view them online at http://www.compassionatefriends.org/Brochures.htm The brochures cover many areas such as: *Understanding Grief When a Child Dies, Understanding Grief When a Grandchild Dies, The Grief of Stepparents When A Child Dies, When a Brother or Sister Dies, Caring for Surviving Children, How Can I Help When A Child Dies?, The Death of An Adult Child* and many others. TCF also publishes a magazine for $20 per year. You can subscribe to the quarterly magazine by contacting the national office. Contact information: The Compassionate Friends, Inc., P.O. Box 3696, Oak Brook IL 60522, Phone: (630) 990-0010, Fax: (630) 990-0246.

Trip's Heavenly Angels (Internet Resource)

Trip's Heavenly Angels is for parents who have lost a child or children through illness, accidents, miscarriage or stillbirth. An active and comforting online forum with chat rooms, message boards and more. Visit them at http://www.groww.com/Heavenly.htm

Unite, Inc.

This national organization, founded in 1975, has 14 groups. They offer support for parents grieving miscarriage, stillbrith and infant death. They have group meetings, phone help, a newsletter and an annual conference. For more information contact Janis Heil, Jeanes Hospital, 7600 Central Avenue, Philadelphia, PA 19111 or call (215) 728-4286.

General Bereavement Support
ACCESS: Air Craft Casualty Emotional Support Services

ACCESS provides comfort to friends and families of air disaster victims and survivors. ACCESS helps people cope with their grief and pain by connecting them to grief mentors who have also survived or lost loved ones in an air tragedy. ACCESS is there for as long as the grieving need support. They can be contacted at 1594 York Avenue, Suite 22, New York, NY 10028, (877) 227-6435. Or visit their website at www.accesshelp.org or e-mail info@accesshelp.org

Bereavement and Hospice Support Netline (Internet Resource)
This is a national online public service directory of bereavement support groups and hospice bereavement services. It's sponsored by the Hospice Foundation of America and the University of Baltimore. You can e-mail the group at bereavement@ubmail.ubalt.edu

Concerns of Police Survivors, Inc. (COPS)
This national assocation provides services to surviving friends and families of law enforcement officers killed in the line of duty. COPS can be contacted at PO Box 3199, Camdenton, MO 65020; or by calling (573) 346-4911 or by e-mail at cops@nationalcops.org

GriefNet (Internet Resource)
GriefNet is an Internet community consisting of more than 30 e-mail support groups and two web sites. Over three million people have visited the website in the last year. A very supportive site. Visit it at http://www.griefnet.org

Grief Share (Internet Resource)
This internet resource provides a comprehensive support group directory, special resources and a bookstore. Additionally, they have a wonderful area about journaling and a thirteen-week-guide with a Christian focus that includes scriptures, ideas for writing and journal pages you can print. Visit their site at http://www.griefshare.org

GROWW (Internet Resource)
GROWW is an independent haven for the bereaved developed by the bereaved. "At GROWW, you will find your partners in pain sharing their experience and strength. We have message boards, resource listings and secure chat rooms hosted by the most loving people on the Internet for all who are grieving." This site has a comprehensive chat schedule and great resources. You can visit it at: http://www.groww.com

Healing Hearts

Healing Hearts leads retreats, workshops and support groups that encourage individuals to explore their personal histories and gain insights and inner peace through the healing process. You may contact them at: (520) 219-8200 or by fax at (520) 219-8200. Or write to P.O. Box 65792, Tucson, AZ 85728-5792. Or you may e-mail them at grief@healinghearts.net or access their web site at http://www.healinghearts.org

Jewish Family and Children's Services (JFCS)

JFCS recognizes that today's fast-paced society does not offer most people the time, place or support to grieve fully when experiencing loss. JFCS has developed a comprehensive, non-sectarian bereavement program including counseling, support groups and educational workshops. JFCS bereavement specialists help people address their losses and experience new satisfaction in their lives. JFCS offers Widow and Widower Outreach and Support, Bereavement Workshops for those coping with the loss of a relative or close friend and individual and family counseling. They offer these services in three California locations. In San Francisco call (415) 561-1212, in the Peninsula call (415) 326-6696 and in Marin County call (415) 507-0564. Or visit their web site at http://www.jfcs.org/bereavement.html

National Self-Help Clearinghouse

The National Self-Help Clearinghouse was founded in 1976 to facilitate access to self-help groups and increase the awareness of the importance of mutual support. The Clearinghouse conducts training activities for group leaders, carries out research activities, maintains a databank to provide information about and referrals to self-help groups, addresses professional and public policy audiences about self-help group activities, and publishes manuals, training materials and a newsletter. They offer many helpful brochures, and you can obtain more information by writing to the National Self-Help Clearinghouse at 25 West 43rd Street, Room 620, New York, NY 10036 or visit their website at http://www.selfhelpweb.org

National Organization for Victim Assistance

This organization promotes advocacy for victim's rights, offers help for crime victims and more. They also provide a 24 hour telephone crises service for victims. The hotline number is (202) 393 6682. To learn more about their resources, visit their web site at http://www.try-nova.com or write to 1757 Park Road NW, Washington DC 20010 or call Phone: (202) 232-6682.

Newsgroup alt.support.grief (Internet Resource)

Newsgroup allows users to post messages on the Internet and receive responses or respond to others. The alt.support.grief offers this to its users. With Newsgroup, however, it's always good to just watch and listen and get a tone for the group before jumping in with posts.

Remove Intoxicated Drivers (RID)

This national organization has 152 chapters in 41 states. Founded in 1978, this project is organized to advocate against drunk driving, educate the public and aid victims of drunk driving. You may contact RID at P.O. Box 520, Schenectady, NY 12301 or call (518) 372-0034.

Sena Webzine (Internet Resource)

Sena Webzine is dedicated to the enrichment of life through developing community awareness of grief and loss issues and promoting the recognition, understanding and support of those experiencing grief and loss. The magazine is a vehicle for the safe sharing of difficult and sometimes painful experiences in all stages of life. Overcoming fear through human compassion and caring involvement is the publication's objective. You can learn more about how to receive the webzine by accessing it online at http://www.sena.org/v1i3masthead.html

The Growth House (Internet Resource)

Although this group's mission deals mostly with improving end of life care, their website has many resources that are valuable to anyone who is grieving. They also have specific pages on suicide. In addition, they offer a chat room. You can visit The Growth House at http://www.growthhouse.com

Thrive.Com (Internet Resource)

This well built Internet site offers many articles on grief and loss. They have an 'ask the expert' section, links to support, chat and resources. This is worth a regular visit for their regularly updated material. Access their site at http://www.thriveonline.com/health/death/index.html

Tom Golden's Grief and Healing Discussions Page (Internet Resource)

This site uses a web message board where you can post and respond to issues of grief and loss. Access the message board at http://www.webhealing.com/cgi-bin/main.pl?

Tragedy Assistance Program for Survivors, Inc. (TAPS)

This is a national organization serving the families and friends of those who have died while on active military duty. You may contact them at 2001 S. Street, NW #30, Washington, DC 20009; or by calling (800) 959-TAPS.

Transformations (Internet Resource)

This well-designed site offers support in many areas, including grief. They offer a chat area and a schedule of events as well as a place to share your thoughts, stories, poetry and more. You can access the site at http://www.transformations.com/contents.html

Support for Loss through Suicide

American Association of Suicidology

The American Association of Suicidology is dedicated to the understanding and prevention of suicide. AAS promotes research, public awareness programs, education and training for professionals and volunteers. In addition, it serves as a national clearinghouse for information on suicide. Their web site also has a comprehensive listing of support groups. Simply click on your state for different groups. You can access this feature at http://www.suicidology.org/survivorsofsuicide.htm Contact information: 4201 Connecticut Ave., NW, Suite 408, Washington, DC 20008, Phone: (202) 237-2280, E-mail: ssilve16@ixnetcom.com

American Suicide Foundation

This national organization offers state-by-state directories of survivor support groups for families and friends of suicide. Contact them by e-mail at or write to 1045 Park Avenue, New York, NY 10028; or call (800) ASF-4042.

Friends for Survival, Inc.

Organized by and for survivors, this non-profit group offers its services at no cost to those who have lost a loved one to suicide. Resources include a newsletter, referalls to local support groups, a list of suggested resources and more. You may contact them at Friends for Survival, Inc., Post Office Box 214463, Sacramento, California 95821. Or call (916) 392-0664. They also have a Suicide Loss Helpline—(800) 646-7322.

Heartbeat

This support organization was formed for those who have lost a loved one to suicide. They offer referals to local support groups and information on starting your own group. You can write to them at 2051 Devon Street, Colorado Springs, CO 80909 or call (719) 596-2575.

Ray of Hope

This group offers information and resources related to suicide and information on starting your own support group. You can write to them at Post Office Box 2323, Iowa City, IA 52244. Or call (319) 337-9890.

SIEC (Internet Resource)

This is a comprehensive site for those looking to help someone with suicidal symptoms or who has lost someone to suicide. Many helpful and informative brochures can be ordered from the site and there are many stories shared as well. http://www.siec.ca/survivor.htm

suicide @ rochford.org (Internet Resource)

Suicide information and education. A very comprehensive source for those seeking to learn and understand more about suicide and its victims. Also lists many support groups.

Support for Sibling Loss

Julie's Place (Internet Resource)

Julie's place is a web site that reaches out to grieving children and teenagers who have lost a sibling. They offer resources, a special remembrance area and many other valuable and comforting resource and communication opportunities for children. Access the site at http://www.juliesplace.com/

Twinless Twins

Twinless Twins is an organization comprised of nearly 1300 twinless twins that gather annually for a conference and encourage each other. Between conferences they telephone, write and e-mail each other. Many twins have found this communion with other twinless twins an immense help in their lives. If you are a twinless twin, call or write to: Twinless Twins Support Group International, 11220 St. Joe Rd., Ft. Wayne IN, 46835 or Phone: (219) 627-5414. You can also visit their web site at: http://serv1-r.fwi.com/twinless/

Suggested Reading

General Books for Adults

A Time to Grieve: Meditations for Healing After the Death of a Loved One by Carol Staudacher, Harper SanFrancisco, 1994—365 daily readings offer comfort, insight and hope. This book is written specifically for people after the death of a loved one, however it is appropriate for anyone who still copes with the effects of a loss of any kind. A great gift for yourself or a grieving friend.

Beyond Grief by Carol Staudacher, New Harbinger Publications, 1987—This book is about understanding and then coping with loss, with clearly stated suggestions for each part of the grieving process. Written both for the bereaved and the helping professional, it combines supportive personal stories with a step-by-step approach to recovery. *Beyond Grief* acknowledges the path, reassures and counsels. Includes guidelines to create support groups and guidelines for helping others. It says to the grieving person: you are not alone, you can get through the pain, and there is a path back to feeling alive again.

Companion Through Darkness: Inner Dialogues on Grief by Stephanie Ericsson, Harperperennial Library, 1993—As a result of her own experience with many kinds of loss, the author offers an intimate, touching guide for those in grief. The book combines excerpts from her own diary writings with brief essays.

Complicated Losses, Difficult Deaths: A Practical Guide for Working Through Grief by Roslyn A. Karaban, Ph.D., Resource Publications 1999—Written by a pastoral counselor, certified grief therapist and death educator, the book deals with losses that are more difficult to cope with than others: suicide, sudden loss, the death of a child and murders among others---losses that evoke grief reactions and symptoms that are more intense and last longer than "ordinary" grief.

Dreams that Help You Mourn by Lois Lindsey Hendricks. Resource Publications, 1997—This book will put you in the company of other mourners and their dreams. You'll learn that dreaming after losing a loved one is absolutely normal. In fact, it's the soul's way of mourning. The book will help you take better advantage of the healing power of your dreams.

I Can't Get Over It: A handbook for trauma survivors by Aphrodite Matsakis, New Harbinger Publications, Inc., 1996—Explains how post-traumatic stress disorder (PTSD) affects survivors of a variety of traumas including disasters, rape, crime and violence. Addresses the survivor directly and helps them self-diagnose to then get appropriate treatment. Includes a variety of techniques and self-help suggestions for safe recovery.

In Memoriam: A practical guide to planning a memorial service by Amanda Bennett and Terence B. Foley, Fireside Books, 1997—Written in an easy-to-read format, this book provides a full range of options to help you choose music, arrange flowers, select a format, prepare a eulogy and invite speakers and offers a wide range of selected appropriate readings.

Life After Loss: A personal guide dealing with death, divorce, job change and relocation by Bob Deits, Fisher Books, 1992—Provides skills for healthy recovery, including how to cry, how to write a goodbye letter, how to deal with emotions and how to cope.

Moving Beyond Grief: Lessons from those who have lived through sorrow by Ruth Sissom, Discovery House, 1994—A religiously oriented book offering stories of persons who have learned to cope with grief and trauma.

The Courage to Grieve by Judy Tatelbaum—This book covers many aspects of grief and resolution. Divided into five sections, it explores the grief experience and creative recovery.

The Dream Messenger: How Dreams of the Departed Bring Healing Gifts by Patricia Garfield. The author writes about the distinctive patterns that she discovered in her research of over 400 dreams. These include images of a journey, dream gifts from the departed, a "soul animal" whose characteristics are associated with the departed person, and images of a "veil" or boundary that separates the living the from the dead. She emphasizes that such dreams are an esential part of the healing process around mourning, providing comfort to the bereaved.

What to Do When a Loved One Dies: A practical and compassionate guide to dealing with death on life's terms, by Eva Shaw, Dickens Press, 1994—Presents excellent guidelines describing what to do when a death occurs. It has an extensive listing of support groups, resources and other sources of help. The approach is extremely detailed and includes sections on dealing with catastrophic deaths.

With Those Who Grieve: Twenty grief survivors share their stories of loss, pain and hope—by Kay Soder-Alderfer, Lion Publishing, 1994—Describes the healing process of grief and its effects, as well as how to find and offer help. The stories of grief cross the lifespan.

Words to Comfort, Words to Heal: Poems and Meditations for those Who Grieve compiled by Juliet Mabey, Oneworld Publications, 1998—This lovely book would make a nice gift to give another or to give yourself. It features works drawn from poets, writers, philosophers and sacred literature. An inspirational anthology that celebrates lives that have ended and offers consolation to those left behind.

Books about Grief Recovery

Grief's Courageous Journey: A Workbook by Sandi Caplan and Gordon Lang, New Harbinger Publications, 1995—Grieving the loss of a loved one is an intensely personal process. This workbook takes the hand of those who are left behind and guides them, at their own pace, along the path of their own healing journey. It provides a compassionate program for coping with day-to-day life and accepting the changes in yourself and others. Guided by a sequence of journaling exercises and suggestions for creating healing personal rituals, you can use the workbook to tell the story of your relationship with the person who died, grieve your loss and safely remember the past. You will also learn techniques for redefining your present life and re-creating your sense of future. The book includes a comprehensive ten-session facilitator's guide for creating a grief support group in your community.

Healing our Losses: A Journal for Working Through Your Grief by Jack Miller, Ph.D., Resource Publications—The author shares experiences of loss in his own life and will guide you to record your memories, thoughts, and feelings about loss in your life. Journaling may be done alone or in a group setting.

Healing the Heart; Letting Go; Therapeutic Stories for Trauma and Stress; Stories to Heal the Grieving Heart (AUDIO TAPES), N. Davis, 1995, 6178 Oxon Hill Rd., Suite 306, Oxon Hill, MD, (301) 567-9297—These audio tapes contain collections of therapeutic stories designed to ease the process of grieving, explain stages of grief, address the intuitive side of the mind and help the listener find what he/she needs within the self. Visual imagery and relaxation exercises are also included.

Managing Traumatic Stress through Art: Drawing from the center by Barry M. Cohen, Mary-Michola Barnes and Anita B. Rankin, The Sidran Press, 1995—Provides step-by-step art experiences designed to help the reader understand, manage and transform the after effects of trauma. Written in a practical, useful style that shows the ways in which art making and writing can assist one's healing from severe trauma.

The Grief Recovery Handbook by John W. James & Russell Friedman (Revised Edition), HarperCollins, 1998—Drawing from their own histories, as well as from others, the authors illustrate what grief is and how it is possible to recover and regain energy and spontaneity. Based on a proven program, this book offers grievers specific actions needed to complete the grieving process and accept loss.

Books for Grieving Men

Griefquest : Men Coping With Loss by Robert Miller, St. Mary's Press, 1999—*GriefQuest* is a book of meditations written for men and the women who love and care about them. This book, written by other men, helps make sense out of the unique challenges that grief and loss force on men today.

Grief Therapy for Men by Linus Mundy, Abbey Press, 1998—This little book acknowledges the uniqueness of male grief and offers men real permission to grieve. It gives a host of practical suggestions for healthy male grief—what to do, what not to do, when to act boldly and when to just "be."

Men & Grief: a guide for men surviving the death of a loved one by Carol Staudacher, New Harbinger Publications, 1991—*Men & Grief* is the first book to look in depth at the unique patterns of male bereavement. Based on extensive interviews with male survivors, it describes the four characteristics of male grief, explains the forces that shape and influence male grief and provides step-by-step help for the male survivor.

When Men Grieve : Why Men Grieve Differently and How You Can Help by Elizabeth Levang, Fairview, 1998— Insightful text on the unique characteristics of men's grief and how they face loss. Includes poetry and strategies for partners, friends and relatives.

Books about the Loss of a Friend

Grieving the Death of a Friend by Harold Ivan Smith, Augsburg Fortress Publications, 1996—The death of a friend is one of the most significant but unrecognized experiences of grief in American culture. This unique new book moves with, rather than against, the natural grief process by exploring its many aspects—the friending, the passing, the burying, the mourning, the remembering and the reconciling.

When a Friend Dies: A book for teens about grieving and healing by Marilyn E. Gootman, Ed.D., 1994, Free Spirit Publishing, Minneapolis, MN—A small, powerful book whose author has seen her own children suffer from the death of a friend. She knows first hand what teenagers go through when another teen dies. Very easy to read, some of the questions dealt with include: How long will this last? Is it wrong to go to parties and have fun? How can I find a counselor or therapist? What is normal?

Books about How to Help Someone who is Grieving

The Art of Condolence by Leonard M Zunin, M.D & Hilary Stanton Zunin, Harperperrenial Library, 1992—Offers specific and wise advice for responding to another's grief. Discusses what to write, what to say, and what to do.

When Your Friend's Child Dies: A Guide to Being a Thoughtful and Caring Friend Angel Hugs Publishing, 1998—A simply written, straight-forward book that will tell you what to say and do when you have a friend whose child has died. And, just as important, Chapter 1 tells you what not to say and why. An early reader described this book as a "slap-in-the-face wake-up call." After reading this book you will know how to comfort a parent who has lost a child, even ten years later.

You Can Help Someone Who's Grieving : A How-To Healing Handbook by , Penguin, 1996—A practical resource that deals with such issues as what to say and not to say after someone dies, how long the grieving period lasts and its many stages, how to write sympathy notes, and how to handle holidays and anniversaries.

Books about the Loss of a Child

A Broken Heart Still Beats: When Your Child Dies edited by Anne McCracken and Mary Semel, Hazelden, 1998—Edited by two mothers who have lost a child, this book combines articles and excerpts—some fiction, some nonfiction—that featured the death of a child. A brief introduction to each chapter, describes a different stage of the grieving process and how it affected their lives.

After the Darkest Hour the Sun Will Shine Again : A Parent's Guide to Coping With the Loss of a Child by Elizabeth Mehren, 1997—This inspiring guide to coping with the loss of a child combines the author's own story with the experiences and wisdom of others who have gone through this tragedy.

After the Death of a Child : Living With Loss Through the Years by , John Hopkins University Press, 1998—Drawing on her own experience with losing a child, an inspirational self-help guide for parents examines the continuing love parents feel for their child, ways to preserve the bond and strategies for coping with loss.

Recovering from the Loss of a Child by Katherine Fair Donnelley, Berkley Publishing Group, 1994—The death of a child is one of life's cruelest blows. This comforting book offers bereaved parents, siblings, and others inspiring firsthand accounts from people who have survived this heartbreaking experience. In addition to healing advice, the book illustrates how such deaths affect family relationships.

The Worst Loss: How families heal from the death of a child by Barbara D. Rosof, Henry Holt & Co., Inc., 1994—The death of a child overwhelms many people. This book describes the losses that the death of a child brings to parents and siblings as well as potential PTSD reactions and work of grief. A very thorough and wise book. One of our favorite books on the topic.

When Goodbye Is Forever : Learning to Live Again After the Loss of a Child by , Ballantine, 1991—In 1985, John and Mairi Bramblett's youngest child, two-year-old Christopher, died in an accident, leaving them and their three older children devastated by shock and grief. Four months later, John began writing this deeply moving and honest story of how he and his family coped with the nearly unbearable pain of losing their son. *When Goodbye is Forever* walks us along the author's path to acceptance and recovery, taking us through the first hours and days of the tragedy, the painful but necessary first outings, and such occasions as Christopher's birthday, and the anniversary of his death. Mairi and the children share their responses to the tragedy as well, showing us the effect such a tragedy can have on the whole family.

General Books for Professionals

Grief Counseling and Grief Therapy, 2nd Ed.: A handbook for the mental health practitioner, 1991, New York, Springer Publishing Company—Details ways to help clients accomplish tasks of mourning to avoid unresolved grief and its complications. A chapter on grieving traumatic losses is included, as are sketches for role-plays in training.

Helper's Journey: Working with people facing grief, loss and life-threatening illness by D. G. Larson, Research Press, 1993—Designed for volunteers, counselors and clergy who work in direct caregiving roles with survivors and those facing death. Gives practical suggestions as well as exercises and activities designed to develop coping skills.

Helping the Bereaved: Therapeutic interventions for children adolescents and adults, by A. S. Cool and D. S. Dworkin, 1992, New York, Basic Books—This professionally oriented book focuses on therapeutic interventions with bereaved individuals and groups. Gives therapists specific therapeutic techniques including development of ethical wills and rituals. It also addresses the development of groups for children and adults.

Living Beyond Loss: Death in the family by F. Walsh and M. McGoldrick (Eds.), W.W. Norton, 1995—This book aimed at professionals, looks at how the field of family therapy treats death and discusses the family impact of death and loss. It uses both systems and developmental perspectives.

The Many Faces of Bereavement: The nature and treatment of natural, traumatic and stigmatized grief by G. Sprang and J. McNeil, Brunner/Mazel, 1995—Written especially for professionals, this book provides an overview of traumatic grief and specific situations leading to traumatic grief (e.g. murder, critical incidents). It includes assessment protocols, debriefing strategies and treatment interventions.

Book for Children, Teens and their Caregivers

A Taste of Blackberries by Doris B. Smith, Harpercollins Juvenil Books, 1992 (8-9 years)—The author conveys the experience and feelings of an eight-year-old boy whose best friend Jamie dies unexpectedly. The boy and his family, along with Jamie's family, deal with the myriad of questions and feelings engendered by this unexpected event.

Bart Speaks out: Breaking the Silence on Suicide (ages 4-12), by Linda Goldman, MS, Western Psychological Services, Los Angeles, CA—Bart, a lovable terrier, misses his owner Charlie, who has just died. But Bart's grief is complicated by the silence that surrounds Charlie's, death. Sad and puzzled, Bart gradually comes to understand that Charlie has committed suicide. This workbook will give children an opportunity to explore suicide openly, to resolve their grief by breaking through the barriers of shame and secrecy that typically cloud this subject. Workbook exercises dispel myths about suicide, provide age-appropriate facts and explanations, and show children how to express their feelings.

Beat the Turtle Drum by Constance C. Greene, 1976, The Viking Press, NY (10-14 years)—In this touching story, the effect of the sudden death of an 11-year-old child on her older sister and parents is told with warmth and sensitivity.

Bereaved Children and Teens: A Support Guide for Parents and Professionals by Earl A. Grollman, Beacon Press, 1996—Explores the ways that parents and professionals can help young people cope with grief. Topics covered include what children can understand about death at different ages, the special problems of grieving teenagers, how to explain Protestant, Catholic, or Jewish beliefs about death in ways that children can understand, and more.

Breaking the Silence: A guide to help children with complicated grief by Linda Goldman, Western Psychological Services, Los Angeles, CA—Designed for both mental health professionals and parents, this book provides specific ideas and techniques to use in working with children who have suffered psychologyical trauma from violence, homicide, suicide or other traumas. Explains how to break the silence and then how to help children recover.

Coping with Death and Grief by Marge Eaton Heegaard, Lerner Publications, 1990—Includes stories about young people, grades 3-6, who deal with grief. Provides facts about death that are developmentally based.

Don't Despair on Thursdays! (ages 4-12) by Adolph Moser, Ed.D., Western Psychological Services, Los Angeles, CA—This gentle book lets children know that it's normal to grieve in response to loss and that grief may last more than a few days or weeks. Offers practical suggestions that children can use, day by day, to cope with the emotional pain they feel. Young readers will be comforted by the reassuring text and colorful illustrations.

Goodbye Rune (ages 5-11), by Marit Kaldhol and Wenche Oyen, Western Psychological Services, Los Angeles, CA—Rune and Sara are best friends, until the day that Rune accidentally drowns. This is a sensitive account of a child's first experience with death, Sara asks her parents endless questions, and their patient answers help her come to terms with the loss of someone special. She comes to realize that, through her memories, Rune will always be with her. Explores death and grief in terms children can understand.

Helping Bereaved Children, edited by Nancy Boyd Webb, DSW, Western Psychological Services, 1999—This book for therapists includes therapeutic interventions for children who have suffered a loss. Individual chapters focus on such topics as, death of a grandparent, father or mother, accidental sibling death, suicide of mother, violent death of both parents, traumatic death of a friend, sudden death of a teacher, and more.

It happened to me: A story for child victims of crime or trauma, **Something bad happened**: *A story for children who have felt the impact of crime or trauma*, **All my feelings**: *A story for children who have felt the impact of crime or trauma* by D. W. Alexander, 1992, Huntington, NY, Bureau for At-risk Youth—These coloring/workbooks are designed for early elementary school students. They identify the various components of PTSD and help with healing.

Life & Loss: A guide to help grieving children (Preschool through teen), by Linda Goldman, Western Psychological Services, Los Angeles, CA—Helpful information using photographs, children's drawings, essays, anecdotes and other simple techniques. Gives all the tools you need to help children through the grief process. Includes, how to recognize various kinds of loss, avoid blocked feelings, the four psychological tasks of grief, and how to commemorate loss among other topics. Offers a guide to community and national support groups and a list of materials addressing specific kinds of loss.

Lifetimes: A beautiful way to explain death to children by Bryan Mellonie & Robert Ingpen, Bantam Doubleday, 1987—A moving picture book for children of all ages that lets us explain life and death in a sensitive, beautiful way. With large color illustrations, it tells us that dying is as much a part of living as being born.

Part of Me Died, Too: Stories of creative survival among bereaved children and teenagers by Virginia Lynn Fry, 1995, Dutton Children's Books, NY—Eleven true stories about young people who experienced the loss of family members or friends in a variety of ways including, murder, suicide and accident. Includes writings, drawings, farewell projects, rituals and other creative activities to help children bring their feelings out into the open.

Straight Talk About Death for Teenagers: How to Cope with Losing Someone You Love by Earl A.Grollman, Beacon Press, Boston, MA, 1993 (13-19 years)—With reassurance and compassion, Grollman explains normal reactions to the shock of death, the impact of grief on relationships, dealing with pain, funerals, and much more. Includes a place for readers to record their memories.

Talking About Death: A Dialogue between Parent and Child by Earl A. Grollman, Beacon Press, 1991—How do you explain the loss of a loved one to a child? This compassionate guide for adults and children to read together features an illustrated read-along story, answers to questions children ask about death, and comprehensive lists of resources and organizations that can help. Helpful for children from preschool to preteen.

The Good Mourning Game by Nicholas J. Bisenius, PhD and Michele Norris, MSW, Western Psychological Services, Los Angeles, CA—Using an artistically designed game board, this resource is a wonderful therapy tool for children who've suffered a loss. The board illustrates nature's basic cycle, which, like the grief cycle, moves from stormy intensity to relative calm. It can be played by a therapist and one to three children in usually about 45 minutes.

The Grieving Child: a parents guide by Helen Fitzgerald. Fireside, 1992—Compassionate advice for helping a child cope with the death of a loved one. Also addresses visiting the seriously ill, using age-appropriate language, funerals, and more.

The way I feel: A story for teens coping with crime or trauma
It happened in Autumn: A story for teens coping with a loved one's homicide by D. W. Alexander, 1993, Huntington, NY, Bureau for At-risk Youth—These short books which include space for completing exercises, are part of a 6-volume series designed for teens exposed to crime and trauma.

What on Earth do you do When Someone Dies? (ages 5-10) by Trevor Romain, Western Psychological Services, Los Angeles, CA—Someone you love dies, and your whole world changes. Written to and for kids, this little book offers comfort and reassurance to children who've lost a loved one. It answers questions children often ask such as, Why? What next? Is it my fault? What's a funeral? It is still okay to have fun? Will I ever feel better? Includes a list of practical coping strategies.

When Something Terrible Happens: Children can learn to cope with grief (ages 6-12) When Someone Very Special Dies: Children can learn to cope with grief by Marge Eaton Heegaard, Woodland press, 1992—These two books teach basic concepts of death and help children, through their workbook format, to express feelings and increase coping skills. Children use their own personal stories to complete the pages as they draw events and their accompanying feelings.

Books about the Death of a Mate

How to Go On Living When Someone You Love Dies by Therese A. Rando, Ph.D., 1988, New York, Lexington Books—Includes suggestions for ways to deal with sudden or anticipated death. Offers self-help techniques to work on unfinished business, take care of the self and when to get help from others. Leads you through the painful but necessary process of grieving and helps you find the best way for yourself. Offers guidance to help you move into your new life without forgetting your treasured past.

Grief Expressed: When a Mate Dies by Marta Felber. Lifeword, 1997—This compassionate workbook guides you through the process of grieving the death of a mate. Sensitive writing and practical exercises help you to address issues such as loneliness, building a support system, managing sleepless nights, finances, self-nurturing and much more. The author has drawn from her own counseling background, as well as her self-healing after the death of her husband.

Widow to Widow: Thoughtful practical ideas for rebuilding your life by Genevieve Davis Ginsburg, M.S., 1995, Fisher Books—The author writes from her own experience as a widow and therapist. The book is frankly honest and attempts to dispel myths, disputes the rules and encourages the widow to begin her new life in her own way and time.

When Your Spouse Dies: A Concise and practical source of help and advice by Cathleen L. Curry, Ave Maria Press, 1990—This short book deals with a variety of practical topics within a spiritual framework. Includes topics such as advice on loneliness and sexuality, financial priorities and planning and good health practices, among others.

Living with Loss: Meditations for Grieving Widows by Ellen Sue Stern, 1995, Dell Publishing, NY—This book, small enough to fit in a purse, is full of supportive and empowering reflections. This daily companion is designed to help you cope today, cherish yesterday and thrive tomorrow.

Books about the Loss of a Parent

How to Survive the Loss of a Parent: A guide for adults by Lois F. Akner, Catherine Whitney, 1994, William Morrow & Co.—Therapist and author, Lois Akner, explains why the loss of a parent is different from other losses and using examples from her experience, shows how it is possible to work through the grief.

Losing a Parent: Passage to a New Way of Living by Alexandra Kennedy, Harper San Francisco, 1991—Based on the author's personal experience, she writes on topics such as keeping a journal, saying goodbye, tending to your wounds and the "living parent within you."

Losing a Parent: A personal guide to coping with that special grief that comes with losing a parent by Fiona Marshall, 1993, Fisher Books—Offers comforting and inspiring advice for helping one cope with the different and difficult effects of loss. The author includes insightful and practical strategies to use in dealing with the surviving parent and other family members. Looks at the impact of the sudden death of a parent as well as terminal illness. It also includes suggestions on how to locate help and inheritance issues.

Mid-Life Orphan: Facing Life's Changes Now That Your Parents Are Gone by Jane Brooks. Berkely Books, 1999—Many mid-life orphans feel isolated, even abandoned, when their parents die, but they also learn how to cope and extract life lessons from their experience. This book focuses on a loss that has been a fact of life for centuries, but has moved to the forefront as baby boomers, who represent 1/3 of the U.S. population, are forced to deal with this age of loss.

Motherless Daughters: The legacy of loss by Hope Edelman, Delta, 1995—Includes stories of women whose mothers have died early in their lives and how the absence of a mother shapes one's identity.

The Loss That is Forever: The Lifelong Impact of the Early Death of a Mother or Father by Maxine Harris, Ph.D., Plume, 1996—Explores the impact that early loss of a parent has on every aspect of development. Who one becomes, how one loves, how one parents, and what one believes about the world, are all shaped by the experience of this loss. Provides comfort and guidance for coping and shows how the human spirit can survive and master this loss.

When Parents Die by Edward Myers, Penguin, 1997—Offers compassionate advice to adult sons and daughters coping with the death of a parent. Discusses the psychological responses to a parent's death such as shock, depression and guilt, and offers suggestions on how to manage these feelings.

Books about Suicide

After Suicide, John Knox Press, 1980—the author writes, "This book was written for persons struggling in the aftermath of losing a family member or close friend to suicide. It is written in conversational style and is ideal for mental health professionals and others who care about suicide survivors."

Healing After the Suicide of a Loved One Fireside, 1993—The authors address the special needs and emotions of the survivors and those affected by the suicide of a loved one. It explores the natural grief, and the added guilt, rage and shame that dealing with a suicide often engenders. Includes a directory of worldwide support groups.

No Time to Say Goodbye: survivng the suicide of a loved one by Carla Fine, Doubleday, 1997—Suicide is something most people are unable to talk about, which makes the pain all the more unbearable. Written by a suicide survivor, this book explores the overwhelming feelings of guilt, shame, anger and loneliness that are shared by survivors. Offers guidance to those who were left behind and are struggling to pick up the pieces of their shattered lives.

Silent Grief: Living in the Wake of Suicide (The Master Works Series) by Jason Aronson, 1997—The authors present a practical book to guide friends and families of suicides through a program of grief recovery to mental health. To be of special interest to parents and educators of teenagers.

Why Suicide? Answers to 200 of the most frequently asked questions about suicide, attempted suicide and assisted suicide by Eric Marcus, Harper San Francisco, 1996—No matter what the circumstances surrounding suicide, those of us who are affected are left with difficult and disturbing questions. This book provides thoughtful, comprehensive answers to 200 of the most frequently asked questions about suicide, attempted suicide and assisted suicide.

Books for Helping Professionals

Coping with Trauma: The victim and the helper by R. Watts & D. J. de L. Horne, Australian Academic Press, 1994—This readable, practical book examines the nature of trauma and the impact of traumatic experiences on both victim and helper. Includes chapters on traumatic accidents and large-scale road accidents that often result in sudden, traumatic death and complicated bereavement reactions.

Trauma and Transformation: Growth in the aftermath of suffering by R. G. Tedeshi and L. G. Calhoun, Sage Publications, 1995—This book is designed to help readers focus on positive outcomes of trauma and traumatic loss. It looks at ways to help survivors of traumatic loss examine and change their belief systems, to cultivate compassion and understanding, and includes a model of personal coping.

Where am I now?
parting notes from the authors

Brook Noel...

Pam and I have been working like crazy to finish the draft of this book. This was my last section left to write, and believe it or not, the day it came up in my to-do pile marked the second anniversary of Caleb's death (October 4, 1999). It's interesting—last year I couldn't function at all. I went away by myself. This year I find I can still function during this anniversary, though I feel more like a robot than a human.

I am proud of the strides I have made. My mother, myself and a few close friends have started a water-ski tournament in my brother's honor. We held the first tournament this past summer. It feels good to keep his interests and passions as part of our lives.

As for me, specifically, I'm doing all right. In many ways, I haven't yet fully felt my loss. I still tend to run from my pain instead of feel it—but writing this book has helped me to quit doing that. It's taught me to explore the full range of my feelings—though I still have a way to go.

I'm not afraid of death, or of life, anymore. I've developed a trust in the processes and cycles of Nature and the Universe. I don't fully understand these 'life forces' on most days, but I've learned to trust in their unfolding as I am able.

I've emerged from the dark cocoon of acute grief and come to a place where the grief now "lives with me," smaller in size, but molded into my being. Grief has taught me to laugh, enjoy and be present for every moment.

Where am I now? I'm surviving and rebuilding. At one point you could have tried to convince me that something good would come from my loss and I would have laughed at you! But now, I see it. This loss has given me life—through the death of my brother, I have learned how to live.

Pamela D. Blair...

It's been nine years since George's death. I'm married to a great guy. I'm a therapist specializing in loss and transition—death and divorce specifically. My son, Ian is in college. He is a musician and works part-time as a shift manager for Starbucks Coffee. My daughter Aimee gave birth to a beautiful son, Derek, who is now eight-years-old. He will never know George except through his mother's eyes. She remembers the unconditional love, the trust, the playfulness of the man. I'm not sure what Ian remembers. My guess is he remembers catching the ball with his dad at Yankee Stadium, and visiting his dad at work in the camera store and the family trip to Disneyland. Me? I remember the bitter sweetness of our too short marriage, the hugs he gave, the miracle of the child we made together, the day the life sustaining machines were shut down—the day the new memories stopped forever.

I still feel the loss. I also feel the new life it gave me. In every loss there lies a hidden possibility. It stays hidden until one shakes it loose—like the lost sock that ends up in the corner of the newly washed fitted sheet. It's there—you just need to ruffle up that sheet a bit and out it comes.

Where does sudden loss take us? It takes us to places we never asked to visit. It take us on uncharted, mysterious, unfamiliar journeys to the depths of our souls, where we clatter and crash about, slog through the molasses of grief and come out the other side. That's all. I am here to tell you that one can survive that mess and come out the other side and that although death surely ends a life, it never ends a relationship.

May you see light where there was only darkness, hope where there seemed nothing but despair, may your fear be replaced with faith and insight, may you feel some victory in the defeat and a sense of the sacred web into which we are all woven. Most of all may you stay in tune with your capacity to love life even as you are engulfed by death.

Appendix

This Appendix includes several worksheets and guides to help you in various parts of the grief process. Use these as templates or springboards for ideas of your own.

The Memorial Service

When the person in charge of the memorial service does not know the deceased, consider filling out this form and giving it to them. Keep a copy for yourself. The information included on the form will be an aid in creating a meaningful service. The form will also be useful if the person in charge knew your loved one.

If at all possible, do not fill out this form alone. Ask friends and family to contribute information. If your loved one had a career, chances are they have a resume in a file somewhere. Their resume may help fill in some of the blanks.

INFORMATION TO PROVIDE TO
THE PERSON (OR CLERGY) IN CHARGE

Name of deceased: Age:

Cause of death: Date of birth:

Religious background (if any):   Date of death:

Type of service the deceased would have liked (i.e. quiet, casual, formal, offbeat):

Those who would like to participate:

Family background:

Education:

Career (or career aspirations):

Club memberships or affiliations:

Activities or hobbies:

Relationships:

What kind of books did they read:

What kind of music did they enjoy:

Favorite bible verse or inspirational verse:

Favorite poet or poems:

Favorite charity/charities:

NOTES:

The Eulogy

You've been asked to deliver a eulogy. What now? According to Terence B. Foley and Amanda Bennett (*In Memoriam*, Simon & Schuster, 1997), "The most important thing to remember when delivering a eulogy is that it is a gift. A gift for you to be able to speak about a family member or friend before those who also loved and respected him...It is not a performance, nor will it be judged as such. Your job is to be thoughtful and genuine..."

This form should get you thinking about those things that were most important about the deceased. As you deliver the eulogy, do not rush, take your time. If you decide to use humor, make sure it is done with affection. Avoid jokes and stories that would embarrass those present. If you lose your composure, give yourself a moment of quiet, take a deep breath or a drink of water, and go on.

FORM FOR DELIVERING A EULOGY

My relationship with the deceased:

I've known him/her for how long:

How we met:

What I remember most ...

What was best about them:

What was eccentric about them (presented with affection):

Kindnesses I received from the deceased:

What would the deceased say about the events today:

Integrating what we learned from this person into our own lives is a constant memorial and source of comfort for the family. Therefore, consider the following three questions:

What did I learn from this person (through example or teaching):

How do I plan to implement what I learned from them:

What words of wisdom would the deceased want us to remember:

NOTES:

A Checklist of Calls to Make

The following list can be a useful reference for calls that need to made. Give this form to your support person to help you complete the calls.

☐ Call a support person to help you. Give the support person this list and let them work through it and ask questions as necessary.

☐ Choose a funeral home to assist in arrangements. Set date and time for funeral and memorial services.

☐ Contact a clergy person to officiate services. If a mediator is needed, contact them as well.

☐ Select pallbearers for the funeral if you will be having a burial.

☐ Make a list of people who need to be notified. Obtain the deceased's address book for phone numbers and other people to notify.

☐ Contact the newspaper for the obituary. An obituary typically includes: age, cause of death, place of birth, vocation, college degrees, military service, outstanding work or achievments, list of survivors in immediate family, time and place of services.

☐ Choose a memorial or charity for any gifts or donations.

☐ Notify all insurance companies—social security, credit union, trade union, fraternal, military, standard life, credit card, etc. Check for income from any of these sources as well.

☐ Call all debts in a timely manner. Insurance may cancel out some debts. For other debts ask for a payment plan.

☐ If the deceased lived alone, contact the landlord and utilities. Select a group of people to help move the deceased's belongings from the apartment/home.

☐ Contact a lawyer and the executor of the will, if a will is in place. If there is no will, contact a lawyer for guidance.

Friends Support Group Invitation

The letter that follows is an example of a creative response to the need for support. The following invitational letter was written to family and friends by the deceased's sister, Karen. Kathleen's death was a suicide which occured after a long struggle with cancer and mental illness. The letter was written on stationary with this quote imprinted in the corner: "What we call the beginning is often the end. To make an end is to make a beginning. The end is where we start from." ---T. S. Eliot

Dear Family and Friends,

During the past few weeks I have had the opportunity to speak with some of you regarding the impact of Kathleen's death on your life. These discussions have served to assist me in dealing with my grief.

Some of you mentioned that you've been so busy that you've hardly had time to feel, much less deal with the loss. Many societies throughout the world have rituals built into their communities to facilitate the difficult walk through grief. Our "progressive" society has only begun to realize it's shortcomings, and in efforts to counter the emotional isolation, society has assigned the task of assisting us with our grief work to counselors and mental health care (bereavement groups). These are valuable, however, I'd like to propose that another helpful way might be for the members of Kathleen's community to come together to talk, sit, just be together, in an effort to promote healing.

The nature of Kathleen's death has left us all with many questions. In discussing these issues with some of you privately, it has come up that talking about the issues together may assist us all in finding peace.

I have enclosed information our family received from the Albany Medical Center the night Kathleen died. We have found it helpful to review this information regularly in an attempt to monitor our healing.

If Kathleen had been a participant in a hospice program, they would be offering a program for bereavement for the family and friends to have a framework to evaluate progress along the grief walk. Her mental illness was indeed terminal. In an effort to create a structure for us to walk in our grief I'd like to host the following afternoon gatherings.

Also, my family is trying to piece together a historical outline of Kathleen's life, birth to death. We would find it helpful to hear your experiences with Kathleen so we can add them to the tapestry we hope to create.

Thank you all for taking the time to call and talk. I look forward to further discussions and insights.

Schedule of Bereavement Gatherings:

3:00-5:00pm at 134 Ridge Avenue

(for those of you who wish to stay after,

soup and sandwiches will be served)

Saturday, January 27 — 3 month anniversary of Kathleen's death

Saturday, April 27 — 6 month anniversary of Kathleen's death

Saturday, July 27 — 9 month anniversary of Kathleen's death

Saturday, October 26 — 1 Year

The first year of feeling the void and figuring out ways to compensate is the most difficult. If you cannot attend these gatherings, I would request that you make time to remember the memories.

I'd appreciate an RSVP call.

For those of you who experienced Kathleen's association with the Native American culture, you may recall her referring to their custom of communication to "all my relations."This demonstrates the understanding that we are all part of a network, a web, a community. When the fabric of the web is broken, loose ends flap around until the members can come together and mend the space. How we choose to repair the hole will depend on who we are and what we will bring to offer each other. Thank you all for your willingness to offer and obtain comfort. The hope is that the memories which cause pain in the initial blow can, in time, serve as great comforts and a means for our own growth.

Blessings to all.

In light and love,

Karen

Bibliography

Adrienne, Carol. *The Purpose of Your Life Experiential Guide.* William Morrow, 1999.

Akner, Lois F. Whitney, Catherine (contributor). *How to Survive The Loss of a Parent: A Guide for Adults.* Quill, 1994.

Albertson, Sandy. *Endings and Beginnings.* Random House, 1980.

American Association of Retired Persons Brochure, *Frequently asked Questions by the Widowed.*

American Association of Retired Persons Brochure, *On Being Alone.*

American Association of Retired Persons web site article, "Common Reactions to Loss."

American Association of Retired Persons Brochure, *When an Employee Loses a Loved One.*

Anderson, George and Andrew Barone. *George Anderson's Lessons from the Light : Extraordinary Messages of Comfort and Hope from the Other Side.* Putnam, 1999.

Balch M.D., James F. and Phyllis A. Balch C.N.C. *Prescription for Nutritional Healing.* Avery Publishing Group, 1997.

Bowlby, John. *Loss: Sadness and Depression.* Harpercollins, 1980,

Bozarth, Alla Renee. *A Journey Through Grief: Specific Help to Get You Through the Most Difficult Stages of Grief.* Hazelden, 1994.

Bramblett, John. *When Goodbye Is Forever : Learning to Live Again After the Loss of a Child.* Ballantine, 1997

Breathnach, Sarah Ban. *Simple Abundance: A Daybook of Comfort and Joy.* New York: Warner, 1995.

Challem, Jack. "Relief for Chronic Fatigue: How NADH Can Help." *Let's Live,* October 1999. pp 48-50.

Chevallier, Andrew. *The Encycloped of Medicinal Plants.* Dorling K indersley, 1996.

Childs-Gowell, Elaine. *Good Grief Rituals: Tools for Healing.* Station Hill, 1992.

Coffin, Margaret M. *Death in Early America.* Thomas Nelson, 1976.

Collins, Judy. *Singing Lessons : A Memoir of Love, Loss, Hope, and Healing.* Pocket Books, 1998.

Compassionate Friends brochure, *Caring for Surviving Children.*

Compassionate Friends brochure, *The Death of an Adult Child.*

Conway, Jim. *Men in Midlife Crisis*. Chariot Victor, 1997.

Curry, Cathleen L. *When Your Spouse Dies: A Concise and Practical Source of Help and Advice*. Ave Maria Press, 1990.

Cunningham, Linda. *Grief and the Adolescent*. TAG: Teen Age Grief.

Dahl, Dolores. *Suddenly Alone*.

Deits, Bob. *Life After Loss : A Personal Guide Dealing With Death, Divorce, Job Change and Relocation*. Fisher, 1992.

Doka, Kenneth J (editor). Kenneth, Kola J. (editor). Hospice Foundation of America. *Living With Grief After Sudden Loss : Suicide Homicide Accident Heart Attack Stroke*. Taylor and Francis, 1996.

Edelman, Hope. *Motherless Daughters: the legacy of loss*. Delta, 1995.

Editors of Prevention Health Books. *Prevention's Healing with Vitamins*. Rodale Press, 1996.

Edward, John. *One Last Time: a psychic medium speaks to those who have loved and lost*. Berkley, 1999.

Ericsson, Stephanie. *Companion Through the Darkness : Inner Dialogues on Grief*. Harperperennial Library, 1993.

Flber, Marta. *Grief Expressed: When a Mate Dies*. Lifeword, 1997.

Fine, Carla. *No Time to Say Goodbye : Surviving the Suicide of a Loved One*. Main Street Books, 1999.

"Final Details." Brochure by The American Association of Retired Persons.

Fitzgerald, Helen. *The Mourning Handbook : The Most Comprehensive Resource Offering Practical and Compassionate Advice on Coping With All Aspects of Death and Dying*. Fireside, 1995.

Friedman, Russell and John W. James. *The Grief Recovery Handbook : The Action Program for Moving Beyond Death Divorce, and Other Losses*. Harpercollins, 1998.

Freud, Sigmund. From a letter to Ludwig Binswanger who had lost a son.

Fry, Virgina Lyn. *Part of Me Died, Too: Stories of Creative Survival Among Bereaved Children and Teenagers*. Dutton, 1995.

"Forgotten Mourners." The Journal News, July 29, 1999.

Fumia, Molly. *Safe Passage : Words to Help the Grieving Hold Fast and Let Go*. Conaris Press, 1992.

Gibran, Kahlil. *The Prophet*. Random House.

Ginsburg, Genevieve Davis. *Widow to Widow: throughtful practical ideas for rebuilding your life*. Fisher Books, 1995.

Gootman, Marilyn E. *When a Friend Dies: A Book for Teens About Grieving and Healing.* Free Spirit, 1994.

Gordeeva, Ekaterina. Swift, E.M. (contributor). *My Sergei: A Love Story.* Warner, 1997.

Gray, John. *Men Are from Mars, Women Are from Venus : A Practical Guide for Improving Communication and Getting What You Want in Your Relationships.* Harpercollins, 1992.

Grollman, Earl A. *Living When A Loved One Has Died.* Beacon Press, 1995.

Golden, Tom LCSW. "A Family Ritual for the Year Anniversary." Tom Golden Grief Column.

Goldman, Linda. *Breaking the Silence: A guide to help children with complicated grief.* Western Psychological Services.

Gootman, Marilyn. *When a Friend Dies: a book for teens about grieving and healing.* Free Spirit Publishing, 1994.

Goulston, Mark MD and Philip Goldberg. *Get Out of Your Own Way.* Perigee, 1996.

Halifax, Joan. *The Fruitfull Darkness: Reconnecting With the Body of the Earth.* Harper Sanfancisco, 1994.

Harris, Maxine. *The Loss That is Forever: The Lifelong Impact of the Early Death of a Mother of Father.* Plume, 1996.

Hays, Edward M. *Prayers for a Planetary Pilgrim: A Personal Manual for Prayer and Ritual.* Forest of Peace Books, 1998.

Heegaard, Marge Eaton. *Coping with Death and Grief.* Lerner Publications, 1990.

Hendricks, Lois Lindsey. *Dreams that Help You Mourn.* Resource Publications, 1997.

Henricks, Gay. *The Learning to Love Yourself Workbook.* Prentice Hall, 1992.

Hewett, John H. *After Suicide.* Westminster John Knox, 1980.

Johnson, Elizabeth A. *As Someone Dies: A Handbook for the Living.* Hay House, 1995.

The Journal News. "Forgotten Mourners: after the death of a brother or sister, family members often don't realize the extent of the siblings' grief." July 29, 1999.

Kennedy, Alexandra. *Losing a Parent: Passage to a New Way of Living.* Harper San Francisco, 1991.

King, Marlene. "The Surrogate Dreamers." *Intuition.* January/February 1998.

Kolf, June Cezra. *How Can I Help? : How to Support Someone Who Is Grieving.* Fisher Books, 1999.

Kubler-Ross, M.D., Elisabeth. *On Children and Death: How children and their parents can and do cope with death.* Simon and Schuster, 1997.

Kushner, Harold S. *When Bad Things Happen to Good People.* Avon, 1994.

L'Engle, Madeleine. *Sold into Egypt : Joseph's Journey into Human Being.* Harold Shaw, 1989.

Lerner, Harriet. *The Dance of Anger : A Woman's Guide to Changing the Patterns of Intimate Relationships.* HarperCollins, 1997.

Livingston M.D, Gordon. *Only Spring: On Mourning the Death of My Son.* Marlowe & Company, 1999.

Marshall, Fiona. *Losing A Parent: A Personal Guide to Coping With That Special Grief That Comes With Losing a Parent.* Fisher Books, 1993.

Matsakis, Aphrodite. *Trust After Trauma : A Guide to Relationships for Survivors and Those Who Love Them.* New Harbinger Publications, 1998.

Matsakis, Aphyodite. *I Can't Get Over It: A handbook for trauma survivors.* New Harbinger Publications, 1996.

Matsakis, Aphyodite. *Survivor Guilt.* New Harbinger Publications, 1999.

Mabe, Juliet. *Word to Comfort, Words to Heal: Poems and Mediations for Those Who Grieve.*

Mechner, Vicki. *Healing Journeys:* The Power of Rubenfield Synergy. Omniquest, 1998.

Melrose, Andrea LaSonder (editor). *Nine Visions: a book of fantasies.* Seabury Press, 1983.

Mental Health Association in Waukesha County. "Grief After Suicide." Pewaukee, Wisconsin.

Miller Ph.D., Jack. *Healing our Losses: A Journal for Working Through your Grief.* Resource Publications.

Mitchard, Jacquelyn. *The Deep End of the Ocean.* Penguin, 1999.

Mothers Against Drunk Driving Brochure, *We Hurt Too.*

Noel, Brook. *Shadows of a Vagabond.* Champion Press, 1998.

Noel, Brook with Art Klein. *The Single Parent Resource.* Champion Press, 1998.

Northrup, Christiane. *Women's Bodies, Women's Wisdom: Creating Physical and Emotional Health and Healing.* Bantam, 1998.

Nouwen, Henri J. *Reaching Out : The Three Movements of the Spiritual Life.* Image Books, 1986.

Nuland, Sherwin B. *How We Die: Reflection on Life's Final Chapter.* Vintage, 1995.

Overbeck, Buz and Joanie Overbeck. "Where Life Surrounds Death." Adapted from Helpng Children Cope with Loss.

O'Neil, Anne-Marie; Schneider, Karen S. and Alex Tresnowski. "Starting Over." *People* magazine, October 4, 1999. p 125.

Prend, Ashley Davis. *Trancending Loss: Understanding the Lifelong Impact of Grief and How to Make It Meaningful.* Berkely, 1997.

Rando, Therese A. Treatment of *Complicated Mourning.* Research Press, 1993.

Rando Ph.D, Therese *A. How to Go on Living When Someone You Love Dies.* Bantam, 1991.

Rich, Adrienne. "Tattered Kaddish."

Rifkin, Jeremy. *Time Wars: The Primary Conflict in Human History.*

Rilke, Rainer Maria. *Letters to a Young Poet.* WW Norton, 1994.

Rosof, Barbara D. *The Worst Loss: How Families Heal from the Death of a Child.* Henry Holt, 1995.

Sachs, Judith with Lendon H. Smith. *Nature's Prozac : Natural Therapies and Techniques to Rid Yourself of Anxiety, Depression, Panic Attacks & Stress.* Prentice Hall, 1998.

Sanders, Dr. Catherine M. *Surviving Grief.* John Wiley, 1992.

Schiff, Harriet Sarnoff. *The Bereaved Parent.* Viking, 1978.

Shaw, Eva. *What to Do When A Loved One Dies: A Practical and Compassionate Guide to Dealing With Death on Life's Terms.* Dickens Press, 1994.

Sheehy, Gail. *Passages.* Bantam, 1984.

Staudacher, Carol.A *Time to Grieve : Meditations for Healing After the Death of a Loved One.* Harper San Francisco, 1994.

Staudacher, Carol. *Beyond Grief : A Guide for Recovering from the Death of a Loved One.* New Harbinger Publications, 1987.

Staudacher, Carol. *Men and Grief : A Guide for Men Surviving the Death of a Loved One : A Resource for Caregivers and Mental Health Professional.* New Harbinger Publications, 1991.

Stearn, Ellen Sue. *Living With Loss : Meditations for Grieving Widows (Days of Healing, Days of Change).* Bantam, 1995.

Stearns, Ann Kaiser. *Coming Back: Rebuilding Life after Crisis and Loss.*

Stoltz PhD, Paul G. *Adversity Quotient : Turning Obstacles into Opportunities.* John Wiley & Sons, 1999.

Tatelbaum, Judy. *The Courage to Grieve.* HarperCollins, 1984.

Temes, Dr. Roberta. *Living With an Empty Chair : A Guide Through Grief.* New Horizon, 1992.

Viorst, Judith. *Necessary Losses : The Loves, Illusions, Dependencies, and Impossible Expectations That All of Us Have to Give Up in Order to Grow.* Fireside, 1998.

Walsh, Froma. *People Magazine.* "Starting Over."

Webb, Denise, Ph.D. "Supplement News." *Prevention*, October 1999. p 61.

Westberg, Granger E. *Good Grief.* Fortress Press, 1971.
Zarda, Dan and Marcia Woodaard. *Forever Remembered.* Compendium, 1997.

Worwood, Valerie Ann. *The Fragrant Mind.* New World Library, 1996.

Zadra, Dan (compiler) and Marsha Woodard. *Forever Remembered.* Compendium Publishing, 1997.

Zunin M.D., Leornard M. and Hilary Stanton Zunin. *The Art of Condolence.* Harperperrenial Library, 1992.

Mailing List

The Authors maintain a mailing list for announcements about appearances, future works and their projects. You may mail you address, for inclusion on their mailing list, to:

Brook Noel and Pamela Blair
c/o Champion Press, Ltd.
8689 North Port Washington Road
Suite #329
Milwaukee, Wisconsin 53217
Or fax (262) 692-3342
Or e-mail info@championpress.com

Contact the Authors

You may also write the authors at the address above or e-mail Brook Noel directly at brook@championpress.com.

Internet

To learn more about the authors and their projects visit http://www.championpress.com

About the Authors...

Pamela D. Blair, Ph.D.

Pamela D. Blair, Ph.D. is a psychotherapist and pastoral counselor with a private practice in Hawthorne, NY. She has been a faculty member at many prestigious learning facilities such as the New York Open Center in New York City, Wainright House in Rye New York and the Interface Institute of Cambridge, MA. She is the director of the Divorce Resource Network, and former publisher of the *Surviving Divorce* newsletter. As a therapist, she is known for her innovative personal growth workshops and support groups. Her spiritual-oriented programs provide a forum for participants to gain an understanding of their losses and to successfully recreate their lives.

A frequently invited guest on TV, cable and radio talk shows, Dr. Blair has appeared on CBS TV and was a regular columnist for *Single Living* and writer for *American Woman*. She is currently a contributing editor to *Divorce Magazine* and to *SingleParents Magazine*.

Dr. Blair holds a Ph.D. in Philosophy and a Masters in Metaphysics from the American Institute of Holistic Theology, and a divinity degree from The New Seminary in New York, NY.

Brook Noel

Brook Noel is the author of six other highly-acclaimed books including, *Back to Basics: 101 Ideas for Strengthening Our Children and Our Families* and *The Single Parent Resource*. Noel regularly conducts workshops on parenting and writing and has taught or lectured at Cedars-Sinai Medical Center, The Los Angeles Times, Washington State University and many others locations. She is a frequent guest of radio and television. Her work and commentary have appeared in many media outlets including *Woman's World*, *The Denver Post*, *Our Children* (magazine of the PTA) and *Parent's Journal*. Visit her web site at www.brooknoel.com. She can be e-mailed at brook@championpress.com

Healing Exercises – Part One

In this interactive, online course, you'll complete 10 different exercises that help you move forward through grief and resolve open issues. These exercises can be completed again and again after the class to further your healing. Brook Noel will comment on work you choose to turn in and encourage you in your journey.

Class length – 6 weeks   Cost $49

Now What? Living After Loss

This class offers a solid foundation for anyone wondering how to go on after loss. You'll learn what to expect physically and emotionally and how to take your first steps toward healing.

Class length – 3 weeks   Cost $19

Rituals to Honor Your Loved One

Rituals are a wonderful way to keep the memory of your loved one with you. This class will introduce you to different types of rituals and guide you in creating one of your own.

Class length – 4 weeks   Cost $29

When Will the Pain End?
Working through Unresolved Grief

Throughout this 10 week course, you'll learn about the different stages of grief and how to recognize which of your life losses have not been grieved completely. You'll learn exercises and tactics to heal and work through unresolved grief issues, which are the most common causes of sadness and depression. This is the perfect class for anyone who is having difficulty moving forward after a life loss.

Class length – 10 weeks   Cost $99

The Healing Journey: Writing through Grief

In this writing-intensive class, you'll learn how to write the story of your loss and discover its meaning. You'll create a record of your cherished memories and discover how your loved one is still in your life today. When you complete this class you will have a very special chronicle of your relationship with your loved one.

Class length – 12 weeks   Cost $129

How to Create Your Own Support Group

In this class you will be given assignments that will lead to the creation of your own support group by the completion of the course. You'll decide what type of support group you want to start (online or in-person), create materials to help spread the word and learn how to successfully guide your support group meetings.

Class length – 8 weeks   Cost $79

Basic Strategies and Exercises for Healing

In this interactive, online course, you'll complete 4 different exercises that can help you on your grief journey. You will also learn what to expect on your journey and strategies for coping.

Class length – 3 weeks   Cost $19

Take a step toward healing.
Enroll today at www.griefsteps.com

OTHER BOOKS TO HELP YOU ON YOUR JOURNEY...

Grief Steps:
10 Steps to Regroup, Rebuild and Renew After Any Life Loss

by Brook Noel

ISBN 1-891400-35-5
224 pages $14.95

Facing the Ultimate Loss:
Coping with the death of a child

By Robert J. Marx & Susan Davidson

Hardcover 1-891400- 93-2
$23.95
Softcover 1-891400-99-1
$14.95

I Wasn't Ready to
Say Goodbye:

Surviving, coping and healing after the sudden death of a loved one

by Brook Noel and Pamela D. Blair, Ph.D.

ISBN 1-891400-27-4
$14.95

also available …
I Wasn't Ready to Say Goodbye…a companion workbook

ISBN 1-891400-50-9
$18.95

To learn more visit

www.griefsteps.com

Additional books in the GriefGuides Series
Watch for these additional titles being released in 2004. Visit www.griefsteps.com for more information or to place your order

Grief Guides are short, concise guides to assist those who are grieving specific areas in their grief journey. Each GriefGuide is $8.95 US

Surviving Grief: A Compassionate Guide for Your First Year of Grieving

Coping With the Loss of a Partner

Coping With the Loss of a Child

How to Help Someone Who Is Grieving

Surviving Holidays, Birthdays and Anniversaries: Strategies for Coping During Difficult Days

Coping with the Loss of a Sibling

Coping with the Loss of a Parent

Resource and Support for Those Who Are Grieving

Grief Exercises that Help Ease the Pain

Helping Children Cope with Grief

To order any of the products on pages 57-61 by mail, send a check or money order to Champion Press, 4308 Blueberry Road, Fredonia WI 53021. Please include $3.95 shipping and handling for any books ordered and $1 for each additional book. No shipping or handling is necessary for the online classes. Use your visa or mastercard to order online at www.griefsteps.com